SAGE was founded in 1965 by Sara Miller McCune to support the dissemination of usable knowledge by publishing innovative and high-quality research and teaching content. Today, we publish over 900 journals, including those of more than 400 learned societies, more than 800 new books per year, and a growing range of library products including archives, data, case studies, reports, and video. SAGE remains majority-owned by our founder, and after Sara's lifetime will become owned by a charitable trust that secures our continued independence.

Los Angeles | London | New Delhi | Singapore | Washington DC | Melbourne

DEMOCRACY, CIVIL SOCIETY
―― and ――
GOVERNANCE

DEMOCRACY, CIVIL SOCIETY ——— and ——— GOVERNANCE

GHANSHYAM SHAH

Los Angeles | London | New Delhi
Singapore | Washington DC | Melbourne

Copyright © Ghanshyam Shah, 2019

All rights reserved. No part of this book may be reproduced or utilized in any form or by any means, electronic or mechanical, including photocopying, recording, or by any information storage or retrieval system, without permission in writing from the publisher.

First published in 2019 by

SAGE Publications India Pvt Ltd
B1/I-1 Mohan Cooperative Industrial Area
Mathura Road, New Delhi 110 044, India
www.sagepub.in

SAGE Publications Inc
2455 Teller Road
Thousand Oaks, California 91320, USA

SAGE Publications Ltd
1 Oliver's Yard, 55 City Road
London EC1Y 1SP, United Kingdom

SAGE Publications Asia-Pacific Pte Ltd
18 Cross Street #10-10/11/12
China Square Central
Singapore 048423

Published by Vivek Mehra for SAGE Publications India Pvt Ltd and typeset in 10.5/13 pt Berkeley by Zaza Eunice, Hosur, Tamil Nadu, India.

Library of Congress Cataloging-in-Publication Data

Names: Shah, Ghanshyam, author.
Title: Democracy, civil society and governance/Ghanshyam Shah.
Description: Thousand Oaks: SAGE Publications India Pvt Ltd, [2018] |
   Includes bibliographical references and index.
Identifiers: LCCN 2018046263 | ISBN 9789353281793 (print (pb)) | ISBN
   9789353281809 (e pub 2.0) | ISBN 9789353281816 (e book)
Subjects: LCSH: Civil society—India. | Democracy—India. | Representative
   government and representation—India. | Social structure—India. |
   Economic development—Social aspects—India. | Poor—Political
   activity—India.
Classification: LCC JQ281.S48 2018 | DDC 300.954—dc23 LC record available at https://lccn.loc.gov/2018046263

ISBN: 978-93-532-8179-3 (HB)

SAGE Team: Abhijit Baroi, Vandana Gupta, Shobana Paul and Nishant Dhawan

To
Aarav, Aashna and Shama

Thank you for choosing a SAGE product!
If you have any comment, observation or feedback,
I would like to personally hear from you.

Please write to me at **contactceo@sagepub.in**

Vivek Mehra, Managing Director and CEO, SAGE India.

Bulk Sales

SAGE India offers special discounts
for purchase of books in bulk.
We also make available special imprints
and excerpts from our books on demand.

For orders and enquiries, write to us at

Marketing Department
SAGE Publications India Pvt Ltd
B1/I-1, Mohan Cooperative Industrial Area
Mathura Road, Post Bag 7
New Delhi 110044, India

E-mail us at **marketing@sagepub.in**

Subscribe to our mailing list
Write to **marketing@sagepub.in**

This book is also available as an e-book.

CONTENTS

List of Illustrations ix
List of Abbreviations xi
Preface xvii

Introduction 1

1. Civil Society: Historical Background 25
2. Civil Society Organizations and Social Activists 51
3. Civil Society and Education: Reproducing Hegemony and Inequality 71
4. Self-employed Workers and Their Empowerment 109
5. Legal Recourse and Collective Struggles of the Subalterns 129
6. Social Movements of the Non-poor 153
7. Narmada Dam: Development and Displacement 171

Epilogue 202

Bibliography 212
Index 231
About the Author 239

LIST OF ILLUSTRATIONS

TABLES

4.1	Distribution of Employed Persons in Gujarat in 2000 and 2016 (in %)	111
4.2	Average Monthly Earnings (in Rupees) of Self-employed in Rural and Urban Gujarat (2015–2016)	111

FIGURES

I.1	Society, State and Civil Society: Interrelationship	16
3.1	Enrolment by Social Groups at Different Levels of Education in Gujarat (2014)	83
3.2	Gender Parity Index 2011–2012 (Gujarat and India)	85
3.3	Net Attendance Ratio at Different Levels by Household Income	86
3.4	Decadal Growth of Educational Institutions in Gujarat and India	88
3.5	Enrolment by Management of Institutions at Different Levels (2011)	97

LIST OF ABBREVIATIONS

AISHE	All India Survey on Higher Education
ALA	Agricultural Labour Association
AMC	Ahmedabad Municipal Corporation
AMS	Antyodaya Mahila Sangh
ANA	Anand Niketan Ashram
ARCH	Action Research in Community Health and Education
ASAG	Ahmedabad Study Action Group
ASER	Annual Status of Education Report
AWAG	Ahmedabad Women's Action Group
BJP	Bharatiya Janata Party
BSC	Behavioural Science Centre
BSM	Bhil Seva Mandal
CA	constituent assembly
CAG	Comptroller and Auditor General
CBSE	Central Board of Secondary Education
CM	chief minister
CPI(ML)	Communist Party of India (Marxist–Leninist)
CRZ	coastal regulation zone
CSJ	Centre for Social Justice
CSO	civil society organization
CSS	Centre for Social Studies
CSV	Chhatra Sangharsh Vahini
CSWI	Committee on the Status of Women in India
DAINE	Development Alternatives Information Network

DFID	Department for International Development
DHS	Dalit Harijan Samaj
DPAP	Drought Prone Areas Programme
DPEP	District Primary Education Programme
DRDA	District Rural Development Agency
EIA	Environment Impact Assessment
EMRS	Ekalavya Model Residential Schools
EPA	Environmental Protection Act
EPH	environmental public hearing
FCRA	Foreign Contribution Regulation Act
FDI	foreign direct investment
FIR	first investigation report
FLA	Free Legal Aid
FWWB	Friends of Women's World Banking
GER	gross enrolment ratio
GoG	Government of Gujarat
GoI	Government of India
GPI	Gender Parity Index
GRA	Grievance Redressal Authority
GSHSEB	Gujarat Secondary and Higher Secondary Education Board
GSP	Gujarati Sahitya Parishad
GVT	Gramya Vikas Trust
HCS	hegemonic civil society
HSS	Halpati Seva Sangh
IAS	Indian Administrative Service
ICSSR	Indian Council of Social Science Research
IDPAD	Indo-Dutch Programme on Alternatives in Development
IIM	Indian Institute of Management
IIPLS	The Indian Institute for Paralegal Studies
ILO	International Labour Organization
IMR	infant mortality rate
INSAF	Indian Social Action Forum
ISID	Institute for Studies in Industrial Development

IWDP	Integrated Wasteland Development Scheme
JHRS	Jamin Hakk Rakshan Samiti
KBS	Kinara Bachao Samiti
KGBV	Kasturba Gandhi Balika Vidyalaya
KVs	Kendriya Vidyalayas
LAHRC	Legal Aid and Human Right Centre
LAM	Lok Adhikar Manch
LAS	Lok Adhikar Sangh
LEP	low-fee private
mcf	million cubic feet
MDM	Mid-Day Meal
MGNREGA	Mahatma Gandhi National Rural Employment Guarantee Act
MHRD	Ministry of Human Resource Development
MMR	mother mortality rate
MP	Madhya Pradesh
NA	Narmada Abhiyan
NABARD	National Bank for Agriculture and Rural Development
NALSA	National Legal Services Authority
NAPM	National Alliance of People's Movements
NAR	net school attendance ratio
NASVI	National Alliance of Street Vendors, India
NBA	Narmada Bachao Andolan
NCA	Narmada Control Authority
NCERT	National Council of Educational Research and Training
NCF	National Curriculum Framework
NDS	Narmada Dharangrast Samiti
NEP	National Educational Policy
NFSA	National Food Security Act
NGO	non-governmental organization
NIAS	The Netherlands Institute of Advanced Studies
NID	National Institute of Design
NPCIL	Nuclear Power Corporation of India Ltd
NPE	National Policy on Education

NPG	Narmada Planning Group
NREGA	National Rural Employment Guarantee Act
NRLM	National Rural Livelihood Mission
NSS	National Sample Survey
NSSO	National Sample Survey Office
NUEPA	National University of Educational Planning and Administration
NVs	Navodaya Vidyalayas
NWDT	Narmada Water Dispute Tribunal
OBC	Other Backward Class
PAFs	project-affected families
PAP	project-affected people
PDI	Policy Development Initiative
PIL	public interest litigation
PMVP	Pushtimargiya Vaishnav Parishad
PPP	public–private partnership
PSS	Paryavaran Suraksha Samiti
PTR	pupil–teacher ratio
PUCL	Public Union of Civil Liberty
R&R	Rehabilitation and Resettlement
RBI	Reserve Bank of India
RCS	radical civil society
RSS	Rashtriya Swayamsevak Sangh
RSSS	Rajpipla Social Service Society
RTE	Right of Children to Free and Compulsory Education
RTI	Right to Information
SAL	social action litigation
SCs	Scheduled Castes
SEC	Secondary Education Commission
SETU	Centre for Action and Knowledge
SEWA	Self Employed Women's Association
SEZ	special economic zone
SGSY	Swarnajayanti Gram Swarozgar Yojana
SHG	self-help group
SIR	Special Investment Region

SIS	Servants of India Society
SMC	Surat Municipal Corporation
SSA	Sarva Shiksha Abhiyan
SSC	Secondary School Certificate
SSP	Sardar Sarovar Project
SSST	Sadguru Water and Development Foundation
STFC	SEWA Trade Facilitation Centre
STs	scheduled tribes
SVS	Shramik Vikas Sansthan
SY	Sangharsh Yatra
TISS	Tata Institute of Social Sciences
TLA	Textile Labour Association
ToI	*Times of India*
UEC	University Education Commission
UNDP	United Nations Development Programme
UNHCR	United Nations High Commissioner for Refugees
UP	Uttar Pradesh
VHP	Vishwa Hindu Parishad
VIAS	Vedchhi Intensive Area Scheme
VKA	Vanvasi Kalyan Ashram
VKS	Vadodara Khetmajur Sangathan
WB	World Bank
WWB	Women's World Banking

PREFACE

While teaching public health at Jawaharlal Nehru University, I got interested to explore the concepts of civil society and governance, and their relevance in understanding the political process. In fact, I owe my interest in the theoretical and operational aspects of governance to I. P. Desai, who used to tell me in the 1970s that mere ideas are not enough; what is important is to find out ways and means by evolving strategies and methodologies in a given socio-economic milieu so that ideas can be actualized. (At that time, the concept 'governance' was not in our vocabulary.) In the 1990s, I was grappling with these twin notions not only in the context of public health but also with the larger concern with democratic transformation under an onslaught of the neoliberal economy projected as a fait accompli. This political economy depoliticizes society and also breeds the social Darwinism mindset.

To problematize the concept of civil society in the Indian context, I began to reflect on my association with the Lokayan project of the Centre for the Study of Developing Societies (CSDS), Delhi, which provided me with an opportunity to have a dialogue with social activists and observe the work of NGOs in different parts of the country. Though I agree with Rajni Kothari that the State has given up the task for social transformation to build a humane egalitarian society, I, however, did not share his romantic formulation of decentralization and civil society, wishing away the prevailing socio-economic power structure as an alternative of the State for social transformation. Granting that the present political parties do not have an ideology to combat neoliberal economy, and they are primarily interested in capturing political power and not in social transformation as envisaged in Indian Constitution, how realistic it is to expect civil society to transform the State and Society? Can civil society be above historical and the contemporary socio-economic forces? In a stratified society, how can civil society become democratic and accountable to the people? The present study is an endeavour to explore these questions.

During my stay at NIAS (the Netherlands Institute of Advanced Studies), I began to get acquainted with the literature on civil society. To get an empirical picture, I undertook a field study on 'civil society and the poor', sponsored by IDPAD (Indo-Dutch Programme on Alternatives in Development) during 2005–2007. The material presented in this monograph on a profile of NGOs and activists, microfinance, watershed management, legal aid and public interest litigation was collected during that project. I then carried out a study on urban governance with Navdeep Mathur between 2008 and 2010. The project was sponsored by Ford Foundation. Later, during my tenure as National Fellow, ICSSR (Indian Council of Social Science Research), I reworked on these two themes and the historical aspect of civil society. I wrote a manuscript, 'Democracy, Civil Society and Governance', and submitted it to ICSSR in 2015. The present book is a revised version of this work.

I am grateful to NIAS for providing me with a very congenial, Indian-ashram type of free atmosphere, which gave me time to reflect on my thinking. I thank IDPAD and Ford Foundation for their support, enabling me to carry out my fieldwork. I sincerely thank ICSSR for awarding me a National Fellowship and the Centre for Social Studies, Surat, for offering me an affiliation during the tenure of the fellowship. Without their support, I would not have been able to prepare this book. I especially thank Pravin J. Patel, Chairperson, Centre for Social Studies (CSS), for his moral support, and Satyakam Joshi, Kiran Desai, Vimal Trivedi, Seema Shukla, Ashok Pawar, Harish Jariwala and Ashish Nigam for their help in facilitating this study. I also thank Varsha Bhagat Ganguly, Kiran Nanavati, Persis Ginwalla and Jignesh Mewani, who provided valuable help as co-researchers in the fieldwork during the course of different studies. I also thank SAGE editorial team for careful copyediting of the manuscript.

While carrying out a study with Navdeep on urban governance, and in the subsequent years, I always gained from his input in my understanding of civil society and governance. For several years, Jan Breman and I have shared our field observations and concerns on the contemporary situations around the world. He has also read the draft of this study and offered valuable comments. Suhas Palshikar, Rajeev Bhargava, Neera Chandhoke and Sudha Pai were kind enough to read some chapters and offer their valuable comments. I thank all of them.

I have been toying with the subject for many years and have incurred the debt of several scholars and social activists who shared with me their insight, ideas and observations. They include the late Rajni Kothari and Anil Bhatt, Dhirubhai Sheth, Sukhadeo Thorat, Indira Hirway, Rita and Abhijit Kothari, and Harsh Mander. I have always been benefited in my understanding of the complex grassroots situation and common sense of people from the late Bhagirath Shah and Babubhai Desai as well as from Martin Macwan, Achyut Yagnik, Anil Patel, Girish Patel, Rajni Dave, Sarup Dhruv, Hiren Gandhi, Prakash Shah, Rohit Prajapati and several other activist friends. I thank all of them.

While writing this study, I frequently faced a dilemma whether I should write this monograph or not. My wife Kalpana, as always, shared my confusion and predicaments. Every morning at teatime, we used to discuss one argument or another, or part of the chapters. Without her support, I would not have been able to complete this work.

INTRODUCTION

Although the Indian Constitution has accepted the Westminster model of a democratic political system, it has gone far beyond the utilitarian philosophy of the liberal democracy of the West. The political system is the outcome of a popular mass movement dominated by the upper strata (predominantly the higher- and middle-caste–based middle class), oriented in Western education. In the course of the anti-colonial movement, the notion of democracy was articulated to mean the original notion of democracy—the rule of all the people rather than the Western liberal notion of the rule of the propertied class or the Marxist notion of rule by the proletariats. 'It had not been transformed by liberal individualism, nor made over on the definite class pattern of Marxism' (Macpherson 1973, 24).

The Congress, which led the movement, was more of a platform for India's freedom than a coherent ideological party. Its social character in terms of economic interests and outlooks was amorphous (including feudals, capitalists, social conservatives, sectarians, modern educated liberals, socialists, Gandhians, anarchists, etc.). However, the social democrats' version of the Western liberal ideology of the post-war era and Gandhi's moral principles for *daridranarayana* (espousing that service to the poor is equivalent to service to God) rooted in an imagination of Indian culture were the guiding spirits in mobilizing masses at different stages of the movement. As early as 1934, the Congress Working Committee declared that the party stood for 'a genuine democratic State in India where political power has been transferred to the people, as a whole, and the Government is under their effective control'. In fact, in 1931, in the First Round Table Conference, Ambedkar demanded a separate electoral system for the depressed classes and also adult franchise irrespective of property and education (Sekhar 2013).

In 1939, the party expressed that the constituent assembly (CA) should be elected on the basis of adult suffrage, but it did not pursue the matter when the CA was formed. Perhaps the elite were not serious in their proposal, and did not pay attention to the required administrative machinery to prepare the electoral roll and conduct the elections (Shani 2018). Be that as it may, the assembly was constituted of those who were elected by property owners and/or educated adults, and the representatives of the erstwhile princely rulers (Austin 1966). The overwhelming majority of members were from the upper and dominant middle castes and classes. Notwithstanding such composition, given the politicization of the people on the eve of Independence regarding the State–individual relationship and the notion of citizen's rights, the nature of the Constitution document may not have been substantially different even if the CA was comprised of elected members.[1] Most of the members were public figures who had been engaged in public discourse on the 'idea of India' embedded in the socio-economic–cultural milieu with inherent contradictions. Simultaneously, they were engaged in articulating ethical values for social relationships and also in confronting, negotiating and contesting the colonial state on political as well as social affairs. They were social activists of the time at the national or regional level.

On the eve of Independence, there were four broad overlapping tendencies in political thinking about economic production and distribution, pluralism and a secular idea of society, and individual freedom/autonomy in the context of social practices and the State: (a) Gandhian, socialist and liberal social democrat; (b) Marxist–communist; (c) liberal—the pro-private enterprise; and (d) conservative cultural (albeit Hindu) nationalist.[2] Communists at that time considered Independence as fake, and rejected parliamentary democracy. They did not, therefore, participate in the debates on Constitution-making. The Congress party represented various political tendencies in different degrees. The conservatives and business industrialists did not spell out their worldview and plan for India's development. The Hindu nationalists were actively working for the dominant Hindu *rashtra* (nation) and rejuvenating 'cultural traditions', and were against the proposed formation of Pakistan. They were dominated by the conservative upper-caste elite and traders. The business industrialists pleaded that the new State should play an active role in encouraging the development of industries. In 1948, considering their capacity for investment and the need for resource mobilization, a section of them prepared a plan, called the Bombay Plan, for the establishment of centralized planning. The plan called for the imposition of economic controls, development of heavy industry and introduction of radical agricultural reforms (Kochanek 1974). The Socialist Party prepared a draft constitution in 1948 which demanded the 'extension of public ownership' and enhancing the State's initiative 'in restructuring the society and economy'. A section of Gandhians pleaded that the State should adopt 'a policy calculated to (a) remove caste ... social inequality; (b) prevent social exploitation of masses, and (c) minority problems...'. They proposed that all the land be acquired by the State, if necessary, and 'every citizen shall avoid, check and if necessary, resist exploitation of man by man...' (all quotations are cited in Palshikar 2008, 152).[3] Liberal social democrats had more or less the same position (Karnik n.d.). A difference among them was related to the extent and nature of the State intervention in production, terms of trade between industry and agriculture, and the distribution of goods.

Following the Congress' commitment, the Indian Constitution provides adult franchise irrespective of gender, creed, caste and education. The right was given with a faith that irrespective of their education, place of residence and socio-economic status, the average Indians have an understanding of their interests and aspire to be free from any kind of discrimination. It had been hoped that voting power would make them citizens asserting their voice for freedom and equality. The architects of the Constitution adopted the adult franchise

> [W]ith an abundant faith in the common man (and woman) and the ultimate success of democratic rule, and in the full belief that the introduction of democratic government on the basis of adult suffrage will bring enlightenment and promote the well-being, the standard of life, the comfort, and the decent living of the common man. (Cited in Austin 1966, 46)

The 'spirit' in which the Constitution was drafted was to bring a 'social revolution'. Of course, the active members of the CA had a different vision of the revolution but, for the sake of consensus, the dialogue on differences was avoided. The Constitution, in its objectives, provided guarantees securing

> (1) to all the people of India justice, social, economic and political; equality of status, of opportunity, and before the law; freedom of thought, expression, belief, faith worship, vocation, association and action, subject to law and public morality; and (2) wherein adequate safeguards shall be provided for minorities, backward and tribal areas, and depressed and other backward classes.

There was an overall normative thrust towards equality for all. Dr Ambedkar, and several socialists and Gandhians, wished that the draft of the Constitution should mention the nature of the economic system (socialist/Gandhian) that the State should follow to attain the well-being of all. In fact, Ambedkar asserted,

> All of us are aware of the fact that rights are nothing unless remedies are provided whereby people can seek to obtain redress when rights are invaded.... I do not understand how it could be possible for any future government which believes in doing justice socially, economically and politically, unless its economy is a socialist economy. (Cited in Jeffrelot and Kumar 2018, 127)

However, neither he nor others insisted on the issue of mode of production and exchange. Perhaps they wanted to avoid any controversy. Or perhaps they felt that they were not united in their perspective and did not have enough strength to carry out their agenda, and most of the liberal members, who dominated in the articulation of their views, hoped that the 'modern' State with the Westminster model would be a 'welfare' state. Their hope was based on their ahistorical reading of 'Western liberal democracy' which had during that period a 'welfare state' posture. They were satisfied with broad principles as spelt out in the Directive Principles to the Indian State to foster liberty, equality, fraternity and justice. The Constitution has provided a number of positive and negative rights to build a society for the common good (Austin 1966). Also important is the fact that unlike Western liberal constitutions, the Indian Constitution has accepted the notion not only of individual rights but also with certain provisos and community rights. It has legally abolished the practice of untouchability and also accepted affirmative action with a view to providing a helping hand to the traditionally deprived communities in order to eradicate discrimination and the caste system. Among the CA members, there were several critics, both liberal and conservative, of 'affirmative actions', but they did not assert their position except expressing their dissent. It was hoped that in 10 years' time, with economic prosperity and equality, the country would not need 'affirmative action' as everyone would have enough opportunities to develop.

To strengthen these provisions, some members emphasized that 'democracy needs to be extended from the political to the economic and social spheres'. Dr Ambedkar reiterated the need for social and economic democracy. He eloquently reminded the members of the CA,

> We must make our democracy a social democracy as well. Political democracy cannot last unless there lies at the base of its social democracy. What does social democracy mean? It means a way of life which recognizes liberty, equality and fraternity as the principles of life. These principles of liberty, equality and fraternity are not to be treated as separate items in a trinity. They form a union of the trinity in the sense that to divorce one form from the other is to defeat the very purpose of democracy. (Austin 1966, 196–197)

Nehru also conceded that the concept of political democracy needs to be advanced to economic democracy. However, the strategy and modus operandi for attaining this objective did not work out, except for making provisions for affirmative action for Scheduled Castes (SCs) and Scheduled Tribes (STs), and enshrining several directive principles in the Constitution. It was assumed that with industrial development coupled with urbanization, the growth of modern institutions and the expansion of traditional educational institutions, the ethos embedded with ascribed hierarchical values and practices will be eroded and eventually erased. And concurrently, modern values of rationality, universality, equality, justice and secularism will grow at both normative and behaviour levels in social interactions. It was hoped that the elected representatives and their governments would translate the objectives of the Constitution in letter and spirit in the distribution of resources and also protect the rights of the subaltern from being violated by the dominant classes. And with adult franchise, people, particularly the poor, would build pressure on their representatives for their rights. In the process, society will move towards an egalitarian social order.

Adult franchise is the core political right in the process of democratization. However, social and economic inequality, embedded with ascribed feudal values, and widespread illiteracy are definitely a stumbling block in democratic functioning. At the same time, I submit that the absence of democracy has no potentiality to bring social and economic equality. Benevolent dictatorship, either of an individual or of a party, or 'efficient' oligarchy may successfully change the economic structure so as to eliminate economic inequalities of some kinds, and it may also lead towards social equality. But it may not lead to a revolutionary transformation in hierarchical hegemonic values rooted in the dominant culture. Such a regime eventually generates another kind of inequality by creating a privileged class in the political and sociocultural spheres. In such a structure of economic equality, cultural and political inequalities continue; hence, it cannot sustain for long as people have been reduced to subjects/followers rather than citizens. Therefore, people do not develop a stake in the system. It replaces one oligarchy and hegemony with another. It blocks the political path for the people to decide their destiny. We are caught in a dilemma: Democracy in a society with gross socio-economic inequality cannot be effective in accomplishing meaningful participation of all, and non-democracy cannot necessarily build a sustainable egalitarian social order.

A society with gross well-entrenched social and economic inequalities woven in its social fabric cannot wait for the introduction of the democratic system until it attains equality. Nor can it wait until a cultural renaissance ingrained with rationality, humanism, scientific thinking, etc. emerges. That never happens. The progress of these values and democratic systems in the post-colonial countries have to go hand in hand. This is not an either-or situation, nor does one follow the other: A democratic system can come into existence after the prerequisites, that is, equality and intellectual rationality, are met or vice versa. Democracy, I assert, is both an end as well as a means. Greater equality in all spheres strengthens democracy and vice versa. Political democracy with its minimal components—rule of law embedded with citizen's right and the system of elected representation—is a process and has potentialities, at least logical, to build an egalitarian social order. It cannot achieve the ideal on its own. It is possible if the system moves to its logical end, involving people at different levels, which compel the elected representatives to formulate and implement policies that bridge the social and economic gap among the classes. The present system provides an opportunity to the women and men of the labouring classes, have-nots, Dalits, Adivasis, minorities and other marginalized people to participate in electing their representatives, and the latter are compelled to seek the support of the former to get elected. In such a process, civil society, first of all, requires functioning as a watchdog to see that the State observes the minimalist components of the democratic system—procedural aspects related to regular free and fair elections, rule of law and citizens' freedom of expression. Simultaneously, while stimulating and supporting the collective struggles of the oppressed against injustice and encouraging their electoral participation, open-ended efforts have to be made to invigorate consciousness of the oppressed for their rights enshrined in the Constitution and structural (sociocultural and economic) impediments in their emancipation.

STATE-CENTRIC POLITICS

Although the State power cannot bring social changes in all spheres, the role of the State in political decision-making for social transformation is unavoidable. It enjoys law-making and enforcing authority, sovereignty and coercive power over its citizens, irrespective of its professed ideological stand. The State has established control over policy formulation related to the creation and management of the accumulation as well as the distribution of surplus in society (Scott 1998). However, to say that the State is the sole repository of power in society is problematic both on theoretical and empirical grounds. The Indian State is not monolithic. There are several centres and forms of power in society, although without legal authority at macro and micro levels (Foucault 1987). They are interlinked with institutions embedded in sociocultural values that are shaping the lifeworld of the members. In the Indian context, dominant castes/classes and the patriarchy enjoy not only ideological hegemony but also coercive power with or without the tacit consent, or indifference, of the State. The modern liberal state, in theory, does not adhere to the ascribed hierarchy and stands for rule of law. To protect their dominance from the counter-assertion of the marginalized in everyday politics, the dominant castes/classes subtly resist or sabotage legal diktat (not always in their favour) of the State or collude with executive authority at a different level to neutralize the State power. It is more possible when the State's commitment to its own policy related to citizens' rights is already weak and ambivalent.

In practice, the Indian State has accepted, right from the beginning, the coexistence of the democratic system with the market economy controlled by the propertied class for the accumulation of surplus. The architects of the Constitution and liberal public intellectuals hoped that the control of the latter would decline in the course of time with the empowerment—economic and social capabilities to assert one's dignity and rights, and the self-confidence to change power relationship in society—of the people. But those hopes have been belied. The grip of the propertied classes, Indian and multinational, has tightened on the State and society (Frankel 2005). Inequality has glaringly increased manifold, and surplus has been cornered by a small stratum (the rich and upper-middle classes), although the scales of abject poverty—homeless families, infant mortality rate (IMR), maternal mortality rate (MMR), starvation death, illiteracy, etc.—have considerably declined. Karma (ascribed birth status) theory for one's position in the society has almost lost legitimacy among the subaltern. Aspirations for a better life are manifesting across castes and classes. Subalterns, individually and collectively, assert for social justice, their dignity and rights. Thanks to their mobilization and also to the interventions by human rights associations, the rights have been enlarged and have stimulated political consciousness of the traditionally deprived people. Some of these expanded notions of rights such as the right to food, education, etc. have also been legalized, forcing the democratic State to comply in a random manner. At the same time, the vulnerability of the marginalized people in the market remains unchanged, delimiting their life chances for development. Their say in the decision-making process and governance of the public institutions remains symbolic and illusionary.

On the other hand, equality as a social and economic principle has ceased to be on the political agenda of the State since the demise of Nehru. His idea of equality in the socialist framework was of the 'mild and timid variety'. He avoided inevitable conflicts involving negotiations and clashes that are inherent in a socialist project between labour and capitalists/feudal landed classes (Gopal 1976). He and the liberals wished away caste-based values and hierarchy, and prevailing socio-economic dominant forces at macro and micro levels. His political imagination was not accompanied by the required bureaucratic rationality and modus operandi—the nitty-gritty, and the nuts and bolts of everyday administration—for implementing his ideas to improve the condition of weaker sections. He depended upon the Congress party, which was ideologically indecisive for political mobilization, and the bureaucracy, dominated by upper caste that was not committed to social change, for the execution of the programmes. Efforts to restructure and rejuvenate the party for greater democratization had little success. The party had no cadre to mobilize the marginalized communities for successful implementation of land reforms. With new 'development' programmes such as community development and agriculture extension, the dominant castes increased their grip over the local power structure. Although politically aspiring backward castes entered the Congress, they remained on the periphery in the functioning of the party; the class character of the party did not change (Shah 1975). The control of landed, business and industrial classes on the party continued to be strong.

Nehru felt that the administrative structure created by colonial rulers was not suitable to meet new tasks after Independence. However, on the eve of Independence, the first and most important task for Nehru was to maintain the 'security and stability of India'. For that, the status quo in the administrative system was necessary. Nehru was not prepared to take the risk of restructuring the bureaucracy. Like others, he feared that it would create chaos. He invited experts and appointed commissions to seek their recommendations for reforming administration, but a thoroughgoing restructuring of the administration was beyond their terms of reference.[4] Hence, Nehru could not prevent a reproduction of the bureaucratic apparatus and administrative tradition of the British Raj (Potter 1986). He did not build a team of ideologically committed leaders and a cadre within the party (Shah 2018).

After his death, the 'Congress system' was gradually reduced to a platform for faction fight. To get and retain power, all kinds of compromises and negotiations, in the name of political exigency, gained legitimacy. Populist politics gained ground in which 'socialism', *garibi hatao* (eradicate poverty) and *vikas* (development) have become buzzwords for electoral politics. This, however, had provided a space to civil society in public discourse and pro-poor policymaking. Concurrently, capitalist economy has penetrated its tentacles cunningly and quietly. Ironically, all political parties, except the Left, have accepted neoliberal economy as an end of ideology, a fait accompli for human destiny. However, after Nehru, for the first time, Narendra Modi's BJP (Bharatiya Janata Party) government in 2014 has a clear political ideology. It is wielding neoliberalism coupled with cultural nationalism, namely 'Hindu rashtra' as conceived by traditionally upper caste, undermining India's folk plural culture and secular ethos in everyday life. Unlike Nehru, he has a committed cadre, well-conceived strategy and modus operandi to translate the BJP's idea of cultural nationalism while continuing with neoliberal economic policy.

NON-PARTY POLITICAL PROCESS

In the Indian political science discourse, until the early 1970s, the liberal political theorists looked at the State as being 'modern' (against traditional) and engaged in social welfare as envisaged in the Constitution. It is a neutral institution above class interests. In their preoccupation with State–society dialectical relationship, they focus more on social and cultural dimensions than on political economy (Kothari 1969, 1970). When the Congress party split and the 'Congress system' was punctured, Kothari spelled out a path for 'political economy of garibi hatao'. He emphasized that the basic political organizational structure in context of economic life had to be altered (Kothari 1972). But soon it became clear that 'garibi hatao' was more of a rhetoric than a serious agenda to withstand the pressure and power of the macro, including multinational capitalist, and the micro, namely dominant classes/castes, forces. Indira Gandhi's government could not meet the rising expectations of the people. Food scarcity and inflation increased. The economic crisis deepened, and unrest among the people took the form of street protests. The government encountered two mass movements—one in Gujarat and another in Bihar—dominated by the middle classes with catchy slogans of *'Navnirman'* (social transformation) and *'Sampoorna Kranti'* (total revolution). The former was confined to the region in its scale and demand. The state negotiated with the protesters, dissolved the state assembly and called for fresh elections. The later, though largely confined to the region, had nation-wide support, and its demand was largely against the union government which, according to the ideologue of the movement, was the root cause of corruption and centralization of power. Under Jayaprakash Narayan's leadership, it had a broad ideological stance rooted in the Gandhian philosophy of Sarvodaya (universal upliftment; Shah 1977). Negotiation between the State and the leaders of the movement failed. Eventually, an internal Emergency was imposed by Indira Gandhi's government. The State abdicated its democratic process. Later, the Janata Party government failed to provide cohesive leadership and governance. Within three years, thanks to internal bickering, it lost power. The liberals who had conceived the liberal state as an agency for social transformation were disappointed.

This was the period when the notion of market fundamentalism at global level was reviving. The idea of dismantling the welfare state was floated in the Western public discourse. World Bank (WB) President Robert McNamara in the late 1960s declared that the Third World states were not capable and efficient in carrying out development works for the poor. To tackle the problem of rising poverty, the WB involved voluntary organizations in its aid system. The Western countries also followed. As a part of their development aid, they began to support non-governmental organizations (NGOs) labelling them as civil society organizations (CSOs). At the same time, there was simmering disquiet and protests in different parts of the world against the capitalist political system, and questions on the nature of growth were being raised. The Club of Rome's report *The Limits to Growth* (Meadows et al. 1972) stimulated discussion among concerned intellectuals around the world to search for an alternative path. In India, the JP movement was its parallel. Kothari in his *Footsteps in Future, Diagnosis of the Present World and Design for an Alternative* (1975) argued against the nature of development, and he spelt out an alternative path of development.

By the end of the 1970s, political class across the parties had lost credibility in the public eye, although, paradoxically, this was not reflecting in voter turnout. It may be because of their faith in the democratic system. In the early 1980s, Kothari observed, 'Democracy has become the playground for growing corruption, criminalization, repression and intimidation for large masses of the people' (1984, 217). Concerned liberal and radical political scholar activists feel that the received theories of class struggle and revolution were unable to explain the situation and guide for action. Gandhians and radicals of different schools—Indian socialists, radical humanists, Maoists, Leninists, Trotskyites, etc.—finding the Left political parties too weak, bureaucratic and ideologically incapable to comprehend changing ground reality, engaged in a non-party political process to influence the system. They joined the grassroots struggles of the people on several issues that varied from their rights to land and employment to the environment (right to clean natural environment, environmental protection, forest produce, etc.). The non-party political process, according to D. L. Sheth, 'referred to individual actors (social activists) and groups whose intentions and programmes, were essentially political, but eschewed the politics of parties and elections… raising and communicating specific issues of people to the political establishment and compel it to address them, by mobilizing popular support' (2013, 192–193).

CIVIL SOCIETY: IMAGINATION

Conceptual Legacy

In the backdrop of conceptual legacy, a notion of civil society had been reinvented in the public discourse at international and national levels by the WB, media and political theorists in the early 1990s. It was also a time of the collapse of totalitarian communist regimes in Eastern Europe. In that transition, 'civil dissent initiatives' and organizations that played a role in fighting against the authoritarian regimes, and later have been involved in building a new political system, are called 'civil society' by the founders and Western liberal political theorists. In the Western political discourse, the concept of 'civil society' has been used differently in different contexts. The crux of the theoretical debate in different contexts of time and space is about the idealized society around the principles of human rights and the role of the State in advancing and maintaining the society. According to political theorists (Chandhoke 1995; Mahajan 1999), though Greek philosopher Aristotle conceived this notion (Sulek 2010), the concept has been reinvented in modern times after the French Revolution by social contract theorists. In his *Two Treaties of Civil Government*, a mythological construction, Locke (1966) used civil and political society interchangeably. While critiquing the divine right theory of the monarchy, he propounded that the State formation was a contract between people and State to regulate society from a 'chaotic' and 'war of all against all' state of nature. He conceived a 'democratic' society in which the central responsibility of the monarch was to protect the rights of the individual. In the 17th century, private property was conceived as a core right accompanied by liberty and life.

However, gradually, the notion of ownership of private property as a right became a contentious issue. In the 18th century, Rousseau was its critic. According to him, ownership of private property had created inequality.[5] In the early 19th century, utilitarian philosopher Bentham deliberated on the principle of 'greatest happiness of the greatest number' and began to talk about 'virtually universal' franchise, excluding only those who were underage and/or unable to read, and possibly women (Macpherson 1973). Hegel considered that civil society is the public sphere of ideas which has a commitment for 'collective interests'. It acts as a 'counterpoint to the self-interest of modern society' (Chandhoke 1995, 249). It is a moral order (Dhanagare 2005). According to De Tocqueville, civil society is a public sphere where individuals associate to debate social and political matters where the rights of individuals have primacy over all else (Mahajan 1999, 1188).

Marx was a critic of the liberal conception of civil society. He argues that both the State and civil society are rooted in the same material conditions of life. Therefore, 'anatomy of civil society is to be sought in political economy' (cited in Draper 1977, 34). Gramsci, having experienced defeat of the working class movement in Italy in the 1930s, observes: 'State=political society+civil society, in other words, hegemony protected by the armour of coercion' (cited in Buci-Glucksmann 1980, 68). According to him, civil society is much more than a material sphere. It is the ideological and cultural apparatus of hegemony, an educative aspect of the state. Economic production 'creates together with itself, organically, one or more strata of intellectuals which give it homogeneity and awareness of its own function' (Buci-Glucksmann 1980, 75). Civil society, through various social and cultural associations, generates consent among the masses for the capitalist state and the general direction imposed on social life by the dominant classes (Mahajan 1999). Mahajan observes that for Gramsci,

> [T]he preponderance of civil society over the state allowed [W]estern societies to generate consent without relying heavily on direct coercion and domination. By comparison, direct intervention by the state and frequent reliance on the coercive power of the state remained the characteristic features of the east. (Mahajan 1999)

Critiquing the 'economism' of the working class movement, Gramsci asserts,

> [I]t is, therefore, necessary to combat economism not only in the theory of historiography but also in the theory and practice of politics. In this field, the struggle must be carried out on the terrain of the concept of hegemony—as it has been done in practice in the development of the theory of the political party, and in the actual history of certain political parties. (Cited in Buci-Glucksmann 1980, 73)

In other words, he finds a space within civil society to counter the hegemony.

Civil Society: Tentative Contours

With these sketchy narratives on a notion of civil society in the sphere of political theory, I construct my normative-cum-descriptive idea of civil society. The components of civil society are: (a) a public sphere in which discursive dialogue/discourse takes place among the civil society actors on the vision for 'good', 'desirable' society (idea of society/ India), coupled with sociocultural political themes for the common good; (b) secular (non-primordial) civic associations; and (c) social movements foreground moral and ethical principles for egalitarian social system by confronting and asserting the State on issues that are immediately affecting people, related to their rights and basic needs. In the process the movements develop consciousness of people for their rights and obligation for attaining the common good. These components are interrelated, and they function within the constitutional framework for a desirable society as envisaged and outlined in the Indian Constitution.

Society and civil society are not synonymous. Society is a broad, all-encompassing spectrum of social, cultural, economic and political groups. More often than not, different groups pursue private and sectarian interests. Civil society is an autonomous space from society and the State. It is an analytical site that is concerned with the common good where collective interests as against particularistic sociocultural and economic interests have primacy (Figure I.1). For that, it works and negotiates and, if necessary, confronts the State for the protection of citizens' rights and justice. It is the site of contestations of different perspectives and approaches towards a common good.

Civil society is engaged in protecting and expanding democratic values. In this process, as it is also a product of society and historical forces, it has to consciously and meticulously evolve a democratic ethos for deliberation and functioning within and across associations. The core of discourse is to provide a space for dissent and to respect disagreements, with a premise that there is no ultimate truth. In a bid to create universal character, its membership has not only to be open for everyone—female and male across caste and creed—but special efforts need to be made in expanding its space for members of subaltern communities in deliberation and participation in the organizations and movements.

It is a domain where morality and the ethical code of conduct for an individual, public persons and institutions are discursively discussed,

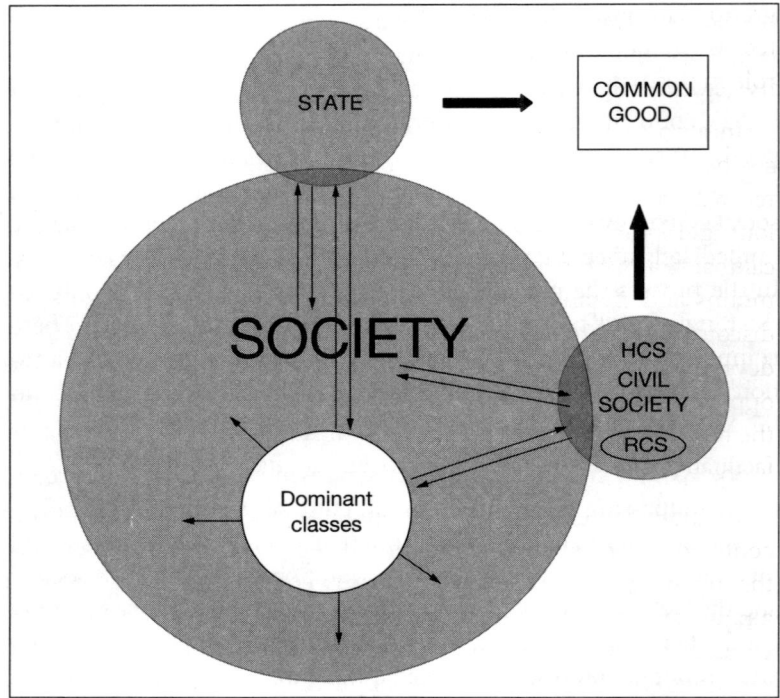

Figure I.1 *Society, State and Civil Society: Interrelationship.*

articulated and disseminated in society. Ethical life, as Hegel suggests, must not be unreflective; 'the individual must consciously understand that his real interests can be secured through universality. And inhabitants must consciously transcend particularity and acquire universality' (Chandhoke 1995, 121). While doing so, civil society requires interrogating and challenging hegemonic values that reinforce hierarchical, primordial and discriminatory values. In the process, counter-values validating equality and liberty have to be articulated, promoted, popularized and practised. With a reflective critical approach, the civil society constantly questions itself, the society, and the State on different situations on various issues concerning the common good. Its primary task is to keep watch on the observance of public morality and raise a voice and confront the State, political parties and sectarian groups subverting democratic, moral cannons. Intelligentsia committed to democratic values and the common good play an important role in this process.

In a post-colonial society like India, embedded within a feudal, socio-economic structure, civil society constantly interrogates the received cultural values that reinforce a hierarchical mindset, behaviour and structure in everyday life. And sustained deliberation and campaign around democratic values in society through various institutions and channels such as education, creative literature, public discourse, etc., are required to be worked out. Pedagogies need to be developed, in Paul Freire's (1970) terms, for conscientization of the oppressed around these values, to evolve a counter-culture contesting the hegemony. Organized struggles against injustice and exploitation facilitate conscientization and unity among the oppressed.

As discussed earlier, in a democratic society, power is not solely confined to the State; there are several centres of power in society at the micro and macro levels. Civil society contests and confronts with a range of powers such as patriarchy, dominant class, caste and religious authority for their anti-democratic values, norms, customs and sanctions which infringe individual freedom. Tentacles of dominant caste(s) and religious sects which strengthen values and relationships that perpetuate inequality in society need to be exposed to the victims. Simultaneously, counter-narratives emerging from subaltern life experiences for mutual sharing as equals need to be articulated through the creative literature and everyday discursive discourse.

Civil society and the State are not opposite to each other. As Mahajan (1999) argues, both together will ensure social equality and non-discrimination along with individual liberty. Both are concerned for the common good as envisaged in the Indian Constitution, though civil society from time to time interrogates the government(s) on its direction and vision on the common good and the priority of programmes. Education is an important agency which the dominant classes in connivance with the State use to perpetuate hegemony. At the same time, it provides a space for civil society to raise questions based on the life experiences of the students belonging to subaltern communities.

The primary task of civil society is to work as a watchdog on the functioning of the State. Civil society has to be up in arms if the State violates the liberty of the citizens and imposes unlawful restrictions on individual autonomy. Concurrently, social activists and NGOs monitor and evaluate government policies from their inception to implementation. In the process, they mediate between the State and various sections of society. Civil society initiates discourse and also interrogates the State's vision on the common good, the path of development, the process of capital accumulation, use of resources, prioritization of programmes, etc. From time to time, it critically deliberates on various issues affecting the marginalized people, and articulates alternative policies and proposals for the empowerment of the have-nots. It campaigns demanding the launch certain policies, mobilizes public opinion, and educates and builds pressure on the political class. While negotiating with the State, civil society also gets involved in policymaking process that provides opportunities to influence the State.

The core function of civil society is to critique the State. However, it need not always be negative of the government and be in a confrontation mode. It needs to get associated with the government in policy formulation and governance for effective implementation of policies that have the potentiality of empowering people. Such involvement provides opportunities to the civil society associations to understand and reflect on the changing ground reality. Engagement of the civil society associations in governance is different from that of the government agency. While availing certain services required for everyday survival, a consciousness develops in the recipients that whatever they get from the State is their right as citizens, and the services have not been doled by the government as their *mai-baap* (benevolent master). In such exercises, the activists unfold the limitations and contradictions of the capitalist system.

With a political agenda for social transformation, civil society gets engaged in political issues—raising problems, aspirations and needs of the people, injustice meted out to them, etc. In order to actualize the rights enshrined in the Indian Constitution, they need to be legalized. This is being done not only by public discourse and advocacy with policymakers but also by conscientizing people by involving them in the lawmaking process. This calls for evolving pedagogies which inculcate subalterns' political consciousness for their rights as citizens. For that, civil society supports protests and struggles against the oppressors in everyday life. While doing so, the participants of the struggles are further conscientized about the politics of the State and dominant classes. Simultaneously, along with protestors, the activists negotiate with the State—the government and judiciary—for enlarging the scope of human rights and their enforcement.

While conceptualizing and codifying justice and human rights, civil society cannot ignore subject matter of mode of production in society and its ramification on power relationships in society. Civil society has to equally address the nature of global as well as Indian capitalism and its intricate relationship with social life. The warnings expressed in the CA are that without social and economic democracy, political democracy remains fragile. The underlying assumption of neoliberal economy is that the Third World is now following something similar to the 19th-century Western utilitarian philosophy. Accordingly, every individual by her/his very nature seeks to maximize her/his own pleasure without any limit. And that is considered as the engine for economic growth, euphonically called 'development'. This premise was questioned by many across the globe in the 19th and early 20th centuries. Mahatma Gandhi rejected the idea that a man by nature is the exploiter of other human beings. Love and harmony are at the core of human nature. According to him, the multiplication of wants does not provide happiness. As a spiritualist, Gandhi strongly believed that material things do not provide happiness. One need not agree with Gandhi's metaphysical views and historical assertion on Indian culture (Shah 2011), but one cannot ignore his ethical position. More importantly, there is a consensus across political perspectives based on scientific facts and conjectures that material productions are not unlimited. Gandhi often reminded us that there is enough in nature to meet our needs but not our greed. Similarly, for a materialistic philosopher like Karl Marx, consumption was not the supreme end of society. He did not advocate the production of all kinds of so-called 'useful things'. He believed that 'the production of too many useful things result in too many useless people' (cited in Fromm 1967, 30). A campaign for self-discipline and reduction of consumption is important for developing sensitivity towards the issue. But it cannot sustain for long with an onslaught of the market which the manufacturers want for maximization of profit. This is rooted in the capitalist economic system. The State promotes the system, treating growth as 'development'. Instead of austerity, simplicity and saving, the State encourages spending through its tax structure, promotion of consumer industries, concessions and protection to capitalist industries. Civil society has to bring back the subject of mode of production in its deliberation, and work out a strategy to combat the neoliberal economy and search for an alternative within a democratic framework.

The present economic system has widened inequality. Inequality in substance hampers effective functioning of the political system and violates the liberty of those who exist at the lower layer of the social pyramid. Greater inequality results in lesser possibilities for effective and meaningful participation of the deprived sections(s) in political processes. They have less access to information, scope for deliberation and choices. Their vulnerability in social, cultural and economic spheres provides them with less space to be equal to those who are in the upper echelons of the systems of production and reproduction. The capacity of the powerful to manipulate the choices of the vulnerable is related to the extent of the gap between the two. Wider inequality hampers possibilities for the deprived to assert their voice.

Civil society's engagement in the political sphere is to negotiate and influence the State, dominant classes and society at large to pursue the common good from the perspective of the poor and exploited. Capturing the State is not its agenda. That is left to the political parties. In that sense, civil society is engaged in a non-party political process which is ongoing, irrespective of the party in power. Its function is to enlarge and strengthen democratic values and institutions.

POSSIBILITIES

My primary interest in this study is to examine the nature of civil society at an empirical level. As it is a site for contestation of ideas, it cannot be monolithic and one-dimensional. Civil society does not exist in a vacuum. It is a product of historical forces and material situations. Class character of the members due to their upbringing and surroundings is reflected in their behaviour and value system in the functioning of civil society, though some reflectively try to overcome their received mindset. The study is focused on contemporary civil society to analyse its sociocultural and ideological character(s), its notion of universality and citizen's rights, its perception of the state and its obligations towards the construction of desirable society. We shall examine the nature of the involvement of the social activists in public life, their activities, and their commitment to individual freedom and equality as well as how civil society operates at an empirical level in legitimizing or interrogating hegemonic values of dominant castes/class, deliberating and contesting development paradigm followed by the State and its alternatives. The extent and nature of their engagement in governance, developing awareness among the people for their rights, and mobilizing and supporting collective actions for their perceived injustice and rights will be probed.

At an empirical level, civil society is not a unified entity. It cannot be so in a stratified society. The unequal strength and position of various socio-economic strata, and the elite with divergent perspectives in a culturally plural, stratified society is reflected in the nature and composition of civil society. It is divided into several segments. The composition of the segments changes from time to time and from issue to issue. Their areas of activities, organizational structures and political perspectives differ. For brevity, we classify these segments into two broad categories. The one which is larger in size may be called mainstream or hegemonic civil society (HCS). We assume that its approach to attain the common good is more or less is in tune with the government of the day. It is indifferent to political economy or is posing to be apolitical. The relationship between the HCS and the State is often, but not always, benign. It functions as an ideological and cultural apparatus of the State and dominant castes/classes. By and large, it tends to tilt towards the status quo in the sociopolitical power relationship in society. On the other hand, the second segment is smaller in size and has less influence on society. Its approach towards the sociopolitical power relationship is somewhat radical (broadly Gandhian/socialist/

Ambedkarist/feminist), and it strives for changing the power relationship in society. Social activists of this segment jointly and separately negotiate and often confront the State as well as dominant castes/classes on various issues and their worldview. The segment presents a counter-hegemonic tendency. We label it as radical civil society (RCS) or peripheral civil society. The boundary between these two segments is fluid, frequently negotiating on different issues. Both the segments of civil society, irrespective of their position on neoliberal political economy, stand for a democratic system and raise voice.

Most of the social activists (including the intelligentsia—litterateurs, academics, media persons, judicial activists, etc.) of civil society (both the segments) belong to the upper strata. Thanks to their socialization in family and community/caste milieu, their life-world is rooted in Pierre Bourdieu's term upper caste/class habitus, though all of them do not necessarily represent the dominant caste/class interests and worldviews. In the process of their involvement with deprived communities, a small section of upper-caste members of RCS is consciously de-class/caste in their approach and get engaged in reflective universality. A small number of traditionally deprived communities—Other Backward Classes (OBCs), Dalits, Adivasis (including de-notified tribes) and socio-economically poor Muslims and Christians—have entered RCS.

Our empirical study is confined to Gujarat, one of the leading states of India in the neoliberal political economy. Since the beginning of the process of modernity under colonial rule, historical writings and printed literature constructed idea of Gujarat as a land of entrepreneurship. Gujarati culture has been repeatedly projected as the land of business where one could, 'sow a rupee, reap a [d]ollar' (GoG 2009). Since the formation of the state in 1960, under the national mixed-economy policy, the state evolved, what Asheema Sinha calls, '[a] bureaucratic–liberalism' model of strategic interaction with the central government to attract investment in Gujarat and also to guide investors (Sinha 2005, 92; also see Hirway, Shah and Shah 2014; Shah 2014). It has also acquired a status of 'laboratory for Hindutva'.

Like all other states, Gujarat is governed by national policies in several sectors. And India's political economy is embedded in a global market and power structure. Therefore, civil society of Gujarat is also influenced by and closely linked with national and international civil society. We shall study Gujarat's civil society in this context. The study is divided into nine chapters. This introductory chapter provides our theoretical framework and the major concepts used for unfolding empirical reality. The next two chapters are on Gujarat's civil society. A historical background of the growth of modern civil society is also provided. And we shall present a broad profile of CSOs and social activists. The third chapter is on formal education. As mentioned earlier, education is an important component of civil society for disseminating democratic values. In the past and present, social activists give importance to education for inculcating ethical values and providing opportunities to the deprived communities for their development. But at the same time, those who control the education system, the State and dominant classes use the education system to reproduce hegemonic values. The chapter examines the spread of education and the process of inclusion or exclusion of the deprived groups in the system. The next chapter is on self-employed workers engaged in informal sector and the NGOs' role in their empowerment. The fifth and sixth chapters focus on collective actions and social movements of the oppressed and other sections of society confronting the State for their rights and the common good. The next chapter is on the role of civil society on contentious issues including paradigm of the present development around the Narmada dam, and formation of a rehabilitation policy for the project-affected families (PAFs) and their resettlement and rehabilitation. The last part is an epilogue highlighting the main features of the contemporary civil society in Gujarat, and its limitations in challenging hegemonic values of the dominant forces and the State.

NOTES

1. The composition of the first elected Parliament was not significantly different from the CA in terms of caste, class, gender and education (Bhargava 2008).
2. However, all of them were not proponents of Hindutva as constructed by Savarkar. They were in favour of status quo in matters related to the economic structure.
3. Gandhi had written Foreword to the document. He wrote, 'There is nothing in it … inconsistent with what I would like to stand for' (Palshikar 2008).

4. Important reports by experts on administrative reforms were by Gorwala in 1951, Appleby in 1953 and 1956, Chanda in 1958 and Krishnamachari in 1962. The two commissions appointed by Nehru were the Das Commission in 1957 and the high-powered committee on administration under the chairmanship of Vishu Sahay in 1961.
5. Rousseau rhetorically puts it, 'The first man who, having enclosed a piece of ground, bethought himself of saying "this is mine," and found people simple enough to believe him, was the real founder of civil society' (cited in Lemos 1977, 37).

Civil Society
Historical Background

The State/political authority had a minimal role in day-to-day social affairs in pre-colonial India. Before the formation of the modern state under the British rule, social organizations at the local level enjoyed considerable independence from the State. The elders of these organizations (ethnic communities) and/or feudal lords/chieftains were regulating customs, rituals and social relationships. The Bombay Code of 1827 enacted by the British rulers recognized caste as a 'self-governing' community and accepted that the court would not interfere in 'internal affairs' of caste (Shodhan 2001). Tribes, Muslims and other religious communities were also granted a similar autonomous status in the social sphere; this legitimized caste and institutionalized religious communities as a 'discrete' category for governance. However, in the inter-community relationship in economic and social spheres, the leaders of the dominant caste/community enjoyed authority over all the inhabitants.

In urban places, different neighbourhoods called *poles* or *lattas* had their locality-based organizations of the residents to regulate civic affairs. At the city level, there were *mahajans*, that is, business guilds, whose members were not always confined to only one ethnic community and religion. In some cases, there were Hindu and Jain as well as Muslim and Parsi trading communities and artisan castes. In normal times, they were primarily concerned with their business interests including fixing wages and negotiating with the rulers about taxes and levies. During the pre-colonial as well as the colonial periods, we get instances from written records suggesting the pre-eminent position of mahajans. They used to submit the demands and grievances of the people to the political authority on behalf of all communities.

In 1844, the city mahajan led a protest of people against the government's decision to raise duty on salt from 8 *annas* (50 paise) to 1 rupee. The bazaar remained close. As the incident happened around the time of the American Revolution in the late 18th century, there was a discussion on the responsibility of rulers towards the citizens and vice versa. Durgaram, a social reformer and one of the leaders of the agitation, declared:

> It is proper for the people to petition the king, but only when the king seeks the opinion of the people before taking action. But if the king does not follow this and instead oppresses his subjects, then the people should fight the king and punish him and hand over the kingdom to another king.... A king must rule in the best interests of his people, he must empathize with his people. But instead of doing this if he opposes people, pauperizes them and favours the subjects in one area so that they may become wealthy at the expense and pauperization of subjects in another area, the people who do not follow the path of righteousness. This does not apply only to the English but to all the kings on earth. Till today, we have seen a number of tyrannical kings both in the world and in our own country. All such kings have been ousted by their subjects. (Cited in Yagnik and Sheth 2006, 73–74)

In 1848, the *mahajan* (administrator) of Surat organized a protest against the imposition of Bengal standard weights and measures on the trading community. In 1878, it also opposed the establishment of a licence tax on local business. The *mahajan* also took up a social issue against the Age of Consent Bill, 1892, prohibiting marriages of children under 12 years (Haynes 1992, 67). Besides playing a leading role in common social and economic issues, a few wealthy persons used their resources for *dan* (charity) as a religious obligation.[1] Dan also adds *abru* (prestige) in the temporal world. It also provides patronage and thereby reinforces the authority of the donor over society (Haynes 1992, 59).

Introduction of Western education by Christian missionaries and a few Samaritan British bureaucrats and merchants was catalytic in arousing aspirations among the educated for social change. The Governor of the Bombay Presidency called a public meeting in 1820 and formed the Society for the Promotion of Education of the Poor. That inspired a few of the city elite to form the Native School Book and School Society in Bombay. The objective of the organization was to spread 'modern', that is, Western, education by starting schools in different parts of the region.

Following the initial years of school education, Elphinstone College came into existence in 1827. The first generation of students belonged to the upper social strata, mainly Brahmins and *Baniyas* (Shah 2002). The college soon became a centre for young students to launch various intellectual activities by forming discussion groups. Initially, their discourse was centred around philosophy—both Western and Eastern—different religions, traditions, civilizations, rationality and social reforms. In the 1840s, the students organized a literary and scientific society *Buddhivardhak* (development of intellect) and a Gujarati *Gyan Prasarak Mandali* (an organization to spread knowledge). Though public space for discourse and reflection was formed, it however took an apolitical stand, avoiding conflict with political authority and religious establishment (Desai 1984, 315).

With the advent of modern education coupled with the printing press and communication technology, a small group of educated literary persons emerged. Embedded in their lifeworld and unreflective universality, they got engaged in creative literature—the writing of poems, stories, essays, novels, etc. By 1830s, Gujarati newspapers and journals also started publications from Bombay, Ahmedabad and Surat. The Gujarat Vernacular Society launched the publication of essays and books on Gujarat's history. The dominant caste leaders, the first generation of college educated, had attempted to standardize the Gujarati language through vernacular press and writing textbooks. While doing so, they considered their caste/community language as being 'correct'/'pure' and the standard for all. By doing so, they excluded several words and constructions used in different parts of the region by different communities. While standardizing Gujarati language, the Brahmin intellectuals excluded not only Muslims and Parsis but also members of other Hindu communities—middle and low castes—and Adivasis (Isaka 2004).

British administrators/ethnographers like James Tod and Forbes encouraged native intellectuals to write a history of their region. They believed that 'after the eighth century, every capital city had been repeatedly stormed and sacked by barbarous, bigoted, and exasperated foes'. These conquerors were ignorant of the local language and were not interested in preserving records. In his *Rasmala*, Forbes divided Gujarat's history into different periods: Rajput (Hindu), Islamic and British. In his narrative, the Hindu period was of 'glorious past', Muslim period was of 'tyranny' and British administration was benevolent. Such periodization has continued in subsequent history writing by hagiographers (Isaka 2002).

The tone and subject matter of the Gujarati literature shifted from the earlier centuries. In the 17th and 18th centuries, literati wrote prose. The poetry of the pre-British period was largely oral. They were not only composed in popular language but their themes were also related to the everyday life of cross-section of the society. The scenario of the literature changed with modern education and press. The newly formed educated class engaged in literary activities and monopolized the field of literature. Some of the writers in search of their identity got engaged in constructing a history of the region, religion and language. In their narratives of Gujarat's history, they attributed great significance to the mercantile tradition of the region. For Govardhanram Tripathi, Gujaratis were 'children of industry and enterprise' (1894 [1958]: 56). Some literati focused their work on social reforms, albeit reforms in customs of their own castes which happened to be Brahmins. Though they claimed to be writing about Gujarati 'society' and region, their worldview was confined to their caste and immediate surroundings. In fact, they use *samaj* (society) synonymously with caste.

The dominant theme of public discourse in the 19th century was *sudharo*, that is, social reform. It was a buzzword with a connotation of 'modernity'. It had different meanings for different propagandists. For Narmadashankar, known as the father of modern Gujarat, sudharo meant 'to increase physical, mental and monetary well-being of people'; for others, it meant advancement in ideas, good and efficient organization, and disciplining the mind (Patel 1988; 232–33). The spread of modern education with a view to bringing social change was a preoccupation of several of them. With the support of British officer Forbes, the Gujarat Vernacular Society, also called Gujarat Vidhya Sabha, was formed in Ahmedabad in 1848. In 1882, Gujarat College was set up in Ahmedabad. During this period, according to Dadabhai Naoroji, a leading political leader of the time, Elphinstone College was the nerve centre for social reform discourse (Seal 1971: 197).

In the sphere of social reform, the focus was on girls' education, widow remarriage, prevention of child marriage, and a transformation of customs and rituals. Later, the National Social Conference was formed in 1887 to co-ordinate social reform activities. A few organizations opposed certain practices in religious places which were exploiting women. Hindu reform organizations such as Prarthana Samaj, Arya Samaj and Brahmo Samaj also came up for reinterpreting Hinduism, replacing folk religion with institutionalized religion. Among them, Arya Samaj took up social issues such as widow remarriage, child marriage, untouchability and caste system.

More often than not, social reform programmes were confined to one's caste. As the reformers belonged to the upper social stratum, the reforms were confined to upper castes and urban areas. As a part of social reform, some upper-caste leaders began to float caste organizations with donations from the wealthy caste members to assist the poor and needy persons of their castes, particularly to encourage them to send their children to schools.[2] Later these organizations became active in regularizing and changing customs and also in providing education facilities to caste students. For example, Nagar Club came into existence in Bombay for providing facilities to Nagar students arriving in the city for appearing in an examination (Desai 1984: 318). With donations from rich persons of their caste, Khadayata Vaniyas created an education fund for their caste students.[3] Similarly, the Visnagara (Nagar) Education Fund was created. It may also be noted that some of the leading 'reformists' of their time did not believe in the caste system as such. But they also got associated with a caste-based association to bring reform from within. They felt that opposition to caste would create resistance and they would not be able to do anything in the sphere of social reform. Some avoided the issue of caste for a tactical reason, namely, to avoid confrontation with the established social power structure. They feared that if they work among the low castes and allow them in their organization without discrimination, they might lose the support of the upper and middle castes. For instance, Sahajanand, the founder of the Swaminarayan sect, said that he would not like to raise the issue of caste because that would create uproar in society and might displease his many followers (Mehta 1986, 18).

At the same time, there were voices from time to time against caste-based hierarchy and closed social order. As early as in 1840, a few youths formed the Paramhansa Mandali in Bombay. Their objective was to oppose idol worship and caste-based discrimination among the Hindus. Its members also included Muslims. It was underground because of the fear that the conservatives might disrupt their activities. A similar organization came up in Surat in 1844, propagating one universal religion and equality among all human beings—the Manav Dharm Sabha founded by a group of English-educated persons (Priyolkar 1945). It advocated that 'there was only one religion of man—the universal religion'. The Sabha published literature 'propagating the idea of unity and equality' of all human beings. Its important feature was the weekly meetings for discussion on social issues. The objective of the Sabha was to create 'enlightenment' as ignorance was the cause of unhappiness and misery (Nilkanth 1879, 62). In 1844, Durgaram asserted that man was not high or low by birth. All were equal (Nilkanth 1879, 59; Trivedi 1934). He also raised voice against *veth* (forced labour) practised by British officers (Chavada n.d.). However, the activities of the Sabha were limited to Surat. The Sabha used to meet once a week for discussion. Attendance varied from seven to seven hundred, depending on the topic. In 1862, one writer asserted for equality in the social sphere. He argued that all thinking persons would agree that all are equal before God's vision, and that everyone should follow according to God's vision. 'But if it is not followed and one does not grant equality and oppressed other fellow men in that can we say that one is following the wishes of God? No'.[4] The topic of Brahmins' oppression of the Shudras was also raised. Hope was expressed that with European education, caste-based discrimination would end.

Such views against the caste system and for equality were confined to a very small group and had limited impact. Narmadashankar has been acclaimed as the father of modern Gujarat, 'rationalism' (opposed to superstitions) and social reforms. His reforms related to widow remarriage were confined to the upper castes, as the practice of widow remarriage was not taboo in most of the communities. In his later life, he was a proponent of Varnashrama Dharma. He argued that inequality of status and ability was hereditary, and the person born as a Brahmin and Bhil cannot 'have equal status as human beings in the affairs of the world' (Suhrud 2009, 66). In fact, lone voices on humanity and equality opposing the caste system were isolated or forced to maintain silence and follow the directives of the caste councils (Raval 1987, 75–76).

By the turn of the 19th century, following the formation of the Indian National Congress, social reform (not confined to caste) organizations came into existence. One of the major groups of Indian National Congress raised the issue related to caste hierarchy and discrimination. They formed the Depressed Class League which was started in Bombay. Dalpatarai and few others started the Aryan Brotherhood, an institution analogous to the Jat-Pat-Torak Mandal (organization against caste system) of Punjab, opposing caste-based discriminations. In 1912, a few anti-caste–minded activists organized an inter-caste dinner. They invited an 'untouchable' to participate. For this, the participants had to face the wrath of the established caste leaders. Later, they apologized for their actions and underwent a purificatory, that is, *prayashchitta* (atonement), ceremony expressing remorse. Moreover, to counter the 'reform' activities, an organization Swa-sudharak Mandali was formed by Manibhai Nabhubhai. It opposed the move for inter-caste dinners, encouraged prayers and day-to-day rituals, prohibited man and woman from sitting together in caste dinners, etc. (Desai 1984, 318).

POVERTY AND INEQUALITY

The prevailing poverty in society was hardly a subject of discourse among the first generation of social reformers. One hardly finds anything printed on this subject till 1867 (Yagnik and Bhavsar 2004). In the mid-1850s, a few social commentators raised the issue of poverty. But it was referred to as poverty of India as against Europe, rather than of the poor within the country. Some argued that the rulers were interested in their own country rather than developing India. There were solitary voices like Durgaram Mehta and Daduba who believed that the reason for the poverty of the country was 'our social system in which only certain people keep arm and fight, and only *acharyas* (priests/gurus) worry about the society and people have not to do anything' (Nilkanth 1879). Occasionally moral duty of rich towards poor was talked about. For instance, in June 1856 *Buddhi Prakash*[5] published an article on 'About the Rich'. It advised the moneyed people that they should not be greedy and proud. They should strive for happiness after birth in heaven by helping the poor. The wealthy person was asked to perform charity to earn *punya* (blessing of God). It is the religious duty of the better off to help those who are in distress. Charity for the poor and needy was repeatedly emphasized as a virtue to get the blessing of God. During famine, such sermons by religious preachers as well as literary persons were expressed. Moreover, philanthropy also became a way for *seths* (wealthy merchants),

> to translate portions of their capital—the resource they possessed in greatest abundance—into authoritative relations with the British rulers.... Influential local men began donating to public causes—education; health care; the building of public facilities like clock towers, water fountains, and public gardens; and relief efforts at the time of plague, famine or flood—in quite significant quantities after the 1860s.... But they rarely abandoned old forms of gift giving, particularly religious patronage, which had long been important to their local status. (Haynes 1992, 121)

With the growth of industries in urban areas, the issue of beggars was a topic for public discussion among a small group of the intelligentsia. For them, begging was the lowest occupation, and everybody was asked to shun that. Those who were engaged in begging, including Brahmins, were asked to get engaged in labour to earn a livelihood. Public arrangements needed to be made for the homeless to provide them with shelter as was being done in England for beggars. The rich were persuaded to make a public home for disabled people as they were maintaining *pinjrapols* (caged shelters) for old and sick animals. Some leading persons including *seths* and social reformers called a meeting in Ahmedabad in December 1870 to discuss the issue of beggars. The district collector presided over the meeting. In the meeting, the Ahmedabad Spinning and Weaving Company offered a place to provide shelter and some assistance for survival to the disabled and old people who were unable to earn their livelihood. A decision was taken to establish a *dharmshala* (rest house for travellers) for the old and disabled. In order to discourage begging, arrangements for food and clothing were also made. However, care was taken to ensure that the food was cooked by a Brahmin so that no one would hesitate to take food (Patel 1988, 198–199). They found a way to express their concern for all without disturbing the traditional social ethos. Their immediate reference group was British officers and their policy. In his study on Surat, Douglas Haynes observes,

> In framing presentations of themselves as public leaders, the English-educated men indicated that their political roles were not confined to the narrow loyalties of caste and religion but embraced the interests of the city as a whole. Implicitly acknowledging the social evolutionary theories of Europe, which posited a universal tendency for societies to move from collectivities organized along local and primordial lines to their own emergence marked a new stage in Surat's political development. (1992, 151)

With the growth of industries in the early 20th century, Ahmedabad witnessed frequent incidents of violent disruption of work in the factories. Long working hours, pathetic living conditions, inadequate infrastructure facilities and low wages were the causes of labour unrest. In the early 1890s, when the mills introduced wage cuts, labour protested and there was an almost complete shutdown of mills. There were two strikes in Surat textile mills in 1882 which were considered as 'the earliest strikes for which authentic data are available' (Lakha 1988, 99). Surprisingly such a wide and frequent unrest of workers did not receive much attention in the public discourse of the educated elite except occasional moralizing to wealthy to donate for the needy to earn *punya* or God's blessings. The agitator workers were advised to shun their habit of drinking.

In the midst of increasing unrest among the unorganized working class, there were stray writings in journals on the poor labouring class. One of the articles in 1895 asserted that 'we should think how to save and rescue the poor and ignorant from the ocean of sin and unhappiness'. The author reminded that 'the reason for our happiness is their all kinds of a labour of the poor...the happiness of others depends on the toiling labour of these workers'. He then reminded that 'as we care for our happiness, we should give thought to the condition of poor. If we do not do that we will close doors for our own happiness' (*Buddhiprakash*, February 1895).

Later, the journal published an article, based on the 1901 census data, revealing that nearly 85 per cent of the population survived on labour and lived in pathetic condition. The author pleaded that they constitute the core of society, and their condition could not be ignored (Desai 1910). Such expressed concerns for the condition of the vast majority were few and far between, but not absent.

Gujarat experienced its worse famine in 1898, called the Chapaniyo Dukar. The death of a large number of poor peasants due to starvation was reported in newspapers and journals. In literary writings, sensitive litterateurs expressed the condition of hardship faced by people. The elite pressurized the government to provide relief to the victims. It was warned that hunger was such a condition in which the most docile people were forced to revolt against the State. Some leaders persuaded the government to use all its resources and also raise resources from England to provide food and water to the poor affected by the famine (Thakar 1899).

PUBLIC INSTITUTIONS

With the formation of the Indian National Congress in 1885 and the National Social Reform Conference in 1886, nationalism and social reform got intermingled. Civic space got expanded. A number of social associations combined social reform with relief work and education.[6] Simultaneously, local organizations were formed to mediate between people and the State, by articulating grievances of the people against public authority and building pressure on the State to resolve them. These organizations were Surat Praja Samaj, the district association, and Praja Hitvardhak Sabha (Society for the Advancement of People's Welfare) in Surat; Dukh Nivaran Mandali (an organization to resolve pain and unhappiness) in Bharuch; and The Ahmedabad

Association in Ahmedabad. These organizations were confined to urban areas. In rural areas, dominant peasant communities, following the Co-operative Credit Societies Act in 1904, had begun to form co-operative credit societies and banks to meet their credit needs and to come out from the clutches of moneylenders (Catanach 1970). Though they began with economic activities, some of the co-operative societies gradually became a nucleus for public activities. They worked as a catalytic agency for middle caste peasants to enter public life.

WIDENING OF CIVIL SOCIETY: EMERGENCE FOR LARGER CONCERN

The process of widening of public space accelerated with the arrival of Mohandas Gandhi in Gujarat. The vocal section of the public arena was waiting for someone like him who could provide leadership in Gujarat. But there was hardly any discussion in any journal or public forum on his magnum opus *Hind Swaraj*, published in 1910 in Gujarati. However, his public activities in South Africa were known in Gujarat. When he was imprisoned in South Africa in 1893 for his campaign against the Asiatic Registration Bill, the Gujarat Sabha organized a public meeting, chaired by Chimanbhai Lalbhai, a textile mill owner in Ahmedabad, and expressed support for him. In 1911, when his name was proposed for the position of president of the Congress, the elite of Gujarat extended their support to him (Mehta 2005). He returned to India for good in 1914. Gujaratis, particularly those who were active in the public arena of Bombay, gave him a warm reception. He then moved to Ahmedabad and decided to settle there for his future public activities. He chose Ahmedabad for three reasons. First and foremost was his own identity as a Gujarati. He believed that it would facilitate him to communicate in his mother tongue with local people. Second, he assumed that as the city was 'an ancient centre of handloom weaving, it was likely to be the most favourable field for the revival of the cottage industry of hand spinning'. Third, he hoped that he would receive monetary support from the wealthy persons of Gujarat (CWMG 1969, 291). Though the first public function in his honour was presided over by Chinubhai Madhavlal, knighted in 1910, recipient of Baronet honour and the first President of Ahmedabad Mill-owners Association (Spodek 2011), most of the businessmen were not warm towards him and were wary of his politics. They were afraid that their association with Gandhi would displease the British and, consequently, their interests might be hampered. He was not surprised by their attitude, as he observed in the *Hind Swaraj*: 'Moneyed men support British rule; their interest is bound up with its stability' (1938, 95). His views on businessmen's interests changed slightly, and he began to see them as torchbearers for social development. He observed in 1917,

> It is my view that until the business community takes charge of all public movements in India, no good can be done to the country.... If businessmen elsewhere start taking livelier interest in political agitation, as you in Ahmedabad are doing, India is sure to achieve her aim. (CWMG 13, 510)

He established his ashram on the banks of river Sabarmati. His mission for political activities was the country's freedom. He believed that it could not be attained without involving cross-sections of society in the struggle. Along with political issues confronting the State, he emphasized on taking up the issues of poverty, marginalization and humiliation. He began by taking up the social issue of the practice of untouchability. He not only embraced the dress code of the poor—a loin cloth—but also adopted a Dalit daughter in his ashram. In his first political conference in Godhara in 1917, he organized a public meeting in a Dalit locality and gave a call to start a school for *bhangi* (lowest of the low, sweeper community) children. With his efforts, a residential school for *atyanjs* (Dalit or untouchables) came into existence in Nadiad. However, a major section of civil society was indifferent to untouchability. In fact, Gandhi was almost warned that he would lose financial support for his views and his action of adopting a Dalit girl. But he did not compromise. He decided to move his ashram to one of the Dalit neighbourhoods in Ahmedabad. In the midst of opposition from the most of the business people and community, one industrialist at the last moment privately came to his help. Later other conservative wealthy Hindus followed (CWMG 10, 333).

Karuna, Seva and Rachnatmak Kam (Compassion, Service and Constructive Work)

Unlike most of the elite of public life of the time, Gandhi did not believe in the separation between social and political issues. From the beginning, his political activities as mentioned earlier were not devoid of social services. Nor did he believe in the precedence of one over another. For him, both—social and political work—should be carried out simultaneously. That was the reason he later emphasized 'constructive work' for the Congress members in general and his disciples in particular. His notion of 'constructive' work was social service based on the principle of non-violence as well as communal harmony. Compassion for the poor and deprived was a guiding thrust of his sociopolitical philosophy. Quoting the Gita, Gandhi used to tell his followers that a true *bhakta* (devotee) of God is one who gets engaged in serving society. He saw God in the poor and called him daridranarayana (espousing that service to the poor is equivalent to service to God).

Gandhi was not the first public figure to focus on service to the poor. The notion of *seva* (service to one's society/community) gained currency in the last quarter of the 19th century due to religious leaders like Swami Vivekananda. In 1905, Gopal Krishna Gokhale and his three friends formed the Servants of India Society (SIS) in Pune. Its objective was to support 'selfless and intelligent' workers who were willing to dedicate their life to serve the public cause— underprivileged, rural and tribal people, relief work in flood, famine and other disasters. 'Its members frankly accept the British connection as ordained in the inscrutable dispensation of Province, for India's good' (cited in R. Srivatsan 2006). Amritlala Thakkar was the first person from Gujarat to join the SIS in 1914. He accepted to devote his life for the service of the deprived. During the first five years, he worked in drought relief work in Uttar Pradesh (UP) and Gujarat, and in welfare work among the labourers of Tata Company in Jamshedpur. In 1918–1919, he worked for drought relief for the Adivasis (tribes) in the Panchamahals district. He then decided to settle in the tribal area to carry out educational and social welfare work to uplift the Adivasis. He invited college students to work among the tribes to impart education during their vacations. Later in 1922, he launched an organization known as the Bhil Seva Mandal (BSM) to work among the Adivasis of the Dahod and Zalod areas of the Panchamahals district. He announced his plan and invited 12 dedicated workers to commit to spending at least three years in the area. Four youths—three from Gujarat and one from Maharashtra—responded to the call. Gandhi also encouraged a few of his disciples to settle in tribal areas as a part of his constructive work to uplift Adivasis so as to bring them into the mainstream life and culture. They were called constructive workers. Like Thakkar, many of them maintained distance from the political programmes of the freedom movement.

Adivasis

The non-tribals, particularly upper-caste Hindus, used to call Adivasis (nearly 14 per cent of the population) as *kaliparj* (black people). Caste Hindus claimed themselves as *ujaliyat* (white people). They looked down on the tribals, often called as *jangali* (literally means stupid and rough, having no 'good' manners). There was some contempt for their habits and culture. Though the Gandhian social workers did not have contempt for Adivasis, they were however not free from cultural bias against the tribal way of life. They had a patronizing attitude towards them. Their agenda for social and economic reform of the tribal belief system and life had upper-caste cultural underpinnings. The reformers believed that social customs, rituals and beliefs of tribals related to their marriage, birth and death were 'backward' and needed changes in the line of the mainstream albeit dominant caste Hindus to which reformers themselves belong. They believed that one of the reasons for backwardness was ignorance. And that could be removed through formal education.

The first residence school—an Ashram school—was started with four Bhil children at Mirakhedi in a small cottage. In a year's time, seven such Ashram schools were started in the area. In the first decade, on an average 500 Adivasi children were taught in these schools. As Thakkar believed that Adivasis were part of Hindu society, he opposed their conversion to Christianity (Navjivan 1926). The BSM's educational curriculum emphasized on imparting religious *sanskar* (moral values). He got Ramayan translated in Bhili dialect and also built a Ram temple in 1926. In his message conveying a blessing to the construction of the temple, Gandhi said:

> [W]ill feel God's presence and resolve to give up eating meat and drinking and be filled with new life. The building of the temple, however, is but the beginning of our service to them, not its end. There are many things we can do to serve them. (CWMG 30, 311; see also R. Srivatsan 2006, 431)

Though BSM initially received financial support from Atyanj Seva Mandal formed by Gandhi, it did not join political activities of the freedom movement. Thakkar believed that social service work had to be kept away from politics. He persuaded his colleagues not to join the civil disobedience movement in 1931.

During this time, political activities for freedom were in full swing. The Congress selected Bardoli to launch a passive resistance movement for 'no tax payment'. Several students of the Gujarat Vidhyapith, started by Gandhi in 1920 to train public workers, reached Bardoli for the work of the proposed Satyagraha. Though the Satyagraha was postponed, two of the activists—Chunibhai Mehta and Jugatram Dave—continued their work in the area. The main activity was to spread Khadi spinning activity among the people. They concentrated their work among the Adivasis who constituted nearly 50 per cent of the population of the district. Raniparaj[7] (Adivasi) Vidyalaya was started in Bardoli Ashram to impart education to tribal boys. In 1929, it shifted to Vedchhi in the mist of the tribal population. In the course of time, Vedchhi became the centre of socio-economic and, unlike BSM, political activities among the Adivasis of the region. Adivasis were mobilized in the 1928 Bardoli Satyagraha (Shah 1974). The activities were focused on (a) khadi, (b) education and (c) economic programme. The concept of spinning and wearing khadi was self-reliance in one's own basic needs. Clothing was one of them. It aimed at providing occupation for livelihood and also to inculcate simplicity and self-reliance in lifestyle. These activities were intermittently disrupted by political participation, which involved imprisonment of the workers and/or confiscation of the ashram by the British government. The main activities of the ashram were social reform related to Sanskritizing their way of life by changing their customs and belief system, like that of the dominant castes, spinning for livelihood and education. The objectives of the education were to develop (a) awareness and consciousness for self-dignity and freedom from tyranny of landed class,[8] (b) skill to learn livelihood and (c) intellect. Post Independence, the activities of Gandhians have continued to remain the same—to bring the Adivasis into the mainstream albeit upper-caste Hindu culture (Gandhi 1962). These activities created a small upward mobile Sanskritized class in the pre-Independence period, but the Gandhians could not penetrate tribal society. Participation of the Adivasis in the Bardoli Satyagraha was negligible despite the concentrated efforts of the Gandhians by invoking traditional tribal idioms (Shah 1974). In the 19th and early 20th centuries, they had often revolted against imposition of British and Maratha administrative regulation which was encroaching forest land. They struggled against the dominance of non-tribal traders, Hindu reformers and Christian missionaries by employing different modes of resistance (Hardiman 1987).

Ex-untouchables

As mentioned earlier, Gandhi gave priority to uplift a socially outcaste community called *achhut* or atyanj. Under the guidance of Gandhi and the initiative of Thakkar, the Atyanj Seva Mandal was launched in 1921. Thakkar was its chairman. It was active in propagating against the practice of untouchability. Later it became a part of the Harijan Sevak Sangh in 1932. Parikshitlal Majmudar and Mama Fadke worked among the Dalits, teaching them cleanliness and other 'reformed' (Sanskritized) habits. They also introduced some economic and educational activities.

In 1932, Gandhi renamed Atyanj as Harijan, 'a man of God'. Gandhi told 'Harijan' workers that instead of confronting caste-Hindus they should reform themselves by changing their habits and lifestyle. He and other Gandhian workers advised them for 'promoting cleanliness and hygiene, improving scavenging and tanning method, giving up carrion, beef and liquor, abolishing practice of untouchability among themselves and sending children to schools' (CWMG 57 1932, 411).

At the same time, alternative approach to untouchability and caste system was in vogue since the mid-19th century. By this time, a section of the depressed classes was asserting their political rights. In Pune, Kamble from the depressed classes formed an Indian National Anti-revolutionary Party to work against the Congress and to support the British rule until the complete removal of untouchability and the overthrow of the school of *Chaturvarna* (four-fold Varna system) had been achieved (Zelliot 1969). In the 1910s, when Gandhi's leadership began to emerge, Dr Ambedkar was also emerging as radical Dalit leader in Maharashtra. In 1919, he submitted a memorandum to the government demanding voting rights for the depressed classes. In 1920, he started a fortnightly *Muknayak* (silent protagonist) to give voice to the problems of Dalits. The next year, he established Bahiskrut Hitkarini Sabha (Organization for Welfare of the Untouchables) to which few Dalits from Gujarat were attracted and became active. In 1925, Ambedkar declared a manifesto of human rights for the untouchables. He provided an alternative worldview than that of Gandhi's to the restive Dalits of the first generation of the textile workers. Under Ambedkar's influence, a few Dalit organizations, outside the orbit of the Congress, were formed in different cities such as Ahmedabad, Navsari and Baroda. Disregarding Gandhi's advice for repentance, self-improvement, self-pity and waiting for compassion of the dominant classes, they asserted for equality in status. In 1928, Shri Dariyapur Atyanj Hitvadhak and Subodhak Mandali and Dariyapur Navyuvak Mandal were formed that later started hostels for Dalit students. In 1931, when Dr Ambedkar visited Ahmedabad, they organized a reception in honour of Dr Ambedkar. They gave him *manpatra* (felicitation letter) with the following citation:

> We feel very happy and joyous to welcome you in the capital of Gujarat and we find no words to express our joy.... We are grateful to you for your self-sacrifice and tireless labour in launching continuous struggle. Looking to the behaviour in the past and today of the upper caste Hindus towards us it is easy to understand that if we want to have our existence today and the free India we have to stand on our own feet and strengthen the struggle for our rights. They call us Bhai (brother) but we smell selfishness in it. This is the best opportunity for them to strengthen their position. Where

is so called equality?... Our children are not allowed to get admission in the schools. Is this equality? Even in this just British raj they behave in this way what would be their behaviour in the free India? In this situation we have to learn ourselves to demand independently for our rights. We are sure that you will help us in this task. You have awaken us and taught us how to fight the caste Hindus. (Mehta 2003)

Many Dalit activists, including leading Congressmen, though with Gandhi and the Congress, were not discarding Ambedkar's views. A vocal section of Dalits was caught between Ambedkar and Gandhi. They were unable to come out of the hegemonic perspective that many upper-caste persons had worked for their betterment and that they would be would be useful to their caste and future generation by remaining Hindu (Shah 1975). With this perspective, some educated atyanjs under Gandhi's influence formed the Dalit Harijan Samaj (DHS) in 1925 for promoting education and economic activities among their caste brethren. The DHS had the patronage of the Congress party as well as of the Textile Labour Association (TLA). To counter Gandhi's influence, the Ambedkarist Dalits started the Depressed Classes Hostel and invited Dr Ambedkar for its inauguration. But his visit to Ahmedabad was stormy. Some Dalits and non-Dalits shouted slogans at the railway station: 'Ambedkar Go Back'. At the same time, Dalits—both Gandhians and Ambedkarists—organized a public reception of Ambedkar. The Gandhian Dalits, however, made it clear that they were honouring Ambedkar because he belonged to their community and working for their upliftment, and not because of his political views. It was unequivocally emphasized that 'a majority of atyanjs follow Mahatmaji (Gandhi) and the Congress'. An average Dalit was in a dilemma as one of the Gandhian workers and Municipal member used to say to the Congress leaders, 'though we are with you, we feel that whatever Ambedkar is saying is true. We are with you and we also support him' (Mehta 2005). Notwithstanding such dilemmas, most of the Dalits in Gujarat were following Gandhi.

Other Deprived Communities

Ravishankar Maharaj, widely known as a constructive Gandhian worker of Gujarat, joined Gandhi in 1919. His compassion for the poor and deprived was reflected in his dialect, dress and lifestyle, and his work was unparalleled among the Gandhian constructive workers. As he succeeded in persuading some thieves to shun stealing, Gandhi advised him in 1922 to serve 'backward' castes like the Patanvadiya and Bareeya. Gandhi wanted these people to shun their occupation of 'robbery'. He advised them in 1920 that it was better to commit suicide and starve than live by robbery (CWMG 1970, 385). At the same time, he did realize that

> Really speaking the depredations of dacoits are reflections of the theft committed by the rich. The subtle theft of the latter becomes, with the dacoits, physical robbery. The reformers, therefore, will have to take in hand both the rich and the poor, the subtle dacoit and the one who commits physical robbery. Only then can the desired results be achieved. This is the work of 'acharyas', fakirs, sannyasis and the like. They have it in them to become the true protectors and guardians of the morality of society, and it is their job, therefore, to end the evil of dacoity. (Hardiman 1981, 176)

Following Gandhi's direction to work for the deprived communities, Ravishankar felt that 'their (Bareeya and Patanvadias) poverty should be eradicated. Their dirt is removed, their bad habits are changed', and for that he had to live with them. Questions arose in his mind,

> Why should they not indulge in stealing? Have our (upper caste) wealthy people spared any opportunity to exploit them? Why do they not drink and make quarrels? The expenses and labour that we incur for our children for their education and training, have we done anything for their children? What is a wonder if they do not have a wide perspective, they do not have an idea about the country and the world? Has anybody gone and talked to them? (Mehta 1955, 19–20)

Though he acknowledged that moneylenders were responsible for their perpetual poverty and misery, his emphasis was on righteous life and good behaviour (towards moneylenders/dominant stratum) on the part of the oppressed. Maharaj advised the poor and deprived, 'we should create a situation where we need not have to borrow from them. This is possible if we live economically and give education to our children' (Mehta 1955, 99). With such perspective, he tried to mobilize resources to start schools and hostels, but the response from the wealthy class was cool. He then motivated Patanvadias to organize caste *parishads* (conference) to bring social reforms in the community. He gave lectures on the Gita, preaching that the Gita teaches that everyone should do one's duty with sincerity without expecting the fruits of their labour (Maharaj 1984).

Moreover, while working at the grassroots level, a few Gandhian activists experienced limitations of relief work. They felt the need for long-term planning and an institutional approach. But that was not a priority for the leaders who controlled the organizations. For instance, after working in famine relief in 1921, Indulal Yagnik, who had radical views, felt that the activists (constructive workers) should not engage in firefighting during the famine. They should evolve an institutional base among the backward castes. After starting atyanj schools in Godhara, Nadiad and Mirakkhedi, he proposed to start more schools in other areas. Yagnik submitted a budget for these schools to Vallabhbhai Patel, the Gujarat Congress president, demanding ₹5,000. His proposal was turned down. Patel considered that the suggestion of starting a new free boarding school for lower caste students was whimsical. He asserted that though the Congress had launched a campaign against untouchability, it had not given a directive to start expensive institutions. Yagnik argued:

> How long can we go on staring at the defenceless, half-naked Bhils being hurled into hunger time and again on account of scarcity, and robbed by the government and the moneylenders? Instead of digging a well when the fire takes place every year, it is not our duty to educate the children of these people, to prepare service-minded workers from among them and to make them strong enough to self-reliant with their help? If the present destitution and misery of the Bhils are to continue forever, what is the meaning of Swaraj for them? Has not Gandhiji thought of Swaraj from the point of view of the common people? ... how can we uplift the untouchables by merely mixing with them in our meeting and processions? ... Could we develop a powerful new nation by merging the crores of untouchable people merely by explaining to the caste people about the superficial removal of untouchability? (Pathak, Spodek and Wood 2011, 23)

His argument did not convince the Congress leadership. Gandhi also could not help him. Out of disgust, Yagnik resigned as the secretary of the provincial Congress.

RADICAL APPROACH

As mentioned earlier, by the turn of the 19th century, unrest among the newly formed industrial workers was increasing, resulting in spontaneous strikes and disruption of work. The conflict between the workers and the owners worsen in 1917. Gandhi played a crucial role in mediating the conflict between the two in 1918. Under his guidance, labour union called the Majoor Mahajan (or the TLA) was formed. The central thrust of the TLA has been to maintain a harmonious relationship between the capital and labour, which remained a dominant concern of the civil society in the following years (Patel 1988). To buttress the approach, philanthropists, patronized by the industrialists, carried out some welfare work to lessen hardship of the workers. They used to advise workers to lead a simple and religious life and shun vices like drinking.

There were, however, voices of dissent within the mainstream and also on its periphery, raising issues of discrimination and exploitation. Such voices in different tunes and actions were expressed by Ranchhod Das Lotwala, Indulal Yagnik, Sumant Mehta, Kamlashankar Pandya, etc. Lotwala sponsored lectures and writings on socialism between 1914 and 1918. Yagnik organized *guamsta*s (shop attendants), tenants and sweepers for their rights. Sumant Mehta observed that with the growth of textile industries in urban areas of Gujarat, wealth was increasingly being concentrated with a few. A section of the middle class was getting the benefits of such development at the cost of the vast peasantry and urban poor. The newly prospering class of Gujarat had shaped political life to suit their interests. Gandhi's idea of class collaboration facilitating capitalism suited them. Mehta believed that the labour organizations were formed for reforming the labour. It was out of compassion rather than giving them their rights. With such political perspective, he and others organized the conference of the poor and landless peasants and working class of urban areas in 1935 (*Prajabandhu*, 23 June 1935). Patel strongly opposed such views. He wrote to his followers: 'I am confident that seasoned workers of Gujarat will have no time or taste for indulgence in dreams of remote idealism'. He warned socialist leaders not to interfere in his work of Gujarat. At a public meeting in Ahmedabad he gave a stern warning that, unlike Gandhi, who was kind even to his enemies, he would deal roughly with anyone who came in his way and tried to undo what the Congress had done. He did not hesitate to admit that in the struggle for freedom, the well-being of capitalists, landlords and princes should also be enlisted (Shankardass 1988, 118–119). Patel sidetracked and marginalized all workers of the Congress socialist group within the party.

Against such resistance, the Kisan Sabha was formed. Indulala Yagnik, Dinkar Mehta, Niru Desai and Kakkalbhai Kothari were the members of the executive committee of the Gujarat unit of the Sabha in 1936. The Sabha mobilized poor peasants, sharecroppers and tenants in Kheda and Ahmedabad districts and in Saurashtra. Adivasis in general and the *halis* (bonded labourers) were mobilized under the banner of Kisan Sabha on the eve of the Haripura Congress in 1938. Slogans like 'Inquilab Zindabad' (Long live the revolution), 'Kisan Sabha Zindabad' (Long live the Kisan Sabha), 'Adh Bhagni Pratha Nabud Karo' (Down with the system of half of share) and 'Hali Pratha Murdabad' (Death to the system of hali, indentured labour) were raised in public forums. The Congress leadership warned the Congressmen to keep away from the activists of the Sabha and the agitation politics. Gandhi himself was critical of the radical agitators. Radical activists were marginalized in the public life of Gujarat.

LITERARY

On the eve of Gandhi's entry to Gujarat civil society, the Gujarati creative literature was dominated by upper castes, largely educated Brahmins. Like their predecessors of the 19th century, one of their preoccupations was reinventing their collective *aaporakh* (self-identity), the identity of Gujarati language and society. Such endeavour has continued thereafter also (Sitanshu 2008). As these writers belonged to a very narrow upper stratum of society and received modern English education, their exposure to larger societal issues was limited. Their lifeworld was their universe. Considering themselves as creative writers, many believed that they were gifted with ideas and their responsibility was to develop the literature, no matter whether it was read by laypersons or not. The Gujarati Sahitya Parishad (GSP), an association of writers formed in 1905, faced the tension between popularity of their writings and excellence. Govardhanram Tripathi, the president of the first conference of the GSP, said that the purpose of the Parishad would be to expand the scope of the literature and also make the literature popular. But this view was not shared by many others. The chairman of the fifth conference in 1915, Narsinhrao, believed that the GSP should be limited only to learned persons. He believed that they should focus on creating 'pure' literature, free from prevailing affairs in society. Their writings circumscribed with individual romanticism, eulogized ancient Hindu culture, feudal lords' extravaganza and courtier's intrigues rather than the prevailing problems faced by common persons and their aspirations concerned with everyday life. 'They were not affected by the social transformation which is being experienced in India and world over', Umashankar Joshi observed (cited in Mehta 2011). Gandhi called upon the literary persons to write for labourers and toiling people so as to improve their language. In 1936, as the president of the GSP, he once again persuaded them to write about things which village people could understand. His appeal did influence a few who were also participating in the freedom movement. Some of them romanticized village life, some others depicted life of poor peasants, labourers, hawkers, women, etc. They carried Gandhi's idea on poverty and social harmony. Rita Kothari observes,

> As far as the literary manifestation is concerned, poverty in Gandhian literature almost always ties up with nobility. The virtue of nobility is either with the upper-class who despite being rich helps the poor, exemplifying the Gandhian principle of essential goodness and charity, or sometimes with the poor, who despite being poor rises above the rich and withstands temptations…. By eliding over the economic root of poverty, Gujarati literature turns poverty in social problem like betrayal in love, or unhappy relationships an issue that could be sorted out by goodwill. (2004)

Among Gandhians, there were a few exceptions, however, who took a radical position in their writings. Under the chairmanship of Premchand they formed the Progressive Literature Sangh at a national level. Its chapter was formed in Gujarat in which litterateurs such as Ramanlal, Sundram, Bhogilal and Umashankar were active (Mehta

2011). Umashankar in his poem *Jathargani* (hunger) in 1932 asked how long the poor and hungry would tolerate their plight. He indicated that when they revolt, they would smash all the monuments created by the wealthy. Several poems of Meghani caught the imagination of the urban youths, working class and poor peasants. He called upon the starving masses to get awakened to get justice. He told them that the earth is to be ruled by '[t]he true labourers, farmers, miners, physical labourers, and Not for those who have grown fat, and wealthy, and educated by drinking the blood of the poor is this place'.

Post-Independence

After Independence, the literary scenario has not changed much. A circuit of a small group of litterateurs who were radical and addressed issues affecting the common person had sunk in the 1950s and 1960s. Rasiklal Parikh, the president of the 39th GSP's conference in 1963, expressed his anxiety that Gujarati literature was not able to build an organic relation with society. He reminded that when Gandhi in 1920 and 1936 had asked literati to be people-oriented, he did not mean compromise excellence in the creative writing. He asked to create good literature which is also people-oriented. He called for the literati persons to get oriented to people, and to understand their culture and life. But this had not happened thereafter. According to him, the mainstream literati had been alienated from society. They had been influenced by abstract, and most modernist literature developed elsewhere irrespective of their congruence with Gujarati society. Some feel alienation from society and feel that in such a modern life with full of agony, it would be a laughing stock to write about commitment, concerned and ideal (Joshi 2004).

There was hardly any discourse in Gujarat among the public intellectuals on political economy. A large section of civil society which enjoys hegemony because of the scale of activities in public sphere calls its work as apolitical. It does not take a position on contentious issues. There had been no sociopolitical movement focusing on 'the common good' and/or deprived sections of society to influence the mainstream literature. The movements that the region witnessed have been essentially of middle class, focusing on emotional issues such as corruption and the revivalist politics of Hindutva. However, Dalit and feminist social movements that emerged in the 1970s and 1980s created a small circle of creative writers highlighting the issues of injustice, inequality, discrimination and humiliation. They have carved out a space for Dalit and feminist literature. However, though there are a few Adivasi litterateurs, their presence is not yet visible.

CONCLUSION

Public space has expanded considerably during the last two decades, but the dominance of upper castes continues. Members of the middle and lower strata of different castes and religious denomination including women had entered a domain of civil society at different stages before Independence. Their size in terms of number has expanded post Independence but, except for middle castes, their presence is still on the periphery. During the freedom movement and thereafter, most of the voluntary associations engaged in philanthropic welfare work for the marginalized people have remained apolitical. While doing so, they have reinforced traditional hierarchical values. Such constructive as well as political activities randomly produced and reproduced Brahminical and mahajan (mercantile) values. Most of the activists perceive these values as universal and normal. They have compassion for the poor and deprived persons. Empathy towards the oppression is rare, making them unable to see humiliation and agony that the oppressed experience in everyday life. Hence, they do not identify with the subalterns. The poor are often made to blame themselves for their deprivation—lacking education, low motivation and entrepreneurship, and their way of life. While taking the cause of the poor, even demanding justice, upper-caste activists more often than not have a patronizing mindset and approach. Pragmatism and compromise as a norm in public life and social relationship are valued. They avoid discussion on conflict inbuilt in capitalist structure between labour and capital and power relationship and values of patriarchal system. At the same time, the dominance of the upper caste and their hegemony has always been challenged within civil society by RCS, a small segment.

NOTES

1. The concept of charity for others has been rooted in morality preached in religion. It has been taught that 'wealth is fundamentally positive', that it brings certain social obligations. Morality tells: 'If a man gives a hungry man a bread, which is much, all the good work, which he performs through that satiety, becomes as it were his own as if done by his own hand' (quoted by Kulke, 1978).
2. 'Nyatbhaionu Kalyan ichcava Vishe', *Buddhi Prakash* Vol. 4, no. 4, April 1857, pp. 52–55.
3. *Buddhi Parkash,* Vol. 30, no. 4, April 1883, p. 12.
4. 'Amerikana Gulamo vishe', *Buddhi Prakash* Vol. IX, February 1862, p. 47.
5. *Buddhi Prakash*, Vol. III, no. 4, 1856.
6. The concept of charity for others has been rooted in morality preached in religion. It has been taught that 'wealth is fundamentally positive', that it brings certain social obligations. Morality tells: 'If a man gives a hungry man a bread, which is much, all the good work, which he performs through that satiety, becomes as it were his own as if done by his own hand' (quoted by Kulke, 1978).
7. Gandhi called the people living with the wild animals as the *raniparaj*. This has a connotation of brave people.
8. One of the poems spontaneously constructed by students of Sarbhan Ashram was: 'Now we will learn, now we will read books; now we will become free, now we will not tolerate abuse of any one!' (Narayan Desai 1984: 128, 184).

Civil Society Organizations and Social Activists

Civil society organizations are large in number. Some are formed ad hoc around an event/issue and disappear after some time. Several are informal with no identifiable structure and constitution. Their objectives vary from recreation to public policy advocacy, and from delivering services to mobilization for rights. We confine to those voluntary organizations which are non-government and non-profit-making. These are those who profess to engage with government's 'developmental' work, including those which do not subscribe to the government's premise on 'development', and strive for structural change in the political economy and engage in mobilizing people for their rights.

According to the Government of India (GoI), there are 3.081 million NGOs in the country (*ToI* 2014). In Gujarat, over 200,000 organizations are registered with the charity commissioner under the Societies Registration Act, 1860, or the Bombay Public Trusts Act, 1950.[1] Of them, nearly 17 per cent are registered as religious organizations. Many caste associations[2] have also been registered under this category. The available data do not tell us how many of them are active today and what their activities are. The majority of them do not submit an annual financial statement as required by the Act.

In an exploratory survey in 2008, we found that some of the registered organizations were untraceable. It was found that several of the charitable trusts formed in the memory of family members are defunct after the registration. For some, registration of the organization is a device to stash funds from family assets to save on taxes and, at the same time, to oblige relatives by distributing school texts and notebooks, etc., to their children as a 'public purpose'. Such activities enhance their social status of doing charity.

Gujarat has a relatively higher number of development NGOs as compared to most other states in India. According to the Development Alternatives Information Network (DAINE) directory, the number of NGOs in proportion to the population is higher in Gujarat than in other states excluding Delhi, Chandigarh and the small states in the North East. According to the Ministry of Home Affairs, GoI, 26,404 NGOs were registered under the Foreign Contribution Regulation Act, 1976 (FCRA), until 2000.[3] Of these, 16,590 declared that they received funds from foreign donors. The highest number of such organizations (2,638) was in Tamil Nadu. Gujarat stood at number eight, with 761 NGOs receiving ₹2.72 billion.

In 1980s, we (with Das) carried out a survey of 252 NGOs to capture a broad profile of the functionaries working in the field of 'development' in general and focusing on poor in particular. I have updated this survey by collecting information from 79 NGOs that had not been covered earlier. Eighty-seven per cent of these had come into existence after 1988. For the present chapter, we have collated both data.

COVERAGE OF POPULATION AND ACTIVITIES

Development NGOs cover a small area, barely 3 per cent of the villages. A majority of them (53 per cent) work only in rural areas; only 6 per cent confine their work to urban areas. The remaining 41 per cent work in both rural and urban areas. Most of them carry out a number of programmes related to economic activities around the issues of livelihood—land, wages, skill development, self-employment, credit, etc.—and also health, education and water. Health care is the main concern for one-fifth of the NGOs. Some are engaged in issues of water (drinking and irrigation) and environment. However, a few organizations focus on rights- and development-related issues of a specific social section, such as women, Dalits, Adivasis and de-notified tribes, and/or specific occupational strata, such as salt workers, migrant farm and non-farm labour, construction workers, etc. These organizations have also formed a network federation to support each other, and share experiences and resources. Most of the organizations profess that 'awareness building' is a part of their activities. The meaning of 'awareness', however, varies from providing information about the schemes and procedures to get benefits to developing consciousness about the right of an individual as a citizen.

THE PERIOD OF THEIR FORMATIONS

The participation of voluntary groups in community development programmes, such as building tanks and channels, forest plantations, etc., is not a new phenomenon. During the colonial period, they built schools and health centres and provided relief at the time of natural calamities. As discussed in Chapter 1, during the freedom movement, the Gandhian constructive workers formed voluntary associations for the welfare of the poor. A few public-spirited Samaritans had also undertaken health care programmes by starting hospitals for the poor. Education was another major programme for many. Besides these programmes, in some urban areas, organizations for literary activities and discussions on public issues have been common. However, a number of NGOs have proliferated since the early 1970s, with the WB's emphasis on non-government actors in development. As mentioned in Introduction, the WB's development aid began to be routed through the NGO sector. Several international funding agencies had begun to give generous financial support to NGOs. After the Emergency, the Janata Party government actively encouraged voluntary groups to participate in rural development. The Seventh Five Year Plan called upon the voluntary agencies to get involved in the implementation of government programmes, particularly in the rural areas.

In the mid-1960s, with the development of agribusiness and agro-based industry, a few industrial houses felt the need to accelerate the process of rural development so as to expand their market. The leading industrial houses such as Tata, Shaw Wallace, Mafatlal, Hindustan Lever, etc., formed voluntary organizations to provide credit loans to cultivators, advice on improved methods of cultivation and technical know-how for developing minor irrigation. In 1977–1978, the process accelerated under the aegis of the Janata Party government, as the

Shivaraman Committee recommended taking advantage of the managerial and technical resources available to industrial houses for rural development. The government introduced Sections 35CC and 35CCA of the Income Tax Act, 1961, which provided financial incentives to corporate and co-operative sectors for undertaking rural development programmes and also for promoting them through other agencies. The expenditure incurred was considered as part of the normal expenditure of the company/co-operative. Several companies formed various NGOs and launched rural development programmes. In 1978, around 300 companies in the country registered NGOs to take advantage of tax concessions. An outlay of ₹800 million was approved for companies undertaking rural development directly, and for those who did so through NGOs. However, later when the provisions in the Income Tax Act were amended in 1983, which according to them curtail their 'freedom', some of their NGOs became defunct or began to undertake limited activities.[4] Under corporate social responsibility under the Companies Act 2013, several corporate houses have floated NGOs to undertake welfare programmes. From the late 1980s, Hindu culturists have formed NGOs to create Hindu consciousness and revive India's glorious traditions. They undertake welfare programmes to reach the poor. A handful of organizations have also come up after the 2002 communal carnage to build communal harmony, and also to get justice for the victims of the massacre.

BROAD OBJECTIVES OF THE NGOS

'Equity, dignity and social justice' are the stated goals of several development NGOs[5] that we focus in this study. Their mission, as many of them mention in their brochures and other documents, is to build an 'equitable living environments where all residents and vulnerable people have access to health, education, essential infrastructure services and livelihood options, irrespective of their economic and social status'. The objective of the organizations working in the field of environment is to work for sustainable development in general and 'sustainable management of natural resources for livelihood' in particular. All these organizations speak of empowerment and capacity building of the vulnerable sections of society. They also mention the community's/people's participation in the planning and execution of programmes. Women's organizations aim at gender equality. For instance, Sahiyar's objective is to attain equal status for women by constructing a society that is free from exploitation, inequality, injustice and coercion. Organizations that focus on the Dalits have the similar objectives to build an egalitarian society. Besides working for social justice and human rights, they extend their support to the struggles of the subalterns and specifically launch struggles against discrimination in general and the practice of untouchability in particular. A few organizations work for a minority community, focusing on welfare programmes related to education, rational thinking, health, livelihood and also legal aid to the victims of the 2002 carnage.

Several activists are perturbed with the rising inequality in society. With a few exceptions, all of them are critical of globalization and liberalization. But they hardly deliberate and evolve strategies to combat a neoliberal economy. At the most, their concern is about how to evolve a mechanism that can help the deprived persons to cope up with the situation. They have the most tangible goal for their target group. For instance, the goal of the Self-employed Women Association (SEWA) is

> [T]o organize women workers for full employment and self-reliance. Full employment means employment whereby workers obtain work security, income security, food security and social security (at least health care, child care and shelter). By self-reliance, we mean that women should be autonomous and self-reliant, individually and collectively, both economically and in terms of their decision-making. (http://www.sewa.org/About_Us.asp)

Many NGOs call themselves Gandhians. It broadly means that they emphasize on non-violence as a creed, and work for the welfare of the poor and for maintaining harmony among different communities. A few profess to work for a structural change in the political economy. Some others do not claim any ideological position; they prefer to call themselves pro-poor. They have a professional approach to deliver welfare services efficiently. Over and above, there are several organizations sponsored by religious sects. They are engaged in managing education institutions with government funds. They serve all, irrespective of caste and creed, but in their perspective, their interests and welfare of their believers precede over 'the common good' of all. We have excluded them in our notion of civil society as they are primarily based on primordial interests and confine their activities to their caste or community members.

Gandhian Approach to Rural Development

In the 1920s, some Gandhian workers formed voluntary organizations for 'rural development' focusing on health care, education, spinning and weaving, etc. They continued and expanded their activities after Independence. Soon after Independence, a handful of individual Gandhians adopted one village and settled there for its reconstruction. One of them was Babalbhai Mehta. He was called a *prakhar gram sevak* (eminent village worker) who believed in the reconstruction of a village through people's education. He settled in the village Thamana in the Thasara taluka of Anand district for implementing land reforms (Pandya 2000). Another Gandhian, Harivallbha Parikh, established the Anand Niketan Ashram (ANA) in Vadodara district in 1949 to work among the Adivasis. A group of four young Gandhians formed the Vedchhi Intensive Area Scheme (VIAS) in 1957 for the development of a cluster of villages (Shah and Chaturvedi 1983). Muni (Saint) Bal established Bhal Nalkantha Prayogik Sangh in Gundi with a mission to construct an *ahinsak* samaj (non-violent society). Gandhian organizations who started Ashram schools for Adivasis pre-Independence have continued their work after Independence with government grants and private voluntary donations. New organizations on a similar pattern have come up for tribal education. One of the central themes of the Gandhian ideology is building a self-sufficient village society. They wish to establish *gram swaraj* (village republic). They strive to construct an ahinasak society free from exploitation. The focus of their activities has been formal education, which they believe is an instrument for social transformation. Some of them have taken up ecological issues and evolved appropriate technological tools for agriculture. Their emphasis is on *sajiv kheti* (organic agriculture). A few have taken up the issue of *paryavaran* (ecology). Others join the mainstream 'development' work and carry out programmes as conceived by government/donors. However, their thrust is on changing values in human beings. They harp on Gandhi's concept of 'voluntary poverty', particularly for the haves, and on the principle of trusteeship (Iyenger 2005).

Hindu Nationalists

Since the early 1970s, the Vanvasi Kalyan Ashram (VKA) has started schools in tribal areas. Besides schools, the VKA carries out welfare activities for livelihood and health. Its objective is to assist the tribals for their social and economic development and to imbibe cultural consciousness to be a part of Hindu society. Besides schools in tribal areas, Vidyabharati, sponsored by RSS (Rashtriya Swayamsevak Sangh), runs 345 schools in Gujarat. Its objective is

> [T]o develop a form of national education system which can nurture a generation of youth committed to Hindutva and engrossed with devotion for the nation physically, mentally, intellectually and spiritually to face the challenges of life successfully and whose life is devoted to the rural people of India, tribals (vanvasis) and people living in the mountains, slums to free them from poverty, pain, scarcity, and bad social practices, exploitation and injustice, and make national life equitable, wealthy and cultured. (Cited in Manjrekar et al. 2010, 122)

Professional/Management Approach

Professional social work as developed in educational institutions in the West began in India in the 1930s. The Dorabji Tata Graduate School of Social Work for professional training in social work came into existence in Mumbai in 1936. Later, in 1944, it was renamed as the Tata Institute of Social Sciences (TISS). M.S. University of Baroda established the faculty of social work in the early 1950s. Gujarat Vidyapith was started by Gandhi in 1920. One of its objectives has been to evoke social orientation among all its students and 'cater national needs of rural uplift with a view to promoting education conducive to the grass-root levels of the society'. The separate department of social work under the school of social sciences was formed in the 1970s to train professional social workers with a Gandhian ideology. With the same perspective, Lok Bharati in Sanosara and Vedchhi Vidyapith in

Vedchhi came into existence. With the growth of NGOs, self-financed colleges training social workers have increased to meet their demand.

In the early 1960s, the emphasis on 'professionalism' gained currency. Indian Institute of Management (IIM), Ahmedabad, and later The Institute of Rural Management, Anand, played a catalytic role. IIM came into existence in 1964 with the initiative of noted scientist Vikram Sarabhai and industrialist Kasturbhai Lalbhai. It got support from the Government of Gujarat (GoG). Initially, it was in collaboration with Harvard Business School. The founders did not conceive it 'to be purely a business school'. The objective has been to professionalize some of the vital sectors of India's economy such as agriculture, education, health, transportation, population control, energy and public administration. IIM undertook two action-research projects in the mid-1970s. The first was Jawaja in 1975 and the second was Dharmapur project in 1976. Ravi Matthai, the first director of the institute, initiated the former. The later was carried out by V. S. Vyas, eminent economist, and his colleagues. Dharmapur is one of the most backward talukas of Gujarat. The objective of the Dharmapur project was to prepare a realistic blueprint for rural development to be implemented by the State or by any other agency. The blueprint was prepared and submitted to the state government for implementation. But it remained on paper and the IIM faculty did not pursue it further (Vyas et al. 1976).

Jawaja is now a well-known action-research project in which not only Ravi Matthai and his students as well as colleagues but also other institutions such as National Institute of Design (NID), Ahmedabad, the Weavers Service Centre, Bombay, and Central Leather Institute, Madras have also joined. The basic idea of the Jawaja project was 'to integrate rural education and rural development and to make education an agent of developmental change'. NID got associated with the project to test the relevancy of bringing design education into the rural context. With their efforts, the local leather workers refined their skill and learnt lessons to market their products. Jawaja Leather Association was formed for production and marketing to bypass the local power structure and moneylenders. Despite their efforts, they are dependent on outside market on which they have no grip (Matthai 1985). The project did not address the issues of women, drinking water, education, health, etc. After 1985, there was no one from the institutes to take the project further (Jongeward 2002).

During the 1970s, a section of Christian missionaries was undergoing an ideological transformation. It may be mentioned here that many of them from different denominations were carrying out social services related to health and education among the poor in Gujarat for over two centuries. A few of them, particularly Jesuits, began to emphasize on social action rather than services in the 1970s. They were guided by liberation theology, liberating the people of the world from poverty and oppression (Berryman 1987). They critiqued the international capitalist economic order, which considers profit as the key motive for economic progress, and carries no corresponding social obligation. With this perspective, some Jesuits organizations are working on issues related to social discrimination, land right, livelihood, etc. A few of them run educational institutions and health care centres in tribal areas.

ORGANIZATIONAL STRUCTURE

With a handful of exceptions, all NGOs are registered under the Society or Trust Acts. The founders of these organizations have been three or four individuals. Their governing board/council is also small with an average of nine members. In most of the cases, they are members for life or get nominated again and again. Hence, the main policymakers continue to remain in office since the inception of organizations. Generally, the director/secretary is the chief who is responsible for the day-to-day functioning of the organization, and often she/he is the sole executive-cum-policymaker. She is a face of the organization in public arena; responsible to generate funds, bring projects and carry out the work. In many cases, the governing council is a passive partner, endorsing the policies and programmes conceived by the chief. The day-to-day activities are carried out by activists/workers albeit 'employees'. They continue to work till the project continues and/or at the pleasure of the chief. Most of the second-level cadres are graduates in social work. Functionaries at the grassroot levels are local persons. However, there are a few voluntary organizations not receiving funds from government or foreign funders. They hardly have any paid employee. By and large, they work in a team.

THE SOCIAL PROFILE OF THE GOVERNING COUNCILS OF THE NGOS

According to our surveys, more than three-fourths of the members of the governing boards/trusts are male. Except for a few Gandhian, Dalit and Adivasi organizations, most of the office-bearers of the organizations are not organically related to the community and/or area for which they work. In terms of the social background of the members, they predominantly belong to upper or middle castes. In fact, nearly 70 per cent of the organizations have all their members from these social groups. The proportion of members belonging to Dalit and Adivasi communities is strikingly negligible. In fact, the number of activists belonging to the deprived communities on the governing boards of the NGOs has increased after 1970s. Some Dalit and Adivasis activists have formed organizations focusing on the problems of their communities. Nearly every second activist is a graduate. Only 7 per cent have primary education, mainly from the NGOs formed before the 1970s.

WORLDVIEW OF THE PROMINENT SOCIAL ACTIVISTS OF THE NGOS

In 2008, we interviewed social activists who in our opinion are prominent in the public life of Gujarat. They are actively involved with one or another leading NGO in the field of 'development'. The interviews were non-structured. We talked to them on a variety of issues related to civil society in Gujarat, the problems of the state, their perception of politics and their views on social transformation. Of these activists, one-fourth are old-timers, who began their public life before the 1970s. Most of them have a Gandhian family background or are influenced by the 1974 JP movement. A few of them came from trade unions and socialist leanings. Among the activists of the second category, many have formal training in social work either from Gujarat Vidyapith or other Gandhian institutions, or from TISS. A few have a Jesuit background or are influenced by the training in the Behaviour Science

Centre of St Xavier College, Ahmedabad. Quite a few of them joined an NGO primarily for employment and slowly got interested in public life.

The Main Issues That Bothers Them

Though many activists believe that inequality is increasing in Gujarat, they are primarily preoccupied with the issue of poverty. There is almost a consensus among them that poverty, unemployment and absence of social security are interwoven as one major problem of the vast majority of the people of Gujarat. They believe that the majority of the people do not get enough work and income. Insecurity of work haunts them. The way in which the market has evolved has reduced job opportunities. Traditional occupations have declined, and competition for jobs has increased. 'Gap between the rich and poor has increased significantly than the past', an activist said. Several activists echoed this view in our conversations. A few are concerned with the widening gap between the rich and poor, which makes the poor more vulnerable. According to them: Buying capacity of the rich and middle class has no limits. They set prices and also induce others to become consumerists. The buying capacity of poor even to meet their basic needs is strikingly low.

The activists engaged with NGOs are preoccupied with issues confronting the poor in everyday life. They hardly relate these issues to the larger political economy. For some activists, water is a major issue in Gujarat. One of them said,

> If I have a power I will take water as the first issue to resolve. Because water changes the society, it changes the life that I have seen with my own eyes, I have experienced. If you give water you need not have to give anything. No Charity is required. People have that skill that with the availability of water they will be able to find out their ways. Concentrate on water and land, most part of poverty will be eradicated.

A few of them who view water as the main problem have a fear that, 'Narmada (dam) will not solve the problems. Those who have resources they exploit groundwater and deprive others'. For them, it is the dilemma that on the one hand, 'we need dam for drinking and irrigation water, but on the other hand, there is an unequal distribution of water, and the poor are deprived even for drinking water despite having water...we are feeling helpless'. Along with the scarcity of water, erosion of natural resources like land and forest is the main concerned of some activists. They believe that the poor are losing control over natural resources, their source of livelihood. They are also getting depleted.

Few of them identified 'communal' polarization between Hindus and Muslims as the major problem of the state. This situation under the state ascendancy disrupts social harmony and breeds intolerance. With this, the problems of the poor are sidetracked and are ignored as a non-issue. Moreover, the worst part is that the poor of all communities not only get divided but are also used against each other. Some activists are worried about the increasing adverse sex ratio. 'Proportion of female population is sharply declining. This speaks about our attitude towards women and equality. It also affects social life', a woman activist said.

Causes of Poverty

Different social activities perceive different reasons for the poverty. Some believe that the whole structure of the economy is based on exploitation and injustice. Production is meant to serve the needs of the rich who can afford to buy. 'Our political class has no will to eradicate poverty, they only talk', a middle aged activist said. Another activist who has grown in public life through struggles believed that so long as the nature and objectives of production do not change, poverty will perpetuate. Similar views are also expressed by another activists:

> [E]xploitation is a part of our system....in our development process only those who are well off have prospered. They have become owners of industries. Whereas labourers have continued to remain as labourers ... earlier they were working as agriculture labourers, now they work as industrial labourers ... but there is no substantial difference in their condition. Their social, physical and economic exploitation have increased.

Some others lay blame on the planning and programmes for eradicating poverty. They believe that the planners have a top-down approach.

Resources allocated for the benefit of the poor do not reach the poor because of corruption and mal-administration. 'People are not involved in the planning process', an activist said. Many activists believe that because of moral degeneration in society, greed has become a way of life of the people. Consumerism dominates the needs and priority of the people. A few also blame the poor for their condition. They are poor because of their habits and beliefs in superstitions, their customs and their lack of will to get out of poverty. According to the activists, lack of education among the poor and population explosion aggravate the situation.

Strategy for Resolving the Problems

For most of the activists, 'people's participation' and their empowerment is the best way to resolve the issues of poverty, erosion of environment and for sustainable development. For many, inculcation of moral values in society is the best way to resolve the present maladies of our society. According to them, the rich should accept poverty voluntarily. They are the trustees of the property—factories and farms—and they should behave like that. It will minimize consumerism and will help the poor. Education is the best way to teach moral values. It can be done through schools and training programmes. According to a few, 'self-sufficient' villages is the right way to remove poverty as people will get work in their own villages.

Struggle

The activists are divided on the method to get justice for the poor. A few believe that: 'Without struggle, we cannot achieve anything to ameliorate the condition of labouring poor'. Struggle, that is, collective action, brings unity among the oppressed and develops a consciousness for their rights. However, before launching a struggle, one should ensure that the leaders have assessed their capacity to mobilize a large number of people and to sustain the victims' capacity to struggle for a long period. One should first take legal measures, negotiate with the opponents and build pressure on those who are in power. Some organizations believe in launching struggles wherever possible on the issues of minimum wages, land rights, forest rights and water, and against the practice of untouchability, atrocities on Dalits and Adivasis, women's rights, etc.

The activists involved in carrying out government welfare programmes do not subscribe to the need for struggle. In their opinion, the struggle harms rather than helps the poor, and disturbs peace in society. Conflict is not an answer to resolve the hardship of the poor.

> We do not believe in struggle. We believe in cooperation. *Sangarsh* conflict creates more *sangarsh*, which do not resolve problems. If we try to solve problems with the support and cooperation of the government then we can solve the problems fast and they will have a long-term impact.

Some candidly accept: 'We are partners with the government in development work. We carry out government projects.... No need for struggle.... What we need is to get engaged in advocacy, building pressure on the government for the pro-poor approach'.

Ideology and Management

Though a few believe that efficient management is more important than 'ideology', several others argue that 'ideology' for public work is a prerequisite for management. Several activists held that: 'There cannot be any development without ideology.... We need values. At the same time, we need good management. But the management without ideology would be empty and will not lead us anywhere'. However, very few spelt out what they meant by 'ideology'. For many, ideology means having good moral values and/or commitment to the poor. Some said that Gandhian thought is an ideal path for development. One of them said,

> No social system can exist without ideology. We have accepted the democratic system. Now we have to think on what basis and how to work this democracy? Should it be on the basis of communist ideology or free market capitalist ideology? We have to create a society without exploitation. We should not give any label but we should have an ideology which suits our society for Swarajs for everyone... Gandhian ideology is based on Indian traditions.

For a large number of them, to be 'pro-poor' was their ideology. Generally, they referred to the implementation of welfare programmes as their 'pro-poor' ideology. For a few, 'professionalism is more important ... professional social worker with commitment is important for executing pro-poor programmes, and not an ideology of rightist or leftist'.

Market and Role of the State

Except one, all activists opined that the state should not withdraw from development work and leave it to the market. They were not in favour of privatization of social services, particularly health and education. It is argued that the private investors are concerned with profit and not the welfare of the people. There is an overwhelming opinion that State intervention in favour of the poor is a must in our society. Some asserted that the State should have minimum role in affairs of society. They are not against market but at the same time, they are opposed to free market without state regulation and monitoring. According to them, a free market would ruin the society. Capitalists are not concerned with just society. Sustainable development cannot be attained by the market economy. One of them said,

> Free market means the state of the jungle where might is right would work.... Only rich will have a say in the social matter and the poor have no voice...the poor are caught in the struggle for survival. They are struggling for livelihood, food, shelter, health...they are in a trap of debt.

Several of them believe that

> Civil society does not have a magic to fight against the forces of the dominant classes.... But the civil society organizations have their role and they play their role...they mobilise people and build pressure on the government for pro-poor actions. Whatever that you are seeing (for poor), it is because of NGOs' efforts.

There are few isolated NGOs, mainly sponsored by the industrial houses, that do not subscribe to the role of the State in the eradication of poverty. According to them, state-sponsored programmes strengthen bureaucracy and encourage corruption. People become dependent on the state. The free development of the market would induce economic growth. That would provide enough scope for all those 'who are willing to work'. People should be left to their choices. The Action Research in Community Health and Education (ARCH), though not supported by industrial houses, in fact, an offspring of a Gandhian organization, also subscribes to such view. In 1993, it rejected 'the radical left programme of total socio-economic transformation'. ARCH now believes:

> In a changed perspective, we now hold that only the free trade and free market with their important pre-requisites like private property and the rule of law can take the mass poverty head-on. We visualize the state, not in the role of employer, provider or the benevolent great patriarch. The state should do things that it can do best like upholding the rule of law and plan, if at all, for the market to operate freely and unfettered.

Most of the NGOs do not share this perspective. Except for a few, there is a near consensus among the 'development' NGOs that capitalism is anti-poor. They emphasize the role and the need for state intervention to bring equality in society.

Human Rights Organizations

During the Emergency, a few radical activists realized that civil and political freedom is an important prerequisite to gain economic equality. They formed the Lok Adhikar Sangh (LAS or People's Right Association) in 1976. The LAS believes that

> [T]he human rights of all can become real, effective and meaningful only in a democratic state, economy and society, that the struggle for food and dignified life and for freedom, equality and justice is one and indivisible, and that different human rights groups and organizations working in different spheres of society and at various levels will have to forge a united front and evolve a broad common comprehensive ideological framework to make the human rights struggles a national people's movement for human rights for all. (Patel 2009, 20)

It opposed the Emergency. However, as the organization had been centred on one person's activism, it developed fatigue after active work of two decades. Its work had been confined to courts through public interest litigations (PILs) related to the issues of livelihood, displacement, human dignity, violence, and basic human needs such as health and education, environment, etc. The LAS supported the struggles of the marginalized groups lead by other NGOs. Another civil rights organization, the Public Union of Civil Liberty (PUCL), a part of an all-India organization was launched in 1981. Though it was dormant for a brief period, it was revived in 1993. It is active in mobilizing people on the issue of civil and democratic rights. Besides filing PILs, it frequently organizes demonstrations and sets up fact-finding committees of the citizens whenever human rights have been violated. It gives petitions and memoranda on civil liberty issues. These and many other organizations raise human right issue whenever in Gujarat and elsewhere where atrocities against women and marginal communities take place, and freedom of speech and expression are attacked by the State and/or sectarian organizations. They organize public meetings, processions, demonstrations, etc., to express their protest and to mobilize public opinion. They investigate incidents of violence and atrocities on tribals, Dalits and women and publish fact-finding reports.

INTELLIGENTSIA

Public-spirited intelligentsia includes litterateurs, newspaper columnists, academia, lawyers, architects, doctors, etc., who have from time to time expressed their voice on public issues related to freedom of expression and also the violation of human rights by the State and the dominant economic and social forces. They may be called concerned citizens. Some of them are associated with PUCL and/or some other organizations. A few opposed the Emergency and extended their support to those activists who openly defied the state's imposition of laws. The Gandhian journal *Bhumiputra* flouted the GoI Census Board's regulations during the Emergency. In 1981, PUCL, LAS, and several organizations and concerned citizens opposed the 59th Constitution Amendment facilitating the extension of President's rule beyond one year in Punjab. They formed an anti-Emergency platform. In 1980, the Pushtimargiya Vaishnav Parishad (PMVP) asked the state textbook committee to delete the chapter entitled 'The Age of Narmad' from the Class XI textbook. The portion contained a reference of the 19th-century publicly debated seduction of women devotees by the priests of the Vaishnava cult. The committee did not oblige. Then, under the pressure of the PMVP, the government directed the textbook committee to delete the lesson, and the order was followed. Several litterateurs and other social activists strongly condemned the government's decision. Newspapers' columnists criticized the government. They condemned the government's interference in education and argued that education matter should be above political considerations (Oza 1983). But such protests did not alter the government's decision, and the intellectuals did not pursue the matter. During the same period, another incident happened in which these public intellectuals maintained silence when the freedom of expression of Dalit litterateurs was attacked by the government. It was related to the Dalit journal *Akrosh*. It was confiscated by the government because some of the poems were protesting the atrocities on Dalits (Maheriya 2011).

At the same time, many of the intellectuals protested in 1988 against the government for permitting criminal procedure[6] against the historian Makrand Mehta and the editors of the journal *Arthat* for publishing the article. The research-based article was on 'Sect Literature and Social Consciousness: A Study of Swaminarayan Sect 1800–1840'. The followers of the sect filed a case alleging that the article had hurt their religious feeling. Protests by the intellectuals had no impact on the government. Similar instances have continued in the 1990s and thereafter, but the space for civil society for expressing dissent voice has sunk but has not been erased. Many, but not all, of those who protested in the 1980s against the violation of right for expression have either maintained silence or supported the State and dominant section when the freedom of an artist was curbed by the crowd and the university authority. This was the case of a student artist from M.S. University in 2007. A small crowd barged into the university campus and disturbed internal evaluation examination alleging that the painting of one of the students was hurting their religious feeling. The police arrested the student. His teacher who supported freedom of expression was harassed by the university authority in connivance with the government. Some of the intellectuals and organizations condemned the university's action. Demonstrations protesting against the university and the government's action were organized. Similarly, Ashish Nandy, an eminent social scientist, faced a criminal case for his article in the *Times of India* (*ToI*) in 2007. The article was a critical analysis of the outcome of the Gujarat Legislative Election held in December 2007, and he had commented on 'a sad and unfortunate polarization amongst people of Gujarat'. Ironically, the case was filed against Nandy by Saxena of an NGO called National Council for Civil Liberties[7] alleging that 'the article contained intemperate, distasteful, undue harsh, vituperative and sharp statement showing Gujarat in general and Gujaratis in particular in low light'. With the government permission, he filed an FIR against Nandy. A small section of intelligentsia protested against the government and the petitioner for violating the freedom of expression.

CONCLUSION

CSOs in general and 'development' organizations in particular are heterogeneous in their structure and functioning, scale of operation and influence, and perception on societal problems. They hardly get engaged in discourse on the contemporary political economy, though at a normative level, they oppose neoliberal economy which hampers the interests of a majority of the people. More often than not, their activities are centred on issues which change from time to time. The organizations for human rights often co-ordinate some of these organizations. From time to time, a section of intelligentsias raise their voice for the democratic rights of citizens.

NOTES

1. In 1860, the British government enacted the Societies Registration Act for the 'registration of literary, scientific and charitable societies'. The Bombay Public Trust Act, 1950, is its amended form. According to the Act,

   '[C]haritable purpose' includes (a) relief of poverty or distress, (b) education, (c) medical relief, (d) provision for facilities for recreation or other leisure time occupation (including assistance for such provision), if the facilities are provided in the interest of social welfare and public benefit, and (e) the advancement of any other object of general public utility, but does not include a purpose which relates exclusively to religious teaching or worship.

2. Caste associations are modern phenomena. Caste associations are organized for the 'welfare' of the caste members, and also for a political purpose to build pressure on the government to get certain benefits. Some scholars have treated them as voluntary organizations. See Kothari, Rudolphs. Also see Shah (1977).
3. The main purpose behind the enactment of FCRA was to curb the use of foreign funds and hospitality for nefarious and antinational activities or purposes. The idea was to regulate the acceptance and use of foreign contribution so that the recipient institutions and individuals function in a manner consistent with the values of a sovereign democratic republic.
4. The tax concessions of the companies have been modified in 1982. The Finance Act of 1983 amended Section 35 CCA to provide the National Fund for Rural Development. The corporate sector can also take advantage of this, but with the provision that their contribution have to be first made to the National Rural Development Fund with an indication of the agency and the area and programme they wish to be served with their contributions. See Sen (1985).
5. The objectives of 'development' work foundations and NGOs sponsored by the corporate sectors and professional technocrats do not mention these goals. Instead they declare 'to build an inclusive India', inclusive growth, sab saath badhein, 'to create replicable and scalable models of development through an integrated approach'.
6. According to the Criminal Procedure Code, the permission of the government has to be sought to launch a prosecution under Section 295A of the Indian Penal Code, which deals with an offence to religious sentiments.
7. The organization was established in 1991. Its stated objective is to fight evils that deter the peace and progress of society, in all forms, by all means. It is a strong supporter of the Narmada dam and opponent of the NBA. The organization filed a PIL in the Supreme Court against NBA, charging the andolan with criminal and seditious activities.

Civil Society and Education

Reproducing Hegemony and Inequality

Since the mid-19th century, the spread of formal education had been an important agenda of leading political and social leaders for social transformation. The Indian Constitution has given central importance to education for developing citizenship in a democratic set-up for 'intelligent participation of the masses in the affairs of the country'. Unlike in the past, access to educational institutions is open to students from all strata. Its objective is to reduce social and economic inequality, develop scientific and critical thinking, and inculcate democratic egalitarian values as enshrined in the Constitution among the students. In this chapter, we shall examine the role of civil society in forming education policy, its structure and its contents. To what extent has education played the role of equalizer in the post-Independence period? Does the education system pave a way to social change or does it legitimize and strengthen status quo by reproducing inequality, as Pierre Bourdieu and Jean-Claude Passersion (1977) argue?

COLONIAL LEGACY

In the pre-modern era, formal education in the Indian subcontinent and also in Europe was the prerogative of a tiny section of society, mainly the priestly class as well as ruling families and the dominant mercantile community. During the Reformation period in 16th-century Europe, as written ability gained ascendancy over oral ability, the spread of literacy was a driving force for competing religions to proselytize people. With the rising aspirations of people and opening up of new employment opportunities, the principle of universal and compulsory education gained wide acceptance by the end of the 18th century. Leading public personalities of the time felt the need to develop a 'unified' language with a mission to have the accessibility of 'European culture' to all children. At the same time, some feared that it would be 'dangerous of educating peasants and paupers' (Swaan 1988). In England, the Elementary Education Act of 1870 triggered public discourse, making compulsory education to all a possibility.

The process of modern education in India was first initiated by Christian missionaries in the early 19th century in order to convert and 'civilize' non-Christians. To promote the education of Anglo-Indian children, the members of the Church of England formed a society in Bombay in 1815. Soon after, as mentioned in Chapter 2, the Bombay Native Education Society of 'poor' (albeit belong to upper castes) children was formed. Rather than supporting and establishing elementary schools for the masses, the colonial rulers were in favour of establishing institutions for higher education to cater to the upper classes that enjoyed influence in society (Ambedkar 1993, 99). With this perspective, Elphinstone College came into existence, which (as mentioned in Chapter 2) became a nerve centre of public discussion and activities. However, the education policy that catered the interests of upper castes' elite could not thwart emerging aspirations of not only their poor brethren but also of low castes including the depressed classes. Jyotirao Phule, a lower caste social activist, started three schools in Maharashtra for the depressed classes including girls as well as untouchables in 1852. To meet the rising aspiration from the lower classes in India and the social movement in England for universalization of education, the government formulated a policy in 1854 (Wood's Education Dispatch) that called upon the government to take measures for providing education to the masses. It was expected to raise the 'moral character of those who partake of its advantages', and to supply confident and trusted servants to the government. The policy also aimed at imparting European knowledge in developing modern skill to labour and capital for the development of country's resources and for supplying many articles necessary for British manufacturers (Nurullah and Naik 1943, 160). It also recommended establishing secondary schools in every district. But the government had no commitment for undertaking a responsibility to start and manage education institutions in India. Though it established a few primary schools, the government evolved the grant-in-aid system to encourage local elite to raise resources in establishing and managing schools. With the initiative of local philanthropists, princely rulers and a few urban local bodies started primary schools in some of the large villages and towns. Despite opposition from the upper-caste elite, the government supported the demand of the low caste elite in Maharashtra who collectively mobilized funds to build a school building for their children (Ambedkar 1993, 94). With these efforts, education institutions multiplied, primary schools increased from 1,202 in 1854 to 13,882 in 1882, and secondary schools increased from 169 to 1,363 during the same period. Arts and professional colleges also increased. Less than 1 per cent of the total number of students were from lower castes.

The 1904 Education Policy conceded that primary education received 'inadequate attention and an inadequate share of public funds'. The policy recommended financial support from the provincial governments to local bodies for the extension of primary education. A demand for the introduction of 'free and compulsory' education was mooted in some quarters of civil society. The Gaekwad ruler of Baroda introduced compulsory education in his State in 1906. The Congress leader G. K. Gokhale moved a resolution without success in the Imperial Legislative Council in 1910, demanding 'elementary education free and compulsory throughout the country'. The government, however, acknowledged the importance for expansion and improvement of primary education. Subsequently, most of the British provinces, including Bombay, passed Compulsory Education Acts between 1916 and 1930. The Act was not mandatory; it was left to the local governments to adopt as per their financial and other capabilities. Surat municipal government was the first in the subcontinent to adopt universal and compulsory education in 1919. This was possible because for Surat elite, education had simply become too important a matter for their business and service. Therefore, despite their support for the freedom struggle, they did not respond positively to Gandhi's call for boycotting government schools in the 1920s (Haynes 1991, 198).

However, since the mid-19th century, some social reformers who belonged to upper castes campaigned for girls' education and also started schools for them. Most of them, however, did not envisage women's education as giving them equal rights. They believed that education would enable Indian women—wife/daughter—to learn etiquette so that they could intermingle with British women. An educated women would be able to defend 'traditional cultural values', to be better homemaker, etc. (Shah 1984). Narmad, who is considered the 'father of Gujarat social reform movement', believed: 'By educating the women, the men will benefit. An educated wife will help her husband, he will able to talk to her. And share his joys and sorrows' (Desai, Mazumdar and Bhansari 1998).

In the 90 years from 1854 to India's Independence, the number of educational institutions at all levels increased several times. There were 2,810 primary schools in 1855. Their number crossed 150,000 in 1947. So is the case with the secondary schools—from 281 to 17,258 during the same period. The number of universities increased from 3 to 17, and the arts colleges jumped from 21 to 297. Similarly, the professional colleges also multiplied from 13 to nearly 75. The growth, though impressive, was far below the aspirations of the upper-caste elite. Nearly 10 per cent of the schools were private, catering a tiny section of the well-off class. Forty per cent of the secondary schools, and arts and professional colleges were government-aided. These grant-in-aided schools and colleges were established by the local upper-caste elite by mobilizing resources—land and finances—and tapping government's financial support. In order to get a government grant, founders formed NGOs registered under the 1854 Trust or Society Act. Moreover, as mentioned in Chapter 1, these efforts were supplemented with hostel and scholarship to encourage students of specific castes by their caste organizations.

The Brahmins, particularly functionaries—administrative officers, advisors, etc.—to Maratha and Rajput rulers in the native states, writers and traders were the first recipients of modern English education. In the mid-1850s, most of the teachers in Western India were Brahmins. In 1881–1882, 66 per cent of the college students in Bombay presidency were Brahmins. The trading caste students were nearly 15 per cent, and less than 10 per cent were from the peasant caste, mainly Patidars and Marathas. The situation was the same in Bengal presidency where over 85 per cent college students were Brahmins (Seal 1971). The members of these strata constituted civil society. Despite efforts of Phule, Ambedkar and Sayajirao Gaekwad, the students from lower castes and SCs were few and far between in the 1930s (Chhina Rao 2002; Shah 2002). On the eve of Independence, only 6 per cent of women were literate. Among the students at different levels, there were 30 girls per 100 boys. These girl students were from the upper castes.

POST-INDEPENDENCE EDUCATION POLICY

Though the Indian Constitution entrusted the State with universalization of education, the government gave priority to university and then to secondary school education. In 1948, the University Education Commission (UEC) was formed (Radhakrishnan 1950). After four years, in 1952, the Secondary Education Commission (SEC) was constituted (Mudaliar 1957). Both the reports expressed laudable objectives for university and school education in national development. They emphasized that education is a universal right and should be available to all. They also expressed 'great sympathy with the anxiety of these SCs—and backward communities—to raise their *cultural level*' and pleaded for 'additional assistance'. But except for a cursory mention about the reservation, the commissions did not suggest any methodology, development of curricula and pedagogy to raise the so-called cultural level of the 'backward communities'. Prejudices and biases of the forward communities towards the 'backward communities' were not even mentioned.

However, at that period, a small section of women, largely from the elite class, was vocal about women's position. The authors of these commissions were also familiar with these voices. Granting equality between the genders, they emphasized woman as the 'homemaker'. The SEC observed that there was 'no special justification to deal with women's education separately' and recommended that every type of education should be available to male and female. At the same time, the commission observed: 'An educated girl who cannot run her home smoothly and efficiently, within her resources can make no worthwhile contribution to the happiness and the well-being of her family or to raising the social standards in her country' (Mudaliar 1957, 42). The National Committee on Women's Education was appointed in 1958, chaired by Durgabai Deshmukh. It recommended that the highest priority should be given to establishing parity between the education of boys and girls. Then, the Hansa Mehta Committee (1961) examined curricula and recommend that 'the education of women should be so planned as to enable them to follow a career of their choice *without, in any way, neglecting* their responsibilities for child-rearing and home-making' (emphasis added; cited in Pandey 1996, 342). With this premise, the Committee emphasized the traditional social roles of women as a mother and housewife. It identified certain subjects as 'feminine' and specifically suited for girls (Pandey 1996, 343).

During the 1950s, Bombay state (present Gujarat and Maharashtra) along with a few states such as Himachal Pradesh, Kerala, Bihar and UP had passed Acts making education compulsory. But none of them implemented the Act. In fact, there was hardly any discussion in the corridor of power or civil society on a national education policy in general and universal primary education in particular (Dreze and Sen 2003). Elite of dominant educated strata was primarily engaged in expanding a number of colleges and schools to meet their aspirations.

The first Education Commission was formed in 1964, 14 years after the formation of the Republic. The Commission carried out its task in a changed political scenario. The early euphoria of a free and new India had ebbed by the late 1950s. Dominant interests—industrial-business bourgeoisie, zamindars and newly emerging rich peasants—not only protested openly but also got organized in electoral politics against Nehru's dream for a socialistic pattern of society. At the same time, newly emerged upward mobile middle caste peasants, beneficiaries of Community Development Projects and half-backed land reform, were ignited with aspirations for a 'modern' life in which modern education was the driving force. They wanted to move beyond the agrarian economy and asserted for expansion of educational institutions in rural areas. At the same time, unrest among the lower classes for land rights and minimum wages was mounting. In the mist of this scenario, the Commission spelt out its plan for education from the perspective of a desirable future Indian society for the national development towards a democratic, secular and egalitarian social order. The Commission advocated the introduction of a 'common school system' of public education to attain 'social and national integration' (1966, 14). It repeatedly called upon undertaking 'strenuous efforts' to 'equalize educational opportunity'. That would be enabling an agency to 'the backward or underprivileged classes and individuals to use education as a lever for the improvement of their condition'. Further, in order to mitigate gender and social inequality between the advanced classes and the backward ones—the SCs and the STs—the Commission emphasized a need for 'more intensive' efforts. Like the earlier commissions, except for referring to reservation for SC and ST in accessing education, or rejecting a gender differentiated approach in the contents of education, no attempt was made to spell out any 'special efforts' and strategies to provide equal opportunities to the deprived communities and women. It also did not address the issue of diversity of culture and way of life among a vast majority of the people. It was assumed by the scholars and civil society activists of the 1950s that there would be eventual assimilation (they called integration) of the 'little traditions' of the backward communities with the 'greater traditions' of the dominant culture of the upper castes (Dumount 1980; Marriott 1955; Moffatt 1979; Singer 1959; Singh 1970). It ignored the cultural autonomy that lower social communities were enjoying. There was hardly any effort to spell out the nature of integration of the tribals who have a different historical trajectory, cultural ethos and way of life. At best, emphasis was given on developing communication and agriculture economy, 'including care of forests, improved systems of shifting cultivation, settled cultivation and pasture'.

The Commission asserted that if the existing educational system is changed significantly, the socio-economic and political revolution that society needed would also be *automatically* triggered off' (emphasis added). However, it granted that education alone cannot bring social transformation per se; it hoped and advocated that 'the most effective way of breaking the vicious circle in which we find ourselves at present is to begin educational reconstruction in a big way' (Naik 1982, 52). The Commission emphasized that universal elementary education for the children needed to be taken up on a priority basis. It repeatedly emphasized that to eliminate elitism and segregation in society and to develop social and national integration, 'we must move towards the goal of a common school system of public education' (Kothari 1966, 14).

The government accepted the report, acknowledging the recommendations of the Commission as 'essential for the economic and cultural development of the country, for national integration and for realizing the ideal of a socialistic pattern of society' (Kothari 1966, XII). The National Educational Policy (NEP) was formed in 1968. The main principle of this policy was to provide 'free and compulsory education' to every child, up to the age of 14. It also asked for developing suitable programmes to reduce the prevailing wastage and stagnation in schools. Later, in 1976, with the constitutional amendment, the union government accepted a larger financial responsibility and also pronounced a policy for 'the national and integrative character of education, to maintain quality and standards'. But except for the routine expansion of schools and colleges to meet local demands, the situation remained the same.

Meanwhile, with rising pressure from women civil society activists, the government formed the Committee on the Status of Women in India (CSWI) in 1971. The Committee submitted its report entitled *Towards Equality*. The report observes: 'The deep foundations of the inequality of the sexes are built in the minds of men and women through socialization process which continues to be extremely powerful'. The committee felt that this could be countered by the education system. 'If education is to promote equality of women, it must make a deliberate, planned and sustained effort so that the new value of equality of the sexes can replace the traditional value system of inequality' (CSWI 1975, 281). Though the report (authored by women activists) extensively deliberates on condition of women in the informal sector, it does not dwell upon intersectional difference among women.

During this period, a tiny section of civil society, the Citizens for Democracy, under the leadership of Jayaprakash Narayan and Justice

Tarkunde initiated a campaign for 'Education for Our People'. They believed that educational transformation 'must be an essential part of an egalitarian movement for social transformation'. A group of committed citizens prepared 'A Policy Frame for the Development of Education' (1978–1987). Though the policymakers appreciated the concerns of these citizens, they were lukewarm in taking steps for action. As a lip service, the government revisited the NEP after 10 years in 1986 under the pressure of a rising upsurge among OBCs in different states for their share in education and other sectors. Operation Blackboard (providing at least two classrooms in every primary school) and the Scheme of Restructuring and Reorganization of Teacher Education were introduced in 1987 to spread primary education and provide training to teachers. Later, in 1990, following the implementation of the Mandal Commission's report, the central government revisited the NEP and modified it in 1992.[1] This was in the wake of a clash between 'forward' and 'backward' communities. It reiterated its goal to develop a common school system and provide free and compulsory education of satisfactory quality to all children. The District Primary Education Programme (DPEP) and later, Sarva Shiksha Abhiyan (SSA) or Total Literacy Campaign were introduced to enhance 'universal access and retention, bridging a gap between gender and social groups'.

All these schemes have come under the shadow of structure transformation since the late 1980s. The Seventh Plan (1985–1990) was the beginning of the state's retreat from the social sector, acknowledging that it could not reach all and it seeks the involvement of non-government agencies in 'social development' sectors. Under a neoliberal economy, the private sector was increasingly facilitated to enter the education and health sectors.

These schemes, though important, did not satisfy civil society groups which were demanding universalization of education. Social action litigation (SAL) cases were filed in courts asserting for the 'right to education'. The Supreme Court of India in *Mohini Jain vs State of Karnataka* (1992) reiterated that 'the right to education is concomitant to fundamental rights enshrined under Part III of the Constitution' and that 'every citizen has the right to education under the Constitution'.

A section of civil society at the national level continued its campaign for the right to education as a fundamental right. The activists built pressure on political leaders for the amendment of the Constitution to give education a legal status as a fundamental right. They organized meetings, processions and rallies, and lobbied with the political parties to take the right to education on their agenda. With these efforts, the Constitutional Amendment Bill for the inclusion of education as a fundamental right was moved in the Parliament. But all segments of RCS involved in the campaign were not happy with several provisions in the Bill.[2] The Bill was passed in 2002 as the Eighty-sixth Amendment Act, making education a fundamental right. But it did not spell out modalities for its implementation (Juneja 2003). The campaign of civil society in different parts of the country, including Gujarat, continued to amend the Act and translate it into law.

At last, the Right of Children to Free and Compulsory Education Act (RTE) was passed by the Parliament and became an Act in 2010. It spells out the modalities of the provision of free and compulsory education for children between six and fourteen years of age. The Act also makes a provision that all private schools have to admit 25 per cent of the total students from poor and disadvantaged communities (see Singh 2006; see also Seethalakshmi and Seshagiri 2006). The government agreed to reimburse tuition fees to private schools on behalf of the students belonging to the weaker sections of society who get admission under the Act. The financial burden has been shared between the Central and state governments in a 65:35 ratio for the implementation of RTE through the SSA programme. A major section of the RCS engaged in the long-drawn campaign welcomed the Act. Some of them, however, feared that the government would not effectively monitor its implementation in private schools. And some activists have an apprehension that the Act would not succeed in the universalization of education. They demand a common schooling system as recommended by the Education Commission in 1968, and reiterated in the 1986 as well as 1992 policies, so that everyone gets 'good' education on equal footing. Their campaign in some parts of the country for the common school continues (see Rajalakshmi 2001; Sadgopal 2002).[3] In Gujarat, hardly any CSO was actively engaged in this campaign.

ACCESS, ELIMINATION AND SEGREGATION

With the transformation of political economy embedded in electoral politics during the last six decades, aspirations for the perceived 'better' life across all communities and regions have risen. For most of the people, formal education is the only hope for a better life. A constant public campaign by the State and civil society hammering a message that education is the panacea of poverty and for better chances in life, coupled with the mushroom growth of educational institutions, further boosts the aspirations of people. The quest for education among the parents of traditionally deprived communities for their children is almost universal (Shah, Kalimili and Thorat 2018). Most of them spend money out of their meagre income for educating their children. A few of them even sell their assets to meet the expenditure for their children's studies. Around 60 per cent of the heads of traditionally backward households would like to give a college education to their wards. They believe that education would give them a decent job, generally a government one which gives them security, assured income and social status (Shah, Kalimili and Thorat 2018).

Enrolment

For most children, primary school is an entry point to the educational system. Over a period of time, the growth of a number of primary schools coupled with the Mid Day Meal (MDM) Scheme, free uniform and textbooks to poor students, and also the DPEP and SSA campaign and the RTE, have accelerated the process of enrolment at the primary level. Moreover, state governments have also proactively launched campaigns for enrolment. With such efforts, school enrolment has now reached nearly 100 per cent in Gujarat and elsewhere in the country across the social groups.

Notwithstanding the government's claim of 100 per cent school enrolments,[4] 6 per cent SC and 5 per cent STs children between 6 and 14 years are out of school. Either they are enrolled on paper or they attended school for a while but do not continue their studies. Poverty is one of the main reasons for non-enrolment, chronic absenteeism leading to dropout. The children of inter- or intra-state seasonal migrant labourers' are unable to sustain interest in studies because of lack of facilities at a workplace (Smita 2006). NGOs like Gantar, Setu and others are engaged in running schools for the children of migrant workers, pastoral nomadic communities, etc. They have also evolved the pedagogy to meet the requirements of migrant children. But these NGOs are unable to sustain their work because of their limited human and financial resources.

The gross enrolment ratio (GER) rate at the upper primary has also considerably increased over a period of time, from 67 per cent in 1990–1991 to 82 per cent in 2011–2012. GER in Gujarat at the upper primary level is 78 per cent, lower than the all-India average. GER goes down to 65 per cent at the secondary level and further reduces to 39 per cent at the higher secondary level in India. Gujarat lags behind with 59 per cent at secondary and 37 per cent at higher secondary level. At the secondary level, nearly 40 per cent and at higher secondary level, more than 60 per cent children are out of school system. The GER in higher education in the age group of between 18 and 23 years has considerably increased after 2000 everywhere in the country. By 2000, it was estimated to be around 7 per cent, which reached to 10 per cent in 2005–2006 and 24 per cent in 2016–2017. GER in Gujarat, however, is lower: it is 21 per cent (Pratham 2017).

On the whole, the growth in enrolment at upper primary and secondary levels is slower among the SC and ST than among the non-SC/ST. Among the SC and ST, the growth rate in enrolment is 4.4 per cent and only 1.5 per cent respectively as against 14.2 per cent among the non-SC/ST. As the education level increases, the number of students declines. All those who get enrolled in the Standard VI do not complete Standard VIII. The same is the case with those who pass Standard VIII. This pattern applies to all social groups and genders. But the proportion of getting left out is higher in the country and in Gujarat among the SC, ST, OBC and religious minorities, particularly the Muslim community. The proportion of students belonging to the 'general' (non-SC, ST and OBC) category increases from the primary level to the higher secondary and college levels (Figure 3.1). Except for SCs, the proportion of ST, OBC and Muslims is gradually declining from a lower to a higher level.

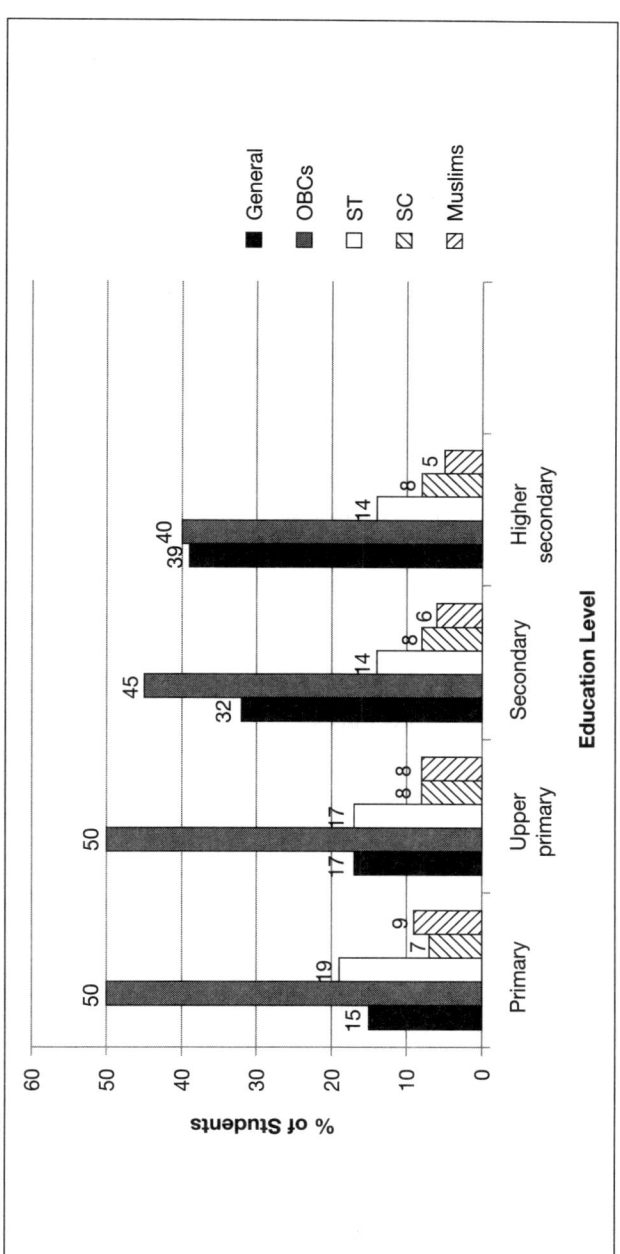

Figure 3.1 *Enrolment by Social Groups at Different Levels of Education in Gujarat (2014).*

Source: ASER 2017.

The gap between girls and boys at the level of enrolment has narrowed down over a period of time. The Gender Parity Index (GPI) at the primary level has increased from 0.41 in 1950–1951 to 1.01 in 2011–2012, and from 0.22 to 0.99 in case of upper primary level (Classes VI–VIII). Figure 3.2 presents GPI at different levels from primary to higher education. On the whole, GPI is lower in Gujarat than in the country as a whole at all levels. The gap in GPI is found in all the communities. It is increasing from primary to higher education in the country as a whole, and also in Gujarat. It is more so among the SC, but in the case of the STs in Gujarat, GPI has improved at the higher level.

Within each social group, the poorer strata—both in urban and rural areas—increasingly gets pushed out from the schooling system as the stage of education increases. The 71st survey round of the National Sample Survey Office (NSSO 2014) shows that at the primary school level, enrolment is nearly universal; net school attendance ratio (NAR) of the high income and the poor is very marginal both in urban and rural areas (Figure 3.3). But the gap increases from secondary to higher education. Only 6 per cent of the children of the poor—the bottom fifth of the population—as against 31 per cent of the richest income group attend educational institutions above higher secondary level in urban India. In fact, over a period of time, with increased privatization of education, the proportion of poor in higher education has declined (Dubey 2009).

Segregation

From the entry point, the students are segregated by the type of schools. Normatively, all state-recognized education institutions function under the common education system with similar curricula and rules. In practice, there are a lot of variations among the institutions with respect to their sources of resources, autonomy, treatment towards students and methods of imparting education. The perception of these differences also accords social status. In terms of management and quality of education, these institutions are of three types: (a) government schools, (b) government-aided schools and (c) private schools.

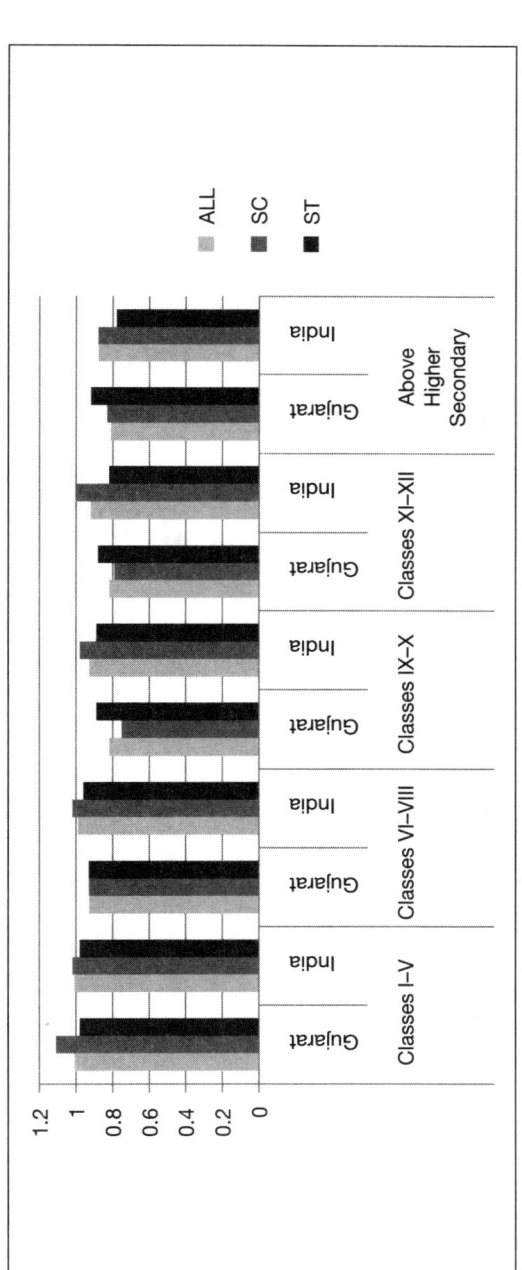

Figure 3.2 *Gender Parity Index 2011–2012 (Gujarat and India).*

Source: For school, GoI (2014); for higher education, AISHE 2014–2015.

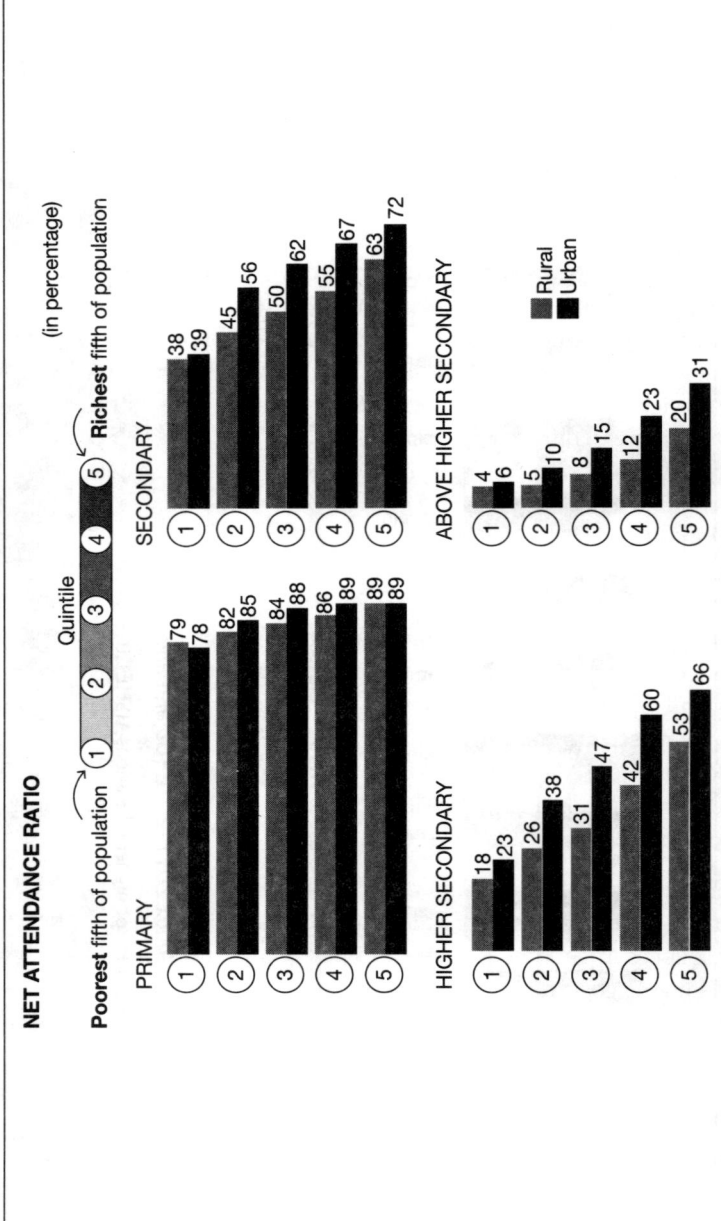

Figure 3.3 *Net Attendance Ratio at Different Levels by Household Income.*

Source: NSSO.

The number of primary and upper primary schools in India has increased from 220,000 to over 1.2 million in the last six decades. In Gujarat, their number has grown from 18,902 to 40,723 during this period. Over 80 per cent of them are government schools that are either managed by the local government or the state/central government. In recent years, quite a few primary and upper primary schools in urban and rural areas have closed down or been handed over to the private organizations despite opposition from some sections of civil society. The State education department enjoys control over schools managed by the local or state government. It decides not only their curriculum and pedagogy but also the strength of the teachers, their qualifications, remuneration and duties, and all terms and conditions of their service. The proportion of private primary and upper primary schools has increased from 3 per cent in the late 1970s to 7 per cent in the early 1990s and to 12 per cent in 2011 (Kingdon 2016). The ratio of government schools has declined, to almost half, at the secondary and higher secondary level.[5] The number of the secondary and higher secondary schools[6] has increased from 173,000 to 230,000 between 1961 and 2011. In Gujarat, they increased from 1,210 to 9,844 during the same period (Figure 3.4). More than one-third of the secondary and higher secondary schools are under private management in the country and Gujarat. The proportion of private secondary schools has sharply increased from 22 per cent in 2000 to 33 per cent in 2014. West Bengal, Goa, Meghalaya, Maharashtra and Gujarat have more than 50 per cent government-aided secondary schools. In Gujarat, they are managed by NGOs.

The number of colleges has increased from 1,500 to over 300,000. The pattern is not significantly different in Gujarat. Twenty-eight per cent of colleges in Gujarat as against 15 per cent at the all-India level are aided by the government. The proportion of colleges under private management is high: 56 per cent in Gujarat and 61 per cent in the whole country. Gujarat has a relatively small ratio of government colleges compared to the country as a whole. More than 50 per cent of the colleges are giving general courses including arts, languages and social sciences. Around 4 per cent of the colleges are providing commerce, science, management, computer application, etc. A majority

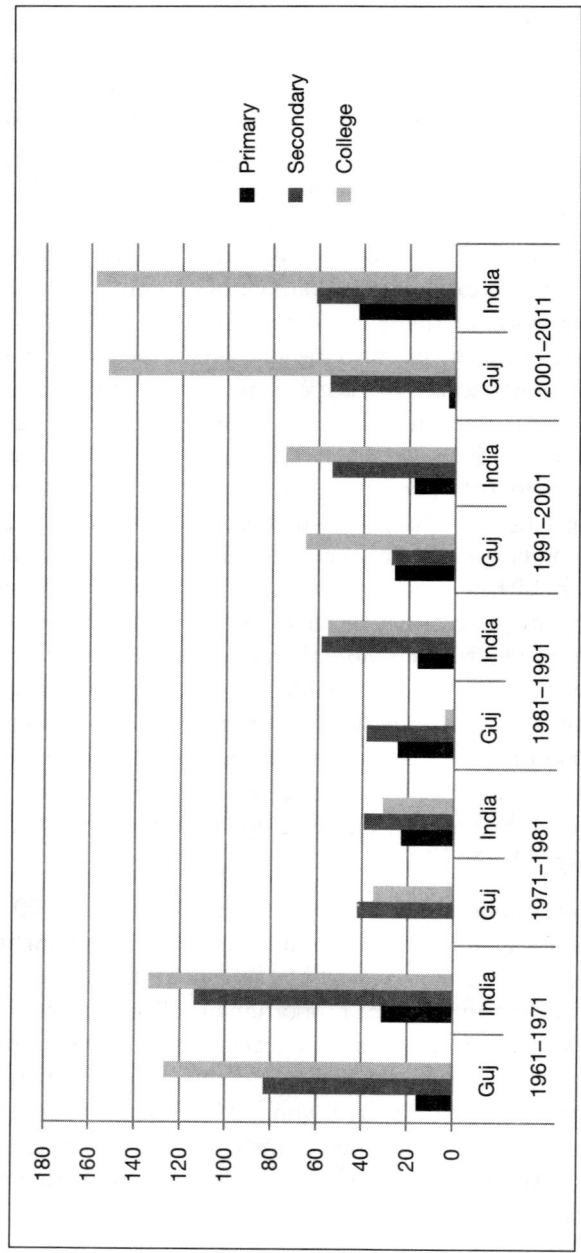

Figure 3.4 *Decadal Growth of Educational Institutions in Gujarat and India.*

Source: NSS 71st round, 2014.

of the remaining impart professional courses. One out of ten colleges are of engineering and medicine (AISHE 2015–2016). In Gujarat, most of the private colleges are in professional courses: engineering, pharmacy and business management. However, a majority of the medical colleges are under government management. Two of them, in fact, have been established and managed by local governments. The Ahmedabad Municipal Corporation (AMC) was the first after Bombay to start a medical college in 1963. Initially the AMC received a donation of ₹150,000 for the college. After nearly 35 years, in 1999, the Surat Municipal Corporation (SMC), one of the richest local governments in India, decided to launch a medical college to cater to the interests of the upward mobile middle class. SMC, however, resolved that it was doing so to meet its objective of *'Bahujan Sukhay, Bahujan Hitay'* (Happiness of the large number of people in the interests of the large number of people). There was some murmur in a section of RCS against the decision as it was catering to the interests of a small section of the middle class. A few argued that higher education was not an obligatory function of the Corporation. But there was no editorial in newspapers or any comments from any column writer. However, municipal members representing labour constituencies were critical of the decision. To pacify them, the political elite decided to start secondary schools for the poorer section of society in June 1999. They are called Suman high schools. The rationale for the decision was,

> [T]hough it is *not an obligatory function* of the SMC to start high school for the students passed from their primary schools, looking to the needs of the poor labouring class who do not afford high fees of the private schools, SMC decided to start high schools. (emphasis added, SMC 2000)

The content and tone of the resolutions for the colleges and schools speak about the perspective and partisanship of the ruling elite. Both are not obligatory functions of urban the local government, but this is specifically mentioned in the case of schools, but not for colleges. Local civil society including RCS silently endorsed such notion of public good as 'normal'. SMC spent ₹747.7 million and ₹150.3 million towards capital and revenue expenditure of the college in the last 10 years—between 1999 and 2008. During the same period, SMC spent ₹8.95 million and ₹85.9 million towards revenue and capital expenditure respectively for these schools. During 2007–2008, SMC spent *revenue expenditure* of ₹1,900 per student for primary schools, ₹2,252 for Suman schools and ₹97,473 for medical colleges.[7] Moreover, in 2009, the SMC created a Science Centre with for the cost of 502.4 million. The admission fee for children in the age group between 3 and 18 years was ₹65.

All government schools, however, are not on equal footing. One per cent of them cater to the middle-class elite. In the past, they were called 'public schools' started by the colonial rulers for the children of military personnel and civil servants. They are modelled more or less on the public schools system in England. In the early 1950s, 14 public schools came in to existence. It was believed that the students of these schools developed 'leadership' qualities. Endorsing this view, Mudaliar Commission observed,

> There are greater opportunities in these schools than in majority of secondary schools for developing certain essential traits of character-including the qualities of leadership, because of the special facilities that they can offer and the close contact between teachers and pupils that is possible in them. (1957, 38)

There were some critics of the view that

> Public school in a modern democracy is an anachronism, that it has not made any material contribution to the educational progress of the country, and, according to some, has tended to produce a type of narrow-minded snob or one who will be ill-fitted to take his proper place in a democratic society. (Mudaliar 1957, 38)

In 1962, these schools were called 'central schools'. Later, the schools were renamed Kendriya Vidyalayas (KVs). The children of defence personnel and of all central government employees, including public sector and Members of Parliament, are entitled to get admission to these schools. They work under the Union Ministry of Human Resource Development (MHRD), registered as an NGO under the Societies Registration Act, 1860. On the same pattern, to meet the pressure from the rural elite, the government started the Jawahar Navodaya Vidyalaya in 1985. Now they are called Navodaya Vidyalayas (NVs);

in 2013–2014, there were 596 in the country and 18 in Gujarat. Both KVs and NVs follow central government curriculum prepared under the Central Board of Secondary Education (CBSE). On a similar model, Ekalavya Model Residential Schools (EMRS) for ST students were established in 1997–1998. As of 2013–2014, around 100 EMRS have come into existence. In order to manage EMRS efficiently, the GoG formed an autonomous society called the Gujarat State Tribal Development Residential Educational Institutions Society in 2000. There are 30 EMRS in the state. Some schools follow the CBSE pattern in their syllabus. Two of them follow the public–private partnership (PPP) model whose management has been given to private organizations: Global Indian Foundation, Singapore, and Navrachana Education Society, Vadodara. They make a high claim of providing management of global standards.

In a bid to appease the deprived communities, the central government started the Kasturba Gandhi Balika Vidyalaya for girls from disadvantaged sections of the society in 2004. In 2013–2014, over 3,500 KGBV were established in the country through state governments. These schools, however, do not have the same facilities as other model schools. In comparison to KV and EMRS, these schools suffer from poor human infrastructure. In Gujarat, many of KGBV do not have teachers with specialization in science and mathematics (Chaudhari 2012).

Although the physical infrastructure of the school building in government schools has considerably improved, 15 per cent of the schools still do not have a drinking water facility and separate toilets for girls. Six per cent of the schools do not have even a blackboard. Around 9 per cent of the primary and upper primary schools had only one teacher in 2010–2011. The same proportion of schools had only one room where students of different standards sat together. The gap in terms of pupil–teacher ratio (PTR) has increased over time. It was 1:24 in 1950–1951 and 1:41 in 2011–2012 in primary schools. In Gujarat, 'out of 43,176 schools in the state, 64 schools having 5,698 students had no teachers and 874 schools had only one teacher as of March 2014 CAG' (2014, 52). The schools in urban areas have relatively more teachers compare to rural areas. The situation in tribal schools is deplorable. In 2014, the test check CAG (Comptroller and Auditor General of India) in five predominantly tribal districts (Gujarat) found that in 5 per cent of primary schools, PTR was not maintained, and in as many as 84 per cent of upper primary schools, PTR was not observed. In one primary school, there was one teacher for 156 students, and in one upper primary school there was one teacher for 363 students. Moreover, at several places, one teacher used to conduct two or more classes together in one room. Sometimes in upper primary schools, teacher of languages was compelled to teach science and maths, and vice versa. Moreover, along with teaching, the government primary school teachers are often assigned a number of extra non-academic duties at the cost of the teaching. Though several RCS activists often demand recruitment of teachers and adequate infrastructure in government schools in tribal areas and slums, they are ignored.

Government-aided Schools

The colonial rulers, as mentioned earlier, encouraged local leaders by providing aid to start schools. The local leaders belonging to upper castes, having clout with the government, took an initiative of starting schools. The same system has accelerated in post-Independence India. As mentioned earlier, more than 50 per cent of the secondary and higher secondary schools, and 28 per cent of the colleges in Gujarat are government-aided. They are created and run by a group of persons called the trustees of the public registered NGOs. They follow the PPP model. To gauge their management structure and functioning, these schools can be broadly divided into four categories: (a) local power elite, (b) social activists, (c) Gandhian and apolitical educationalists and (d) sectarian, established by different religious sects and Hindutva ideologues. An overwhelming number of aided educational institutions fall into the first category. They have been established with an initiative of the local power elite to serve the local community and also create a patronage power network. Most of the founders and executive members of these organizations belong to the upper strata of society. Many of them did not conceive education as a mission to transform individual/society. For them, education provides the skill to get employment, and improve their life chances and social status. Later, some leaders of the deprived communities also followed the same trajectory.

During the freedom movement, Gandhi developed his own vision for education called *nai talim* (new education), linking intellectual and manual work for human development. Gandhians with this perspective started schools and later universities (Gandhi 1962). In 1953, the Bombay government sanctioned Ashram Shala Yojana to legitimize the nai talim education system and provide them with financial support. The Gujarat government continued the scheme after the formation of the state in 1960. These schools cover all the stages of education from primary to higher secondary. They include residential (ashram) and day schools. They constitute less than 1 per cent of the government-aided schools, and are mostly confined to tribal areas. Vidyabharati, an offspring of RSS, a champion for Hindu nationalism, also runs 345 schools, mostly in tribal areas. Some of them are residential, like ashrams, in tribal areas. Hindu religious sects like Swaminarayan as well as Muslims and Christians have also established schools with government grants. Over and above, there are however exceptional cases of public-spirited educationalists who have started schools as their life mission. These schools make efforts to develop the creative potentiality of students. Many of them have been established by social activists and educationalists primarily to cater to the deprived sections of society.

The 1960s witnessed a sudden spurt of secondary schools and colleges, both in urban and rural Gujarat. Middle caste peasants, beneficiaries of land reforms as well as community development programmes began to aspire for new non-farm avenues. The elite, as a part of their social and political patronage network, took initiative in establishing schools with the help of government aid. They developed school and college organizations in the name of public service as their personal fiefdom—hiring and firing teachers at will, getting personalized services from them and using them as political pawns in university and party politics. Several cases of malpractices in the appointment of teachers and other staff and the disbursement of salary came on the surface. That led to unrest among the staff. The teachers union actively pressurized the government for intervention in the matter of recruitment and disbursement of salary, and provide security of job to the staff. The pioneers of the teachers' union were self-styled radicals who were enjoying a position in civil society as intellectuals and social activists. They believed that the governmentalization (then called nationalization) of colleges and schools was necessary for teachers' security and for quality education. The government succumbed to the pressure of the teachers' union and decided in 1973 to pay salary directly rather than in the form of a grant to schools. Later, the teachers' union and political leaders succeeded in codifying rules for appointment of teachers, their promotion and other security measures at par with other government employees. With such regulations, the arbitrariness of the governing bodies of the schools/colleges weakened. But the union did not devote much time to improving content, and the teaching and autonomy of the teachers and institutions. Some of them actively supported the 1974 students' movement against former Chief Minister (CM) Chimanbhai Patel (Shah 1977). A few leaders of the union got co-opted by political parties. Gradually, they themselves became education entrepreneurs, and started schools and colleges with or without government aid.

The government regulations provide security to the teachers and established rule of law; however, the adversary affected institutions, particularly those few working for innovative methods and committed to improving the quality of education. Such governmentalization also affected nai talim schools and colleges following the Gandhian philosophy. The schools established by social activists with little resources to serve deprived communities also find constraints to get committed teachers. A few educationalists engaged in experiments and personal involvement also experienced constraints in recruiting teachers of their choice and getting the involvement of teachers in innovative work, which requires spending more time. Bureaucratization in the management of education has increased and the scope for experiments in education has considerably reduced. Notwithstanding these odds, a handful of grants-aided schools still manage to maintain their distinct identity in governance. A few NGOs also started schools specifically for the children of deprived communities to provide a congenial atmosphere of learning. But they cannot sustain these efforts with the rising costs for human and physical infrastructure, including scarcity of 'devoted' teachers. All of them follow the prescribed curriculum and make little effort to change the content of the textbooks.

Private Schools/Colleges

The number of private secondary and higher secondary schools has increased by leaps and bounds with economic liberalization. The number of private education institutions at all levels has increased since the early 1990s. The proportion of privately managed primary schools increased from 4.1 per cent in 1992–1993 to 8.2 per cent in 2011–2012, upper primary increased from 11 per cent to 16.9 per cent and secondary schools increased from 15 per cent to 40 per cent during the same period (GoI 2014). As private schools cater to the needs and paying capacity of different classes of clientele, their structure and functioning have significant variation. In terms of fees and infrastructure, there are three types of private schools catering to different clients: (a) plebeian, (b) middle class or moderate and (c) elite or upper-class schools.

On average, the tuition fee in the plebeian private primary schools is around ₹5,000 per year. For the moderate middle-class school, the annual fee ranges from ₹3,500 to ₹15,000 and more. The fee for elite schools ranges from ₹15,000 to ₹75,000 plus per year. Fees for secondary and higher secondary correspondingly increase in each category. The middle class, irrespective of social communities, prefer to send their children to 'middle class' private schools. Many of them cannot afford frequent fee hikes by the management. They assert that the state governments should regulate the fees structure and occasionally the government should yield to the pressure of the vocal middle class[8] and a section of civil society. In 2017, Gujarat government enacted the Regulation of Fees Act, putting a cap on primary school fees at ₹15,000, secondary fees ₹25,000 and higher secondary fees ₹27,000 per year. But a few elite schools have gone to the court and succeeded in their plea for higher fees. Some HCS organizations have launched low budget schools called low-fee private (LFP) or affordable schools for poor and low-income strata with a view of providing 'good quality' education (Nambissan 2012; Thakore 2011).

The quality of infrastructure of these private schools differs according to the category. Some schools of the moderate category, which started in the 1960s or before, do not charge 'very high' fees and have a relatively better infrastructure. They were started with the philanthropic purpose of 'social service'. The rest of the schools in this category and a majority of the 'A' and 'C' categories are primarily 'for-profit' institutions. A large number of teachers in the majority of the private schools are not permanent and are poorly paid. Most of the teachers, though educated—SSC (secondary school certificate) and graduates—were not qualified with a degree in education.

Enrolment of Students by Institutions

The proportion of students studying in government schools declines as the level of education increases. At the primary level, 85 per cent of the children studies in government schools. Nine out of ten students at the primary level study in government schools. But their number goes down to 40 per cent at the secondary level and falls further down to 33 per cent at the post-secondary level. On the other hand, the proportion of students enrolled in private institutions increases sharply from 22 per cent at the secondary level to 46 per cent at the higher level (Figure 3.5). Students of the deprived communities also prefer private schools and join wherever it is possible. A majority of them join plebeian schools, and the middle class get enrolled in moderate private schools with a hope to get a good quality education. Only exceptionally bright children of the well-off among them are sent to elite schools.

Medium of Instruction

Students are also segregated by the medium of instruction in school from the primary level. The medium of teaching in most of the primary and upper primary government, as well as private plebeian and middle-class schools, is the regional language. A small proportion of the schools are English medium. Their number, however, has been

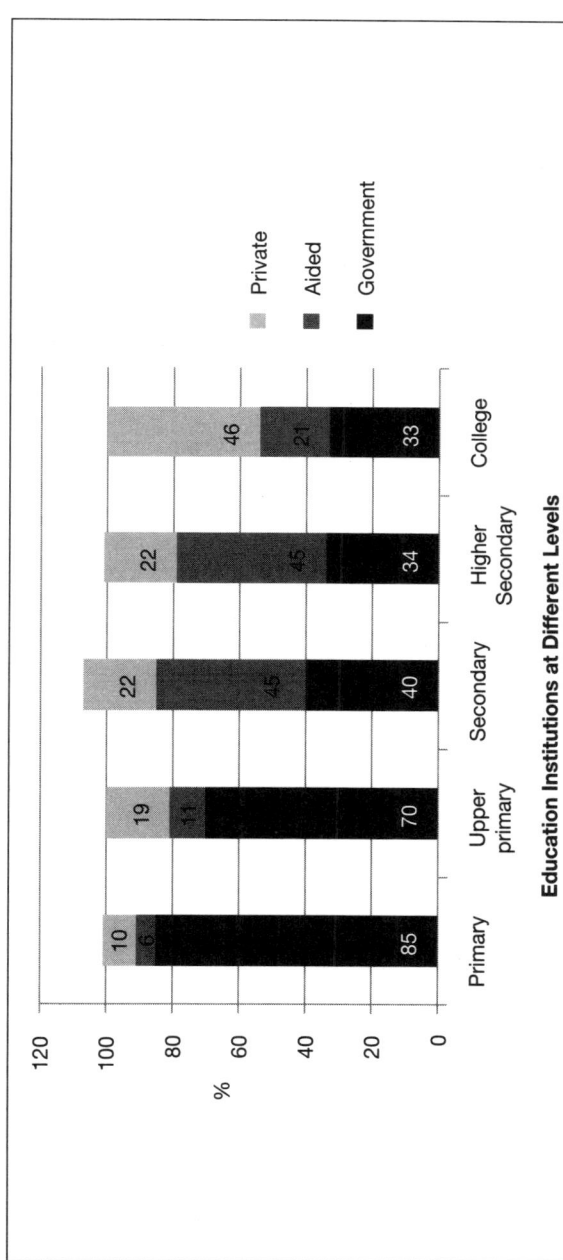

Figure 3.5 *Enrolment by Management of Institutions at Different Levels (2011).*
Source: NSS 71th round, 2014.

increasing with the growth of private institutions since 2000. Civil society in Gujarat is divided on the issue of medium of instruction. A small section is worried about the growth and development of Gujarati language. But another section strongly supports English medium schools. The growth of students studying in English medium is faster from, 6 per cent to 15 per cent, than the all-India pattern, which is from 15 per cent to 25 per cent between 2007–2008 and 2014 (Borooah and Sabharwal 2017, 7). It is increasingly perceived that a student who studies in English medium has better chances of getting 'good' education and employment. Among social circles, English gets a higher status than regional language.

QUALITY OF EDUCATION

For formal schooling, basic skill of literacy and numeracy are the minimum levels of learning. Reading, writing, comprehension of elementary text and arithmetic (computation: subtraction, multiplication and division) are considered as prerequisites for the development of critical analytical thinking. This has been developed as the only parameter to assess the quality of education.

Pratham Education Foundation, an NGO, started work among Bombay slum children to improve the quality of education. It has carried out a survey every year since 2000, covering 21 states on the status of education. According to its report for 2016, the basic ability of a sizable proportion of students studying in primary and upper primary standards class is dismal in Gujarat as well as in other states. In Gujarat, more than 40 per cent of students of Standards III–V were not able to read Class-I level sentences. Their performance in subtraction is worse; only one-third of the students could do subtractions. Though their reading capacity has somewhat improved over the years from 2009 to 2013, the capacity for subtraction has declined both in government and in private schools (Pratham 2015). This is despite GoG's Gunotsav or 'Celebrating Quality' programme since 2009. The programme has been geared to raise awareness among teachers, students and their parents as well as among administrators for the quality of education. A few NGOs and good Samaritans conduct remedial classes for those who cannot afford private coaching. They also run circular libraries to provide books and stimulate a reading habit among the students.

According to the statistics, among the youth in the age group of 14–18 years in rural India and Gujarat,

> [Only 25 per cent] are unable to read basic text fluently in their own language. More than half are not able to do basic arithmetic, division (three digits by one digit) operation. More than half can hardly read English sentences. Even among the youth in this age group who have completed eight years of schooling, a significant proportion (of youth) still lack foundational skills like reading and arithmetic ... substantial number of young people who have completed eight years of schooling have difficulty applying their literacy and numeracy skills to real-world situations. (Pratham 2018)

In other words, they are literate only for namesake. The situation in urban areas is marginally better. Most of these students belong to poor families of the deprived, middle and upper castes.

Comprehension

A recent all-India study of students studying at different levels in government and private institutions shows that an overwhelming number of students (between 60 and 70 per cent) of upper primary and also of secondary schools across the states and communities reported that they found it difficult to 'comprehend' classroom teaching. Some of them reported that the teachers do not explain things clearly to them. Several of them have started believing that mathematics, science and English are 'beyond their ability' to learn. The students are made to blame themselves for their weak comprehension, leading to a loss of self-confidence. Weak comprehension has been reported by SC/ST students as well as non-SC/ST students. The prescribed curricula and methods of teaching are hardly conducive to raise curiosity, and inquisitiveness for learning. Many students from deprived communities find the textbooks and syllabus alien to their everyday life. More importantly, the teacher, who is the heart of the education system, is not equipped and motivated to spend enough time to explain the subjects in the manner that the students can comprehend them (Chauhan 2018; Patel 2018; Shah et al. 2018a, 2018b).

The Gujarat government has converted teachers training college to teachers universities in 2009, with a mission to train teachers who will be 'teachers by choice', and to create a talent pool of enlightened professionals, capable of revitalizing the educational situation in India. But so far, the teachers' training, including their orientation programmes, has not been geared to sensitize teachers towards the children belonging to different sociocultural backgrounds and upbringings. It is not on the agenda of teachers' training and in-service orientation programmes to 'de-caste/class' the mindset of teachers. Also, the student–teacher ratio over a period of time has been widening. Further, more often than not, teachers are overburdened with several non-academic responsibilities. Moreover, their remuneration does not sustain commitment for a long period. The problem is particularly acute in case of teachers appointed on an ad hoc basis in government (including aided) schools/colleges, and most of the private plebeian and middle-class institutions.

The available studies on the quality of secondary education are mainly confined to the performance of students in examinations. This is despite the claim of government as well as of several private schools that they aim 'to promote national unity and integration through cross-cultural learning'. But there are hardly any modules which are used by schools to inculcate or even develop integration among students from different cultural backgrounds. A few elite schools claim that they assess 'students' performance not only from the academic point of view but also in the context of the overall or holistic development of the children'. Or they claim 'quality in education includes a concern for the quality of life in all its dimensions' (ISID 2008). More often than not, these objectives are rhetoric rather than a concerted effort.

Performance of students in an examination is generally taken as a parameter of measuring the quality of education. Comparison of the state boards' results is problematic because of the difference in curricula, style and content of the examination papers and their evaluation systems. On an average, every year, one-third of the students fail in the Class X examination. Of those who pass, more than one-third gets less than 50 per cent marks. Only one-fifth obtain over 60 per cent marks. A majority of them are from urban areas and also from schools which have relatively better infrastructure facilities. The present secondary education hardly develops a questioning mind even in the most moderate or elite schools. Most of the students are forced to parrot information based on textbooks and examination guides. CSOs and concerned citizens often express their dissatisfaction of the examination system, but there have not been any serious efforts to change the system.

Contents

Teaching in schools is mostly centred on the prescribed textbooks. These books are prepared by subject experts under the auspices of the respective state government agencies/boards, private publishers, or non-government cultural and social organizations. They broadly cover the curriculum prescribed by the state government education departments or school examination boards. Besides their political ideology, most of the authors of these books and the policymakers are oriented in dominant caste/class cultural ethos.

Notwithstanding the rhetoric on the importance of education in free India for enlightened citizenship, there was hardly any effort in the 1950s on developing the nature and contents of education. The textbook preparatory committees of different states were left to themselves to prepare textbooks, which more or less reproduced contents of the colonial period in different shades. Only in the mid-1960s did the first Education Commission emphasize on the cultivation of values that are appropriate to a modern, democratic and socialist society including tolerance, willingness to see the other person's point of view, etc. After nearly 20 years, the National Policy on Education (NPE) 1986, stipulated that all textbooks must contain certain common core values mentioned in the first NEP. While preparing the National Curriculum Framework (NCF) in the early 1990s, experts observed the need to understand the 'specific educational needs of learners from different sections of the society with special emphasis on the Scheduled Castes, the Scheduled Tribes and the other socially and economically disadvantaged groups.... The fundamental rights of the disadvantaged groups have to be consciously incorporated into the curriculum' (NCF

2000). But this has more or less remained on paper. Even RCS activists and organizations have not persistently built pressure at the state level for incorporating the recommendation of NCF in the textbooks.

Though since the early 1950s, school textbooks do present the Preamble of the Constitution with its core values of equality, justice and fraternity, they have not been incorporated into social life in the teaching pedagogy. Language and social science textbooks and extra reading material harp on the mercantile values of profit and loss, business competition, and promoting consumer culture and goods. The students are taught that public sectors had been a loss because of the unity of labourers. It is often hammered that professional skills and individual ambition are important for development. And that a high standard of living is the just reward of hard work and intelligence. On the other hand, traditional values of upper castes/classes depicting 'inequality' and hierarchy continue in the narratives, as if they are natural. Critical observations and historical facts on the dominant castes and other powerful segments do not find a place in textbooks. In fact, as we have mentioned in Chapter 2, such narratives like 'the age of Narmad' were deleted from syllabus under the pressure of dominant religious sects. Nirantar, a centre for gender and education, analysed textbooks of five states during 2008–2010, providing a feminist critique of nation and identity. The study finds that textbooks of all the states reinforce patriarchal values. In Gujarat, women organizations such as Ahmedabad Women's Action Group (AWAG), Sahiyar and others frequently protested against the stereotypes used while depicting girls in the textbooks. During the 1980s, the state government positively responded and consulted activist scholars for improving the textbooks. Such efforts have some impact, but the overall thrust of depicting woman as homemaker has not changed. In the civic books, more often than not, a male is still portrayed as a citizen. A woman is primarily pictured as wife and mother than as an individual. 'While women are assigned inspirational roles as nurturers and reproducers of moral values, man retains the hegemonic role in history and development of civilization' (Manjrekar et al. 2010, xii). An imagination of the nation has been constructed from the perspective of the dominant classes and their version of history. The socially determined role of gender and the biases against deprived communities have been hardly problematized. In several states, textbooks glorify the *varna* (caste) system as being a 'unique social structure based on a systematic study of human life' (Manjrekar et al. 2010, 76). The prescribed books hardly discuss the hierarchical and oppressive nature of the caste system and the practice of 'untouchability'. Sociocultural symbols and festivals of upper castes are presented as if universally practised by all Indians. On the other hand, cultural values, idioms and beliefs of the 'little traditions' observed by deprived communities are looked down as being 'inferior'. Most of the supplementary or recommended additional books are not much different. For example, a publisher reprinted children storybooks written by Gijubhai Badheka in the 1930s. According to the publisher, these books were 'the best creative works for ideal education to develop an ideal human being'. A Dalit activist identified more than 35 instances from these stories which make discriminatory and derogatory remarks for castes and for males and females. He raised this for public debate for educators in civil society (Macwan 2004; Shah 2005). A number of intellectuals accused the activist of unnecessarily making this as a caste or gender issue. Some maintained silence; and for a few, these were historical writings and hence there was nothing wrong in their publication (Soni 2005; Vijaliwala 2005). In other words, such expressions are looked at as normal, and not objectionable in the 21st century. In this context, Gujarati HCS has almost maintained a silence on the inroad of Hindutva text and supplementary books in educational institutions.

The students of the deprived communities, particularly from rural backgrounds, relate very little to the contents and language of the textbooks that they are taught from. Women, Dalits, tribals, etc., are almost invisible in history and geography books. Or they are described with upper-caste stereotypes, for example, Adivasis are compared with '*sabhaya*, that is, civilized communities', as if they are not civilized. Class XII textbooks mention that 'they keep faith in invisible and inhuman power'. They are depicted as 'ignorant', and believe in 'superstitions'. Such statements humiliate Adivasis scholars and activists (Vasava 2017). Even if the books do not contain discriminatory representations, the language of textbooks remains discriminatory in their omission of deprived social groups. When the content of primary school language textbooks is meant to be 'applicable to all sections of society', their visuals 'display urban middle-class living', registered in terms of 'appliances (lamp shades, refrigerator, wash basins, etc.) and the clothes worn'. Homogenization of cultural values and behaviour are constructed and normatively legitimized as ideals to be imitated. Lessons on social reform movements largely dealt with reforms related to widow remarriage or sati, which were confined to the upper castes. But the movements by deprived communities against their subjugation by upper castes find little or no space in history books (Manjrekar et al. 2010).

Discrimination

Educational institutions provide an opportunity to the students of different sociocultural family backgrounds to intermingle in an everyday classroom environment and in extra-curricular activities such as sports, picnics, cultural programmes, etc. In a recent study, nearly one-third of the SC and ST upper primary, secondary and college students reported that among three of their best friends, at least one belonged to non-SC/ST communities. They mentioned that they visit each other's homes and eat food there (Shah et al. 2018). Mid-Day Meal (MDM) programme in government schools has played a catalytic role in blurring the caste-driven purity-pollution notion among students of different castes. In the earlier phase of the scheme, upper-caste students avoided taking meals in the school (Shah 1986). But, over a period of time, the resistance of upper castes students against MDMs has mellowed. Many of them, particularly of the poorer strata, have begun to take advantage of the scheme. At the same time, however, students from the upper strata of society are increasingly moving away from government to private schools where MDMs are not served. And segregation of seating arrangement in MDM has not significantly reduced in the schools. More than 80 per cent of SC and ST upper primary students reported that they sit in separate lines while taking their mid-day meals (Shah, Kalimili and Thorat 2018). And nearly one-fourth of the upper primary and one-fifth of the secondary students said that they believe that there is a bias in sitting arrangement in a classroom and they cannot sit anywhere they like. But most of these students do not perceive such arrangements as discriminatory. They treat this as a 'normal'. A handful of students reported a sense of feeling humiliated because of discrimination in their school.

This is, however, not the case with the college students of these communities. They constitute a small but important stratum of these communities, aspiring for 'decent' job, dignity and equality. They have inculcated these values not as much from the school environment but from their own life experiences. Most of them (88 per cent) are the first-generation college students in their families, who somehow managed to survive for more than 12 years in the education system. Almost every second SC and ST undergraduate student of non-elite colleges perceives that she/he has experienced discrimination on the basis of her/his caste and economic status in the institution. The proportion of such students is strikingly higher in elite professional and postgraduate institutions, engulfed with cut-throat competition. In these institutions, the students of deprived communities, having attained relatively better performance, tend to compete with the students of the privileged classes. It was observed in a study of college students of professional courses that as many as two-thirds of them 'experienced discriminatory behaviour in college by classmates, teachers and others in respect to the seating arrangement, taking part in sports and other cultural activities because of their caste identity' (Chuhan 2018). They feel humiliated.

Some of them occasionally also raise questions on the dominant cultural narratives, epistemologies and discourses. These questions often make their teachers uncomfortable. Instead of answering or debating such questions with the students, more often the teachers ignore such queries or reprimand the students by labelling their caste identity. More than 20 SC/ST students of these institutions in the country had committed suicide between 2007 and 2016. The reason for such a desperate act is a sense of humiliation. From the beginning of their entry into these institutions, they are labelled differently and are often reminded of being from 'reserved' category, lacking merit to study the courses they are enrolled in. Some of them were directly or indirectly told that engineering or medicine was not their cup of tea. Some felt that they were discriminated against by not being allowed to take up a project or subject of their preference. The environment in these institutions often makes these students feel that many of their upper-caste teachers and fellow students and administration are biased against them (Rao 2013). They are made to feel, as Rohit Vemula expressed in his suicide note that '[t]he value of a man was reduced to his immediate identity' (Chandru, Shah and Wankhede 2016).

In Gujarat, in the last two decades, children from Muslim community find it difficult to get admission in schools of their choice. They are compelled to study in the schools in their localities. They frequently experience humiliation by the teachers and also their fellow students. There are quite a few poorest of the poor children who still do not have access to primary schools despite the RTE Act. Several private schools find some excuse for not admitting students from poor class under the RTE Act. Among those who comply with the law, a few make such arrangements in a classroom that humiliates these students. As one parent said, 'this insult is a reminder that we belong to a certain economic background who cannot afford education in good school' (*Indian Express* 2015, 'RTE in Gujarat', 9 June).

CONCLUSION

On the whole, the colonial legacy of education system continues in post-Independence India. However, education has spread significantly in the Indian society. Despite repeated phases like equality and justice, it reinforces inequality and hierarchical values in the name of achievement and merit. On the whole, the pedagogy of education and the content used by most of the educational institutions hardly develops critical thinking among students. Despite the eminent and committed public-minded educationists emphasizing the aim of education towards developing an egalitarian social order, education institutions have so far failed in evolving pedagogies and modules to integrate students from various cultural backgrounds into the institutions of learning.

The policymakers and educators, mostly from HCS, by design or default have evolved a hierarchical and discriminatory institutional system that provides 'good quality' education to a select few who can economically afford and enjoy their social status. From the initial stage of schooling, the exclusion process follows two tracks: one of private and the other of government-managed institutions. The former, controlled by the upper strata of society, has expanded in number and has pre-eminence with economic resources as well as sociopolitical capital.

Most of the children of the deprived communities have no other way but to enrol in government-managed schools which suffer from lack of human capital and physical infrastructure. The process of exclusion begins at the primary level, and its scale expands at the higher level. At the primary and elementary levels, the proportion of the traditionally lower and economically poor is substantially larger than the upper castes, thanks to their numerical strength in the country's population. But as the escalator moves up from the secondary level to higher education, their place in the education system ebbs. When they begin to compete with the students of traditionally established strata, they are discouraged, humiliated and marginalized in the institutions of higher learning.

The system reinforces inequality and hegemonic values of the 'greater traditions', and also raise aspirations among the have-nots to be equal to the upper strata. This generates contradictions and tensions. Though the students of the deprived communities imbibe hegemonic traditional values, they particularly at higher level resist the dominance of the upper caste in sociocultural and economic spheres. They resist homogenization. Moreover, education also raises aspiration in the students of deprived communities for their upward mobility, which leads to tension within and outside the education system. Moreover, thanks to increased education, litterateurs from the deprived communities have emerged, not only protesting against discrimination and inequality but also creating a counter-narrative of culture. They have become part of civil society in general and RCS in particular, and encounter tension within civil society.

In the 1950s, the concept of common school was mooted by a small section of civil society. It was repeatedly stressed by the first Education Commission; in the 1970s, RCS organizations campaigned for it. This has gradually become an isolated voice. Educational reform, except for piecemeal and half-baked changes, has never been a priority of any political party and civil society. Though a very small section of RCS continues to campaign for neighbourhood school system, it has failed to develop an effective movement. Ironically, sociopolitical activists of the deprived communities do not show much enthusiasm for this project. That indicates their middle-class mindset, which weakens their organic link with their own community. Though civil society intellectuals and other activists often express their anguish on the state of education in India, there is no systematic discourse and campaign to revamp it. They find ways to give 'better' education to their own children at the cost of the common good. RCS finds that the education system has been hijacked by the private sector with the support of the middle class and HRC. It cannot be improved in piecemeal, and RCS has no capacity to intervene in the situation except for occasional protests.

NOTES

1. See http://mhrd.gov.in/sites/upload_files/mhrd/files/document-reports/NPE86-mod92.pdf, accessed 14 August 2018.
2. The said amendment proposed that Article 21A (fundamental right to free and compulsory education for children in the age group of six to fourteen years) be introduced while former Article 45 (the then existing Directive Principle on FCE) be deleted and Article 51A(k) (fundamental duty on parents) be introduced. In November 2001 the Bill was re-numbered as the Ninety-third Bill and the Eighty-third Bill was withdrawn. The Ninety-third Bill proposed that former Article 45 be amended to provide for early childhood care and education instead of being deleted altogether.
3. See also similar campaigns and protests that have been documented in National Centre for Advocacy Studies (2002).
4. Government data on enrolment and dropout though indicative of a trend is not rigorous. For an instance, according to the government data for 2011–2012, of the total Class I students in Gujarat, 25 per cent belonged to STs, though the ST population in the state is 14 per cent (GoI 2014). CAG test check districts during 2009–2014 also give us a reason to doubt the government data. Iyenger (2014) raises questions on the government figures. See also Berliner (2011) and Ravitch (2010).
5. From 1991, with the restructuring of schooling, higher secondary schools covering Classes X and XI came into existence.
6. The proportion of private recognized (unregulated) schools had significantly increased since the mid-1990s, and they now accounted for 17.4 per cent of all elementary schools. About 2.4 per cent schools are unrecognized (NUEPA 2014).
7. Based on budgets and information on salary provided by SMC on 30 January 2010, per capita expenditure on a student = (Revenue Expenditure + Salary) – Income/Total Number of Students.
8. In 2009, the Tamil Nadu Schools (Regulation of Collection of Fee) Act came into existence. Andhra Pradesh, Karnataka, Maharashtra and Rajasthan enacted similar laws.

Self-employed Workers and Their Empowerment

NGOs carry out a number of welfare and 'development' programmes for the poor out of their own initiative and also in collaboration with the government. In the 1950s and the 1960s, the programmes were related to community development, agriculture improvement, Khadi spinning and weaving, village industries, sewing, pottery farming, literacy and adult education, family planning, etc. From the early 1970s, besides continuing the earlier programmes, they also started programmes in dairy, forest co-operatives, labour co-operatives, housing, health, training village panchayat personnel, carpet making, skill development, watershed, forest product co-operative, self-help and credit, slum development, women and child development, etc. In the 1990s, A. R. Desai observed,

> [T]hese programmes appear like a large departmental store, providing goods and services of diverse, contradictory and even overlapping nature. The inner unity of these diverse programmes appears to lie outside, subverting some deeper purpose of rulers pursuing a particular path than the real needs of the rural poor. (1997, 139)

Except for a handful of organizations, these programmes have been carried out by the NGOs as a delivery agency to meet the prescribed targets, similar to the government departments (Shah and Chaturvedi 1983). However, there have been a few groups which used some of these programmes to conscientize the oppressed to reflect and act, to see the contradiction, and to resist against their exploitation and injustice (Shah 1988).

SELF-EMPLOYED WORKERS

In this chapter, we shall confine to two programmes involving self-employed workers: micro-credit and water-shade. Self-employed workers constitute the single-largest category of the employed persons in India and Gujarat. Their proportion is higher in Gujarat (57 per cent) than the all-India average which was 47 per cent in 2015–2016. In rural Gujarat, they constitute 59 per cent as against 46 per cent in urban areas. However, their ratio in rural Gujarat has slightly declined since 2000, but has increased in urban areas during the same period. In rural areas, a majority of them are cultivators. As against 43 per cent in 1970–1971, 66 per cent in 2010–2011 were small and marginal farmers. A majority of them belong to OBCs, SCs and STs (Dabhi 2017).

Self-employed are of three categories: producers, self-labourers and traders. In production work, the activities vary from cultivation on one's own land in rural areas to manufacturing. The former includes small and marginal farmers and rich peasant; the latter includes large industries employing more than a thousand workers and small micro industries with self and family labour. The activities also include spinning and weaving, embroidery, papad rolling, plate-making, dairy, poultry, fishing and animal husbandry, preparing eatables like Khakhara, pickles, etc. As self-labourers, they sell their skill as a lawyer, medical practitioner, architect, chartered accountant, engineer and so on, and also un/semi-skill labour as a coolie, cart puller, rag collector, carpenter, driver, mechanic of vehicles, gadgets and other machines, etc. And as traders, they own business and companies as well as work as a vendor and petty shopkeeper. Household self-employed activities are largely confined to women. Some organizations have formed co-operative societies of the producers and sellers to share the risk and management. Such variation is reflected in their earnings. Half of the self-employed, on an average, earns less than ₹7,500 per month. Their proportion is strikingly higher (68 per cent) in rural than in urban Gujarat (25 per cent). Less than 1 per cent earns more than ₹50,000 per month. In urban Gujarat, their proportion is 1.4 per cent as against merely 0.2 per cent in rural areas. Those self-employed who earn more than ₹50,000 per month are university-qualified professionals and middle or large business/industry owners. In rural areas, they are middle and rich farmers. Nearly 50 per cent of the self-employed workers are petty producers, vendors and skilled/unskilled labourers with their own instrument. The last category is dicey; it covers casual labourers, coolies and cart pullers and also plumbers, blacksmiths, etc. A large number of women are self-employed as petty producers and traders as vendors (see Tables 4.1 and 4.2).

Table 4.1 *Distribution of Employed Persons in Gujarat in 2000 and 2016 (in %)*

Type of Employment	1999–2000		2015–2016	
	Rural	Urban	Rural	Urban
Self-employed	59.2	41.0	58.2	45.9
Regular salary employed	6.3	34.1	9.0	31.6
Casual labourers	34.5	24.9	32.9	22.5
Total employed	100.0	100.0	100.1	100.0

Source: Hirvey and Mahadevia (2004); GoI (2016).

Table 4.2 *Average Monthly Earnings (in Rupees) of Self-employed in Rural and Urban Gujarat (2015–2016)*

	Rural	Urban	Total
>5,000	41.0	10.3	31.7
5,001–7,500	26.7	14.8	23.5
7,501–10,000	17.5	21.8	18.8
10,001–20,000	11.9	34.1	18.6
20,001–50,000	2.7	17.7	7.2
<50,001	0.2	1.4	0.5

Source: GoI (2016).

SELF-EMPLOYED AND SELF-HELP GROUPS

Credit is a major constraint of the poor, self-employed producers and sellers. Commercial banks and moneylenders are usual sources to get a loan. More often than not, banks do not prefer to give a loan to the poor who do not have property or other assets for a mortgage. The poor have to often accept usury by paying a very high rate of interest to local moneylenders. To mitigate this, an alternative source of credit through self-help groups (SHGs) was innovated in the 1970s. Later, in the late 1980s, international bankers and donor agencies, as well as the States here and abroad, found SHG to be the panacea not only for poverty alleviation but also for making poor entrepreneurs free from their dependency on the State as well as private moneylender support. The underlying assumption is that SHG is the best way for the State to retreat from the social sector. The poor are persuaded to find out their way in the market. Management gurus have eulogized microfinance as 'the hidden wealth of the poor', which needs to be tapped by the market for the benefit of the poor and also the corporate sector. Many development NGOs with the support of donors, bankers and the State are involved in forming and managing SHG.

SEWA AND THE FORMATION OF WOMEN'S CO-OPERATIVE BANKS

SEWA is one of the leading organizations in unionizing self-employed women for their empowerment. It is an offshoot of the Majoor Mahajan Sangh (labour union) founded in 1919 by Gandhi on the principle of class collaboration, maintaining harmony between capital and labour. SEWA is a trade union of self-employed women workers that was registered in 1972. Its goal is to organize women workers, 'for full employment [and] self-reliance with income security, food security and social security'. In fact, before the concept of SHG gained international currency, SEWA from its own experiences evolved an institutional mechanism of the poor self-employed women for helping each other by creating capital of their own to support each other. While working with self-employed women in Ahmedabad, SEWA realized that one of the major problems of vegetable and second-hand garment vendors was debt. They needed small capital to buy the goods in order to sell them, which they borrowed from moneylenders, touts, etc., at high interest—varying from 10 per cent to 25 per cent a month. SEWA approached the scheduled banks, seeking loans for the self-employed. But the banks were not willing to oblige them. As a natural part of the coping mechanism to survive themselves in the situation, an idea of forming their own bank had emerged from their internal dialogue in 1973. They thought that though they were poor, they were many in number, and could collectively help each other with a small saving of everyone (Bhatt 2006, 102–103). Before translating their thought into action, SEWA carried out a survey to know their potential clientele. After assessing the potentialities of saving and risk, the Shri Mahila SEWA Sahakari Bank Ltd. (SEWA Women's Co-operative Bank) was formed in 1974, with an initial share capital of ₹71,320 from 6,287 members. In 2016–2017, its membership reached 471,653 and its working capital was over 3.4 million. It has 13 branches in Gujarat, mostly in Ahmedabad. The bank is a part of a SEWA network of more than 19 organizations. From the beginning, SEWA does not engage merely in providing credit but also provides training and assistance to members to make their loans and savings productive. From time to time, it has also evolved different strategies for extending technical and management assistance in production, storage, procurement, design, and sale of their goods and services. In 2003, the SEWA Trade Facilitation Centre (STFC) was established, to facilitate production and marketing of more than 15,000 women artisans in the textiles and handicrafts sector. Unlike a usual commercial bank, it has innovated affordable devices of repayment to meet the requirements of poor borrowers can afford. It has created a cadre among the members called 'banksathi' who motivate members for saving, identify members who need a loan for their occupation, and assess their capacity—previous liability, regularity of income, etc.—and guide them about procedures of the bank for a loan.

SELF-HELP GROUPS

A year after the formation of the SEWA bank, Elaben participated in the first United Nation's World Conference on Women, held in

Mexico City, in 1975. The conference resolved to create a global support network for women who have entrepreneurial skills but who lack the capital, management skills and confidence to build a viable business. One of the participants Michela Walsh, a US investment broker, established Women's World Banking (WWB), a global organization based in New York, in 1980, which aims at providing finance to female micro-entrepreneurs around the world. In 1982, the Friends of WWB (FWWB) was formed. This was the time when Muhammad Yunus, a professor of economics in Bangladesh, formed mutual-help groups of vendors in villages which eventually became the Grameen Bank in 1983.

In India, the government established NABARD (National Bank for Agriculture and Rural Development) in 1982 with the objective of providing and regulating credit and other facilities for the promotion and development of agriculture and small-scale industries. In 1987, NABARD decided to promote microfinance through SHGs (for women or man), and sanctioned ₹1 million as grant assistance to the credit management groups promoted by them. The Reserve Bank of India (RBI) directed all scheduled commercial banks to participate in NABARD's pilot project of extending loans to SHGs. In 1994, the RBI constituted a working group for studying the functioning of SHGs and NGOs with a view of expanding their activities and 'deepening their role in the rural sector'. In 1999, the government launched the Swarnjayanti Gram Swarozgar Yojana (SGSY), a part of the rural development poverty alleviation programme focusing on vulnerable sections of society. Its objective has been of 'bringing every assisted family above the poverty line within three years, through the provision of microenterprise'. The District Rural Development Agency (DRDA) has become a nodal agency to promote SHGs. Again, to strengthen poverty alleviation programme by improving earlier schemes, the GoI launched the National Rural Livelihood Mission (NRLM) in 2011 to organize the poor into SHGs and make them capable for self-employment.

With the neoliberal economy, the concept of microcredit has become a byword in the vocabulary of development-oriented programmes. The United Nations declared 2005 as the 'Microcredit Year'. Private banks entered in the field of SHGs. In 2005, *The Economist* reported that ICICI had close to 1.5 million customers 'that qualify as deeply poor, and [an] associated loan portfolio of $26m'. Some of the world's wealthiest banks such as City Group, Deutsche Bank, HSBC and ABN Amro have become active players in this field, though the euphoria subsided after the 2008 economic crisis.

According to the NABARD (2014), there were more than 7.5 million SHGs, with the saving deposit of ₹98.974154 billion. On average, the saving of SHG comes to around ₹13,000. In Gujarat, their number is around 200,000, with an average saving of ₹8,000 (Saravanan 2016). Most of the NGOs in Gujarat engaged in 'development' activities are involved in forming SHGs both in urban and rural areas. Seventy-three per cent of the members of SHGs are women. Except for a few, they are linked with commercial banks and FWWB, India.

In order to understand grassroots reality, we carried out a study of SHGs (in 2007–2008) formed by Antyodaya Mahila Sangh (AMS) of the Ahmedabad Study Action Group (ASAG) in Dholaka and Bavala Talukas of Ahmedabad district (Shah 2008). The NGO had organized co-operatives for embroidery and carpet workers. The collected savings were deposited with the SEWA Bank. In due course of time, the SHGs' deposits and loans were linked with FWWB, commercial banks and co-operative credit societies. In 1998, an autonomous federation of the SHGs, registered as AMS, was formed, with a view to encourage women SHG and their leadership.

A majority of the members are small and marginal farmers. Like elsewhere else, the poorest of the poor had either not joined or dropped out from the SHG because of their inability to part some amount regularly from their income, which has been meagre (Das 2000, 37). Eighty per cent of the respondents reported that they almost regularly borrow the generally small amount from someone—relative and friends, moneylenders or employers—every year to buy food-grains during the offseason. Half of them pay interest mostly to moneylenders for such short-term loan. They generally repay as soon as they get their wages or the employers deduct the amount from the wages. Such borrowing from the employer is treated as an advance. In such a situation, a labourer has an obligation to work for the same master, sometimes for lower than the prevailing market wages.

Besides routine borrowing for everyday needs, the poor are forced to borrow to meet certain essential needs. During the preceding year (2004–2005) of the inquiry, as many as 70 per cent of the SHG members borrowed for different purposes from places other than the SHG. Some of them (23 per cent) had borrowed for more than one purpose, and a few (6 per cent) had borrowed three times for different purposes. One of the main purposes of borrowing is to meet social obligations which include marriage, pregnancy, birth and death ceremony, and performance of certain religious rituals. Expenses on such obligations according to them were necessary to be a part of community living. Sickness—particularly major diseases—in the family leads to indebtedness, as health care is very expensive in proportion to the income of the poor. Nearly 22 per cent of the members, borrowed to meet social obligations, buy food grains as well as to pay medical expenses in a year. For minor ailments such as fever, malaria, jaundice, diarrhoea, etc., the patient's family spends on medicine and consultation. Another major purpose for borrowing is to meet the requirements for their agriculture and milch animals. Several of them often require finances to buy fertilizers, fodder, seeds, bullocks, etc. A few borrowed to buy raw material, infrastructure and machinery for their business. Some borrowed to meet expenses of education of their children, repairing of a house, purchase of household things including food grains and clothing, and also for repayment of another past debt (see also Das 2005; Shah 2003).

According to the rules of SHG (in 2008), a member could take the first loan of a maximum of ₹2,000 or double of one's own savings, whichever was less. Beside the membership fee of ₹51, one was required to pay 1 per cent of the loan amount as a service charge and ₹20 as stamp duty if the amount was less than ₹3,000. For the higher amount, the stamp duty was 10 per cent of the loan. One also had to pay ₹2 for a card. Interest was 20 per cent per annum at a flat rate and was required to be paid off in 12 monthly instalments.

An average amount of loan among the borrowers from SHG was ₹6,618. The main purpose of SHG loans had been for buying milch animals such as buffaloes or cows, and/or fodder seeds, fertilizer, insecticides, water, etc. to increase production. A loan amount for such purpose ranged from ₹1,000 and ₹10,000. Some (18 per cent) of the borrowers conceded that they used this loan amount to meet social obligations, but did not mention such purpose in their applications as a loan for a social purpose was not admissible. Three per cent of them used the loan money to repay the earlier debt of moneylenders. This helped them to reduce the burden of interest, and in some cases to get mortgaged land back for self-cultivation. Nearly one-third borrowed for consumption purposes, to purchase food grains and other household things. Fourteen per cent of the borrowers took a loan more of than ₹1,000 for their business. This was to purchase raw material or machinery/equipment. In one case, it was to buy tires for the truck, which the woman's husband purchased with a loan from a commercial bank for transporting goods. Most of them had borrowed less than ₹5,000. Only 3 out of 25 who took a loan for business purposes borrowed more than ₹10,000. In fact, one of them had borrowed ₹100,000 from a bank for his business. Only 5 per cent of the borrowers reported that they could increase their income with the loan, varying from ₹1,000 to ₹3,000 per month.

The loans provided by SHGs were relatively small in the study area; several other studies show similar data (Das 2000; Shah 2003). Nevertheless, meagre sums do, in some instances, provide relief, and in fewer still, help to create 'success stories' as entrepreneurs. But a majority of these successes prove to be temporary: most are unable to withstand the vagaries of the market, and their improved condition is not sustainable in the long run. In the local market, their choice of an enterprise is limited by their skill, raw material and the consumer's buying capacity. Also, people tend to take up the same kind of occupation with the help of the loan. For example, if two women buy sewing machines with their loan, others follow their footsteps. This has also been observed in the case of occupations such as making plates from leaves, grocery, tea, garments and vegetable shops. Their competition disperses and it reduces their income. Many would like to start enterprises that bring in more profit, but in the majority of cases, they lack information about market trends, except their own gut feeling based on observations around on what to produce, how to get raw material, where to sell, etc. Several case studies (Shah 2003) have shown that NGOs and bureaucrats of DRDA do not carry out a market survey. Forward and backward linkages of information, raw material, consumers, competing producers, etc. are not assessed. Hence, more often than not, the investors take a decision on the basis of their past experiences and their observation around local milieu. Consequently, more often than not, they concentrate on the local village market (Shah 2003; VOICE 2008). Even most of the experienced entrepreneurs face difficulties in expanding the enterprise with internal competition and fluctuating market. They are unable to survive against the big players who have more capital, competence and skill to withstand the vagaries of the imperfect market.

For most of the NGO functionaries, SHG is like many other government programmes which enable them to carry on their activities. They are too preoccupied to comply with the procedures and recovery of loans. There are, however, exceptional NGOs committed to improving the economic condition of the poor. They improve procedures for lending, identify forward and backward linkages for enterprise, and train prospective entrepreneurs. But on the whole, they often get disappointed with the ground-level reality where the people without resources have very little chance to compete with dominant forces. Notwithstanding their efforts, a self-employed worker as a producer, vendor or wage labourer gets at best around ₹7,500 per month in urban areas. The notion of the minimum wage per hour or per day is not applied to those who are engaged in home-based self-employment in making eatables, crafts, stitching or other labour-added work. Their bargain power is limited, almost absent, in the fluctuating market and labour surplus situation. With increased competition among workers, sophisticated mechanization, and the vagaries of the weather and the market amongst other factors, available working days and real income have declined. They earn 'too little to live on, too much to die on'. They somehow keep their body and soul together. And the macroeconomic policies for liberalization, as Elaben Bhatt observes, increasingly affect the poor adversely. In despair, they are divided over ethnic, religious, regional and occupational lines, weakening their bargaining powers.

Ela Bhatt says: 'SEWA Bank is not able to control the macro-structural factors, and this is a reality to reckon with' (2006, 122).

While microfinance provides some relief, it does not reduce, let alone eradicate, poverty; it only peripherally touches the problem. Only a few two or three out of a hundred members are able to improve their living conditions, becoming 'success' stories that are often highlighted by NGOs to foster hope among the others. But for many members, this is more of an illusion than a reality. Mahajan rightly observes that a micro-credit loan, 'is at worst an apology for no access to formal credit, and at best a palliate to be used to smoothen consumption'. Meagre help does not improve the condition of the poor; it only helps them to cope with the situation. It is important, however, to remember, as the activists point out, that even the meagre aid provided by the SHGS helps the poor to survive. 'What else can we (NGOs) do?', they ask. Many get disappointed and frustrated, but they do not find any alternative. At the same time, the programme perpetuates hope among many self-employed entrepreneurs, as one woman vendor who is a member of Sewa Bank said to me in 2010: 'You know Ambani was a vendor and became a rich industrialist, we also hope to become a successful entrepreneur'. The scheme legitimizes the capitalist system inculcating aspirations among the poor to be wealthy.

Widespread indebtedness of the poor continues. According to the recent NSSO survey, 2014 reveals that 26 per cent of the rural households in Gujarat reported outstanding cash loans. A majority of these households, around 64.6 per cent, pay more than 25 per cent rate of interest. In fact, one-third of the indebted households pay at an interest rate of 30 per cent or above (Shah 2014).[1] The system of private money continues to thrive.[2]

WATERSHED PROGRAMMES

Gujarat, particularly to its north, the north-western region of Saurashtra and Kutch, and the eastern tribal belt, frequently faces the problem of scarcity of water for drinking and irrigation. Frequent droughts coupled[3] with the erratic monsoon, limited sources for perennial water and depletion of groundwater—thanks to the increasing cash crop (Bhatia 1992)—contribute to the situation. Small and marginal farmers and landless labourers are most affected by water scarcity. In dry and sandy lands, all farmers, irrespective of the size of their holdings, do not produce enough to sustain them and are forced to migrate in search of work during the off-season.

With the passage of time, traditional water management systems which were managed relatively well and assured the provision of drinking water to the villages even during droughts have declined (Hirway and Patel 1994). To meet the frequent water crisis, a few farmers have been innovating different techniques to collect and preserve rainwater, and also recharge their dry wells. One of them is Premji Patel, a middle peasant who has systematically carried out his experiment. He left his business in Bombay and settled in his native village to do farming. In 1968–1969, he innovated a technique of recharging wells by diverting rainwater into the dry wells through a small pit to trap the silt so that only freshwater flows into the well. In 1973, he carried out rooftop rainwater capture in the backyard of his compound. Slowly, a few others followed him in the work of water recharging. They also developed a *khet talavadi* (small pond), that is, check dam, near their farms to conserve rainwater. These pioneers motivated some others, and their number increased in different parts of Saurashtra after the drought spell of 1985–1987. By this time, watersheds (geo-hydrological units draining at a common point by a system of streams) gained currency in the government's area development schemes and were adopted by the drought-prone area programme (DPAP) in 1987. The National Wasteland Development Board put forth its Integrated Wasteland Development Programme (IWDP) in 1989, and emphasis was laid on developing wastelands following watershed method. The Ministry of Agriculture conceptualized the National Watershed Development Programme in rain-fed areas. Besides promoting the economic development of village communities, the programme emphasized the improvement of 'the economic and social condition of the resource-poor and the disadvantaged sections of the watershed community', for 'a balanced development' (Rajora 2002, 11).

This prompted several individuals engaged in water harvesting in Saurashtra to form organizations, register under the Trust Act to get government assistance, and spread their message and widen the group. Some of the widely known organizations are Vruksh Prem Seva Trust (1968), Saurashtra Lok Manch Trust (1989), ORPAT Trust (1993),

Jalkranti Trust (1996), Saurashtra Jaldhara Trust (1998), etc. Hindu religious sects such as Swadhyay Parivar and Swaminarayan Sampraday also actively carry out the work of check dams (Mudrakartha 2012). Many of these organizations receive support from diamonds and textile industrial entrepreneurs settled in Bombay and Surat. A few of them also fall in the category of NGOs to receive a grant from the government under various rural development programmes. In 2000, Gujarat government launched the Sardar Patel Sahbhagi Jal Sanchay Yojana providing a 60 per cent[4] grant for the construction of check dams.

A few other NGOs also came up during this period, focusing on the poor and deprived section in water harvesting programmes. Utthan is one such NGO. The four young women activist-founders were inspired by Professor Ravi Mathai's famous Jawaja experiments. They wanted to initiate a sustainable process of empowerment amongst the oppressed, especially the women. Utthan began its work in Dhandhuka taluka, Ahmedabad district, focussing around the issue of access to a safe and regular supply of drinking water. As against the centralized and expensive pipeline schemes favoured by the government, Utthan focused on smaller, inexpensive, and locally managed schemes and systems. The Aga Khan Rural Support Programme, Sarthee, Medhavi, Anarde Foundation, etc., are also engaged in watershed programmes. In the tribal belt, the first initiative came from Sadguru Water and Development Foundation (SSST) Trust in 1974 for rural development. It is an offspring of a corporate house Arvind Mafatlal (of the group formerly known Mafatlal Group; now, Stanrose Group of Companies), which entered agribusiness in the 1970s as part of its diversification of interests. Besides 'service' to rural areas, its primary objective was to sell 'a whole range of agro-product' to the state for its rural development programmes (Savur 1990, 304). During the drought in the early 1970s, the SSST began philanthropic work, setting up of 'free kitchens', and distribution of seeds and consumption loans to affected tribals in eastern Gujarat. Harnath and Sharmistha Jagavat, trained in social work from MS University, Vadodara, joined the organization and focused their work on irrigation to improve agriculture in tribal areas. With government assistance and the help of engineers, a pilot scheme for constructing a check dam in the village of Shankerpura was planned in 1976, with three more schemes being undertaken over the next four years.

The government's rural development programmes such as the DPAP and IWDP have facilitated the work of Utthan, Sarthee, SSST, etc. They have formed a network called Pravah. Like community-based NGOs, these organizations also construct community lift irrigation, check dams and recharge wells, maintain and deepen ponds, etc. SSST functions largely in the tribal areas of Gujarat, Rajasthan and Madhya Pradesh (MP); Utthan functions in three districts of Gujarat: Dahod, Bhavnagar and Amreli. These organizations are involved in levelling land, bunding farms, social forestry, biogas plants, and horticulture. Utthan focuses on the process of the watershed programme that emphasizing people's participation and gender equality. Though SSST too forms local people's organizations, it is more concerned with providing tangible economic benefits to the tribals. Utthan worked on desalination through reverse osmosis and solar distillation, rainwater harvesting in plastic-lined ponds and roof rainwater harvesting, using highly innovative experiments and providing practical demonstration models. With these initiatives, as many as 166,082 check dams with water storage capacity of 28,408 million cubic feet (mcf) have been built in the state (*ToI* 2016).

Various studies find that with the watershed, new areas have been cultivated in both Kharif and Rabi seasons and soil moisture content has improved. There is an increased preference for growing improved varieties of maize and pulses in both seasons, and for wheat in the Rabi season. The crop yield has also increased, though it is not consistent in all the areas and all the years. Crop damage during the drought years has reduced from what it was in the past. With the check dams as well as the increased length of Narmada canals in Saurashtra region after 2000, ground-level water has increased. The quality of water has also improved; the watershed projects have certainly eased everyday life in coastal areas where salinity and drinking water were two major, acute problems. Women's drudgery in the collection of firewood and water has declined. Distressed migration in the tribal watershed villages has also declined for those tribals who own land and gain the benefit of a watershed.

However, in the non-tribal villages, water resources are controlled by the upper castes. With watershed programmes, middle peasants have improved their economic condition and have also developed their social capital, consolidating their social network. Most of the OBCs and SCs who are landless and small and marginal farmers have benefitted marginally. Though the landless got work at the time of construction of check dams, and their drinking water problem has been somewhat eased, their overall economic condition remained the same. As per the government rule, it is mandatory to form a water committee having members from the deprived communities and women members. In practice, these committees are formed, but dominant caste elite have been reluctant to give place to the poor belonging to SCs and OBCs. Participation of women in village-level activities has not increased, despite efforts of NGOs like Utthan. It has been observed that 'hierarchy of benefits and beneficiaries, with households receiving irrigation benefiting most, followed by those getting on farm treatments like field bunds, and the landless with or without livestock, receiving the least' (PND 2002, 12). A study by the Policy Development Initiative (PDI) and the Gujarat Ecology Commission in 2002 observed: 'As a result, in spite of the positive impact of the watershed programmes on crop production and soil/moisture conservation, *there is no significant reduction in the gender and income inequality in the project areas*' (PND 2001). Even among the beneficiary strata of the watershed, small and marginal farmers (60 per cent) experience difficulties when they face a drought-like situation leading to failure of crops. And even in a normal time as agriculture input has become expensive, they increasingly find it difficult to sustain farming. The majority of them would prefer to give up agriculture and opt for an urban occupation.

STREET VENDORS: ASSERTION FOR PUBLIC SPACE

Since 1971, SEWA has been engaged in organizing vendors for their right to a business that can sustain them. Vendors constitute the single-largest group of self-employed workers in urban areas. They sell all kinds of things: vegetables, fruits, fish, used and new garments, utensils, etc. They sell their goods on the side of the roads, on footpaths and street corners, which sometimes obstructs traffic. The municipality considers this use of public space illegal, and the police, who extort substantial bribes from vendors for allowing them to occupy these spaces, are asked to remove them. Since the early 1970s, with the support from SEWA, their demand is that they should be allowed to use roadsides or be provided a space where they could carry on with their business, and that their businesses have a license so that the police would not harass them. This was around the time when Mumbai's slum dwellers were forced to evacuate footpaths, and social activists were demanding the slum dwellers' right to a life. A PIL was filed in the Supreme Court against their eviction in Bombay. In 1978, SEWA organized a protest march in Ahmedabad against police harassment of the vendors in which about 2,000 vendors participated. The organizers invited the chief minister to address their demands. The first question the CM asked the vendors was why they did not go back to the villages whence they had come (Rose 1992, 69). Later, however, he met with the city superintendent of police and municipal officers asking them to meet SEWA's demands for a designated space for the vendors to conduct their business. Police harassment then declined for a while, thanks to the CM's intervention.

In 1980, the authorities marked the open spaces used by vendors as a parking space. SEWA protested the decision, complaining to the police commissioner about it. The vendors carried on regardless, only to have the police come and evict them. This exercise was repeated every day for a week, during which time the vendors lost out on a significant portion of their earnings. SEWA tried to convince the police commissioner not to evict the vendors on humanitarian grounds. Elaben Bhatt argued: 'Don't these vendors in their bright clothes with their fresh vegetables look much nicer than parked cars?.... Shouldn't we give priority to their earning their living? All they are asking from you is two baskets worth of space' (Rose 1992, 71). Though the commissioner relented and promised to find a way out, nothing happened, and the vendors were again removed the next day. A second week passed. Elaben asked the vendors, 'Shall we brave the police? Are you ready to claim what is yours?' Everyone agreed that it was better to fight than to starve, and they decided to launch a satyagraha on 30 January, Gandhi's death anniversary. Several leaders, including the chairperson and secretary of the TLA, tried to dissuade them from direct action, but it was futile, and the vendors remained firm and occupied their usual space on the 30. Laxmiben, one of the participants, recounted her experience:

> We went to the market early. All the SEWA organizers were with us, and we sat in our usual places. Our baskets were empty though because we did not know what would happen. None of us could afford to lose any vegetables. The organizers stood between and behind us. Many of us were nervous. After everything that had happened to us, we were terrified of the police. I have been badly beaten up many times. Elaben kept reminding us to stay calm. She told us if [they] were arrested, to just go quietly. Five police vans pulled up, full of constables. Pretty soon a crowd gathered, everyone was looking at what was going on. A few people started harassing us and stirring up the situation. The behns [literally, sisters, here used for the leaders] kept reminding us to stay calm. The policemen acted like they were maintaining law and order, but wherever they went, where the fights would start. Also, the shopkeepers were shouting at us. They do not like us here. It was difficult not to fight. This was our place. But we could also see this was just what everyone wanted to happen. If we fought, they would arrest us, and we would be out of the market again. (Rose 1992, 72)

The tussle continued for several hours and traffic was disrupted. The police commissioner failed to persuade Elaben and others, and left in a huff, asking them to manage the traffic. SEWA volunteers managed the traffic for five days. Later, with the initiative of some civil society intelligentsia engaged in town planning, a meeting comprising of SEWA, the vendors, the municipal commissioner and the police commissioner was convened in order to find a solution. A compromise was reached whereby SEWA demarcated a space that would not disrupt traffic which was provided to the vendors. The authorities informally recognized this solution, but the arrangement did not last long, and the vendors again faced police harassment. During this period, P. N. Bhagwati, then the Chief Justice of the Supreme Court and the chairperson of the Committee for Implementing Legal Aid Schemes, invited suggestions from NGOs for amending laws or forming new laws in favour of the poor. Ela Bhatt responded with an angry account of the vendors' hardships:

> Laxmiben had been selling vegetables in Manek Chowk for the last forty years, sitting in the same place where her mother-in-law had sat before her. Each time she was fined—which was three or four times a week—she had to pay 12.50 rupees. She had receipts of the fines she had paid for the past

six years. Shakriben too had been vending, in Manek chowk for the past six years ... there were many women who could demonstrate continuous presence in that market over many years. (Bhatt 2006, 87)

Justice Bhagwati turned her letter into a PIL, and SEWA—four vendors and Ela Bhatt—then filed a case in the Supreme Court against the municipal commissioner, the police commissioner and the State of Gujarat, asserting that by denying licenses to the petitioners, 'the vendors' fundamental constitutional rights to trade was being violated by the municipality' (Bhatt 2006, 88). Neither police nor municipality defended their actions and remained absent from the court. The court ordered the municipal commissioner to issue licenses to all SEWA members in Manek Chowk and to work out a solution for using public space in consultation with SEWA. Until then, the court asked the municipality to provide temporary certificates to the vendors, enabling them to carry out their activities from their current places in Manek Chowk. After a long negotiation, a separate space was identified for the vendors, close to their previous location. There is no permanent solution to this problem yet. The municipality has issued licenses to only 1,000 against the 80,000 vendors in the city in 2004. In 1985 and 1987, in the case of Mumbai and Delhi, the Supreme Court reiterated its position that hawking was a fundamental right.[1] Ela Bhatt laments,

> The court order regarding Manek Chowk survives today as just a document. The municipality drags its feet at every step, even as the next generation vendors takes place, plying their tread in the name of their parents—some dead, some alive. Harassment at the local level continues in Manek Chowk. Vested interests are deep and pervasive—space in this thriving market is at a premium, and the poor are bound to get the short end of the stick unless they can band together to protect their interests. (Bhatt 2006, 88)

Since this struggle, SEWA has continuously campaigned for 'two baskets-worth of space', licenses and identity cards, and social security for vendors, and has built pressure on the Union as well as the state government for the formation of a policy that meets the basic demands of the vendors. In 1986, as a Member of the Parliament, Bhatt moved a resolution on vendors urging the government 'to formulate a national policy for hawkers and vendors by making them a part of the broader structural policies aimed at improving their standard of living', urging that the state to, 'protect their existing livelihood and provide legal access to the use of available space in urban areas' (Bhatt, 2006, 88–89). In 1996, due to SEWA's initiative, various NGOs from 33 cities of the country who were working on this issue met in Ahmedabad to form the National Alliance of Street Vendors, India (NASVI). In collaboration with the Ministry of Urban Development, NASVI organized a national policy dialogue in order to formulate national policy. Again, in collaboration with the Ministry of Housing and Urban Poverty Alleviation, SEWA organized a national workshop in Ahmedabad in 2001, where a national task force that would prepare a draft policy paper was set up, with the Minister of State as its chairperson. After deliberations at various levels, this draft document was finalized in 2002, and sent to state governments for endorsement. The Gujarat government prepared its draft policy on the model of the proposed national policy that gives vendors 'legal status by amending, enacting, repealing, and implementing appropriate laws and providing hawking zones in urban development/zoning plans' (in Bhatt 2006, 98). With these efforts, in 2004, the GoI declared the Street Vendors Policy which was revised in 2009 as the National Policy on Urban Street Vendors. In 2010 the Supreme Court directed the government to prepare central legislation. With all struggles and lobbying, the parliament enacted the Street Vendors (Protection of Livelihood and Regulation of Street Vending) Act' in 2014. The Act provides protection to 'legitimate' street vendors from harassment by police and civic authorities. The local governments are asked to demarcate 'vending zones' on the basis of 'traditional natural markets'. Gujarat government notified the rules in 2016, but schemes have not been formed and vending zones have not yet been created[5]. It is either remained on paper in most of the cities or was inadequately implanted in some cities like Delhi and Ahmedabad (Rai and Mohan 2017). Vendors continue to remain a victim of harassment and eviction (Indorewala 2017).

CONCLUSION

Despite compassion and commitment, coupled with meticulous planning and management of some of the social activists to hold the hand of the poor in providing credit, the programme at the most provides relief to self-employed workers. Few individuals do improve their condition and move up in the ladder, but the rest continue to struggle for survival. This, however, has built confidence among several women to negotiate with the government and the market. This is by no means an insignificant contribution of this collective endeavour. Similarly, the watershed programme and the formation of water committees at the village level by the NGOs have certainly improved groundwater resources. But it has not benefitted the deprived communities and sub-altern women much, except somewhat reducing their everyday drudgery, making getting drinking water less difficult. But on the whole, the women of subaltern communities have not been empowered to have their say in water committees, nor has their vulnerability improved. The beneficiaries of the watershed are those who are middle peasants of the upper castes. They have consolidated their social capital. In the process, their dominance has been consolidated. The case study of the street vendors shows that after a struggle for three decades, they got legal right to have a small space in urban market to do their business. But they are still waiting for the legislation to be implemented.

NOTES

1. See https://counterview.org/2014/12/27/nsso-report-suggests-that-indebted-rural-households-in-gujarat-are-more-dependent-on-informal-moneylenders-than-other-states/, accessed 27 March 2018.
2. See https://www.rbi.org.in/scripts/PublicationReportDetails.aspx?ID=513, accessed 14 August 2018.
3. There were 28 years of drought, famines between 1801 and 1946. Between 1960 and 1970 the state experienced frequent years of scarcity and drought in 1971–1973; and again drought in 1974–1975, 1979–1980 and 1985–1988 (Bhatia 1992, A1–A14).
4. This was later modified as 80:20 for certain regions with tribal predominance, 20 per cent being the local contribution.
5. In the case of Saudan Singh Vs. the New Delhi Municipal Corporation it was declared that 'if properly regulated, according to the exigency of the circumstances, the small traders on the sidewalks can considerably add to the convenience of the general public by making available ordinary articles of everyday use at comparatively lesser price…the right to carry on trade or business mentioned in the Article 19 (1) g of the Constitution, on the street pavements, if properly regulated, cannot be denied on the ground that the streets are meant exclusively for passing or re-passing and no other use'. See Sharit K. Bhowmik. 2004. 'Contesting Urban Space: Street Vendors and the Struggle for recognition'. http://wiego.org/sites/wiego.org/files/publications/files/Bhowmik_Urban_Responses_to_Street_Trading_India.pdf accessed on 27 December 2015.

Legal Recourse and Collective Struggles of the Subalterns

The notion of natural or moral rights has emerged through experiences, social practice and discursive discourse, with different meanings in the course of time in different contexts and in different societies. Some of the natural rights continue to remain ethical codes of conduct and principles, and some others, in the course of time, take the form of social customs and/or State-enacted law in the form of legislation and rules. The laws are enforceable. It is the function and prime obligation of the State to implement the laws that it has enacted. It is the core principle of rule of law. The process of lawmaking is embedded in social morality, practices and public deliberation. Social activists, philosophers and jurists deliberate on moral and ethical aspects of rights in different contexts in the public forum. Some of them also get engaged in campaigning with people and lawmakers in articulating public opinion and in translating moral and ethical rights to legal rights. Having legislation and rules, the civil society builds pressure on the government for the implementation of a law. This process is ongoing from social experiences to deliberation to lawmaking to implementation and back to interrogating law in the practice and experience of law enforcement. This chapter focuses on civil society groups and activists engaged in using the legal agency to provide justice to the poor. Questions that we address are how and which way the law enables the poor to get their rights, and what are constraints in a legal battle that the poor face in getting justice?

There were several movements of peasants in the 19th and 20th centuries till Independence against government-imposed rent and taxes as well as exploitation of peasants by the feudal class. In the course of the struggles, the tillers began to articulate their right as a share in production and also as ownership of land tilled by them. In the process, the demand for land reform legislation and the abolition of the intermediary class between the State and the farmer emerged. Soon after Independence, various state governments including Bombay (including Gujarat), Saurashtra and Kutch enacted the land reforms. In Saurashtra and Kutch, the states rigorously abolished the zamindari system, and tenants were given right to the land. In practice, the upper-caste tenants with their social and political networking and influence received maximum benefits. The tenants and sharecroppers of the lower castes did not get the benefits of the tenancy legislations (Shah 2002).

Following the first phase of land reforms in the 1950s, providing land ownership to the tillers (tenants) and the Minimum Wages Act (1948), radical social activists realized a need for legal literacy and aid to the oppressed so that they could assert their rights. In Gujarat, some voluntary organizations involved in the land reform movement provided legal assistance to the poor tenants to get their right over the land. Sarvodaya activists of the Vedchhi in south Gujarat prepared a simplified version of the Act, its various provisions in non-technical language, so that the poor could understand and know their rights and could fight a legal battle. Such efforts were isolated and did not help most of the tenants of the marginalized communities to get land ownership.

Meanwhile, the different parts of the country experienced the Naxalbari movement of the Communist Party of India (Marxist–Leninist) or CPI (ML) in the late 1950s and the early 1960s. Land grab movements of the socialist and also the assertion of backward castes for political positions in northern India gave a impetus to a section of the civil society of the time. This paved the way for Mrs Indira Gandhi with her slogan 'Garibi Hatao' to get power with a thumping majority. Liberal jurists, academics and other intelligentsia began a search to find ways and means to assist the poor. The radicals who were unhappy with the established Left parties were also in search for a space in the parliamentary democracy. Some jurists and other activists felt a need to provide free legal aid to the poor so that they too could seek justice from the courts. They argued that Article 14 of the Indian Constitution guarantees that, '[t]he State shall not deny to any person equality before the law or the equal protection of the laws within the territory of India'. In 1979, with the amendment of Article 39A of the Constitution, it became the responsibility of the State to provide equal justice and free legal aid to the poor. The amendment states:

> The State shall secure that the operation of the legal system promotes justice, on a basis of equal opportunity, and shall, in particular, provide free legal aid, by suitable legislation or schemes or in any other way, to ensure that opportunities for securing justice are not denied to any citizen by reason of economic or other disabilities.

The Supreme Court[1] stressed that the right to free legal services is an essential ingredient of a reasonable, fair and just procedure for a person accused of an offence, and it must be held to be implicit in the guarantee of Article 21.

In due course of time, with pressure from civil society and pro-common person (*aam aadmi*) judges, the concept of PIL also evolved (Antony 1993). Upendra Baxi (1988) calls it SAL as activists use it as a part of their social action for protecting the rights of the poor. Before PILs gained currency, except in the case of habeas corpus, only aggrieved individuals could move the court for the enforcement of fundamental rights. Justice Krishna Iyer observed,

> Test litigation, representative actions, pro bono publico, broadened forms of legal proceedings are in keeping with the current accent on justice to the common man and a necessary disincentive to those who wish to bypass the real issues on peripheral, procedural short-comings. The public interest is promoted by a spacious construction of *locus standi* in our socio-economic circumstances and conceptual latitudinarianism permits taking liberties with individualization of the right to invoke the higher courts where the remedy is shared by a considerable number, particularly when they are weaker. Less litigation, consistent with fair process, is the aim of adjunctive law. (Cited in Jain 2002, 57–58)

During this period, Jesuit Fr. Joseph Idiakunnel of Rajpipla Social Service Society (RSSS) organized a platform called the Free Legal Aid (FLA) to assist the needy Adivasis. He believed that the spread of knowledge and awareness about the law and the legal system would strengthen the system of rule of law in society. Knowledge of law, according to FLA, was a 'liberating force'. The poor and oppressed can use the law for asserting their rights provided by the State. 'The laws of the State are designed that certain privileges are given to the weakest sections of society, so that they may also successfully compete with the other sections of society' (Kalathil 1978, 7). The FLA organized a training programme for tribal youths in the paralegal field so that it could assist and fight legal battles for the Adivasis. The organization also filed and fought cases for Adivasis against police and forest departments for their atrocities on the poor. Following this model, the Legal Aid and Human Right Centre (LAHRC) was established in 1986 by a Jesuit organization, Surat-based Navsarjan. It works for the tribals in rural and slum dwellers in urban areas. The objective of LAHRC has been to utilize the legal space to ensure the protection and promotion of civil and democratic rights, and uphold human rights, democracy and the rule of law.

Another major programme of LAHRC is to build a team of Adivasi lawyers, both qualified and barefooted (paralegal, without LLB degree). Educational facilities—financial and residential—are provided to Adivasi graduates to pursue their studies in law. It has created a cadre of both female and male lawyers, and it frequently conducts training for the bare-footed lawyers. LAHRC has been collaborating with the Centre for Social Justice (CSJ), Ahmedabad, and the Indian Institute for Paralegal Studies (IIPLS), Pune, for paralegal training.

Jan Vikas is another leading NGO working in legal activism. In 1980, it began with providing training to social activists of different NGOs in the field of human rights. The founder, Gagan Sethi, who earlier worked with the NGO BSC, believes that the law is an important resource for empowering the poor and for bringing social transformation. With the support of the Ford Foundation, a separate unit for social justice called the CSJ was established in 1994. Focusing on 'social justice lawyering', it supports social movements of the people in various parts of the country. While doing this, the law has been used as a tool for building public opinion. With this perspective, CSJ regularly organizes legal training programmes for social activists to create socially committed lawyers for changing power relations in society in favour of the poor. Some of the trainees were inducted into the legal work of different organizations. CSJ has developed law centres in different parts of the state with a team of lawyers, paralegals and trainees. These units work not only for developing legal awareness among the oppressed but also for developing their 'confidence and competencies' to attain equality (Ramaswamy 2017). It also engages with the state mechanism to make *lok adalats* (people-oriented courts) more effective. CSJ worked for the rehabilitation of the victims of the 2001 earthquake as well as of the 2002 communal carnage. It has been actively involved in providing legal help and fighting cases in the court for justice for the victims of the carnage.

CSJ also strives to improve the quality of litigation at the lower courts, legal education and making the delivery mechanism of justice more effective. Along with providing legal aid to an individual, it identifies areas of legal intervention and strives to change existing structures with a view to 'empower' people. It has been instrumental in initiating the implementation of the National Legal Services Authority (NALSA), 1987, in the State of Gujarat. It has contributed to the State Gender Policy and has been consulted by NGOs as well as the government on legislative and policy matters. CJS and other social activists have succeeded in making environmental public hearing (EPH)[2] mandatory before a launching of a project. In order to disseminate legal information, CSJ publishes several journals related to law and social issues: gender and caste-based discrimination and violence, social justice and environment.

The NGOs working for women's rights and equality have legal cells. They assist women victims of rape, sexual abuse, dowry-related crimes and domestic violence. Some of them give training to the police with a view to sensitize them on women's issues. The organizations working for Dalits and tribals also provide legal services to the Dalit victims of atrocities. Notwithstanding these efforts, the cases of violence against women, Dalits, Adivasis and minority communities are increasing every year. Court cases are piling up. Despite a network of legal aid organizations, a number of cases of violence against the poor and marginalized women and men remain unreported. More often than not, a victim avoids taking legal recourse as it is tiring and expensive. Justice in reality remains beyond the reach of many poor people, but social organizations sustain hope among those who are determined to get justice. Therefore, civil society demands judicial reform.

Social Action Litigation

A small radical segment of social activists active in the Navnirman movement in Gujarat and the JP movement in Bihar as well as critics of the Emergency formed the Lok Adhikar Sangh (LAS or People's Right Association) in 1976. Girish Patel, a former professor of law and a lawyer in the Gujarat High Court, was its architect and its spirit. He believes that 'civil, political and democratic rights are not bourgeois illusions, but rather the poor and weak need them more than rich and powerful' (Patel 2009, 11). According to the LAS,

> [T]he human rights of all can become real, effective and meaningful only in a democratic state, economy and society, that the struggle for food and dignified life and for freedom, equality and justice is one and indivisible, and that different human rights groups and organisations working in different spheres of society and at various levels will have to forge a united front and evolve a broad common comprehensive ideological framework to make the human rights struggles a national people's movement for human rights for all. (Patel 2009, 20)

The work of LAS has been confined to courts through human rights litigation. It has also supported several agitations of the poor. It is the only major organization in Gujarat which has fought the largest number of SAL. Some of the cases were filed by its own initiative. In some others, it fought on behalf of other social activists and NGOs. LAS has so far fought more than 50 PILs related to the issues of livelihood, displacement, human dignity, violence, basic human needs such as health and education, environment, etc. After four decades of work, the organization is almost defunct in the 2010s. It won several cases and also lost many in the legal battle. On the whole, Girish Patel believes the experience 'has certainly not been completely negative or totally disappointing or frustrating' (2009, 118).

ADIVASIS' LAND RIGHTS

So far, there have been no large-scale popular social movements encompassing all the poor and the deprived communities in Gujarat and raising the issues of poverty, oppression and exploitation. But there is no dearth of collective struggles, often localized, of the Adivasis (14 per cent) and Dalits (7 per cent) around the issues of land rights, forest resources, wages, discrimination, the practice of untouchability and atrocities. In the late 1940s, soon after Independence, Adivasis and OBCs were up in arms in some parts of the state against the local dominant communities. Individual and collective attempts were made to seize land, which they believed had been encroached from them by the landed and moneylending class. In the 1950s, the Adivasis of south Gujarat struggled to drive out the non-Adivasis from their areas. These struggles did not sustain for a long period against the state's coercive machinery and the hegemony of the dominant classes. However, an organized movement of the Adivasis of Pardi in south Gujarat on the issue of implantation of land reform succeeded after a constant struggle of 15 years from 1953 to 1967. It was non-violent Satyagraha known as Pardi Ghasia (grassland) Satyagraha, led by Praja Socialist Party. It received active support from Gandhian and other organizations. After several confrontations in the form of mass rallies and demonstrations leading to the arrest of several hundred tribals as well as negotiations, the landlords surrounded 14,000 acres of land as a surplus under the Land Ceiling Act of 1961. Eventually, this land was distributed to the Adivasis tenants (Desai 2002). There has been no similar movement by Adivasis in the subsequent period to get land under land reforms.

At the same time, their struggles, though localized, have continued to remain centred on land, against their eviction by the landed class or the government. One of the most striking and long-drawn agitation(s) is of the Adivasis of Bharuch in south Gujarat. The main issue of contention has been their eviction from their land by the landed class and the government for agriculture, industry, irrigation projects, and reserved as well as protected forest and sanctuary. Infringement of their rights over the forest is another issue of their struggles. Violent confrontations with the police and forest departments due to their harassment, terror and beating are not infrequent (Pinto 2002). The state often uses all possible repressive measures to silent the agitating Adivasis. The HCS has always condemned the actions and demands of the tribals and also supported police action against them. Valia and Dediapada areas of the Bharuch district have been labelled by the media as a den of dacoits or the Chambal of Gujarat. However, a few NGOs and individuals have stood by the rights of the Adivasis and their struggles.

Like the Adivasis of Bharuch, the Dangis have all along resisted against the British administration and caste Hindu invaders for taking away their land and forest. Their upsurges were intensified in the 1960s when the government seized their land by classifying the forest land into reserved, protected and unclassified forest. In the mid-1970s, they organized a series of demonstrations demanding allocation of land to the local Adivasis for cultivation. In the 1980s, the Bhumihin Kisan Hakka Sangharsh Samiti was formed which spearheaded several struggles against the State. In some places, the aggrieved Dangis cultivated the 'forest' land without the permission of the forest department. As usual, the State resorted to oppressive measures to oust the tribals from the forest. Several militant activists were jailed and tortured, and quite a few of them were killed in the police firing/encounter. Most of the RCS organizations, not to speak of the HCS kept a distance from the struggle. In fact, several HCS organizations raised a hue and cry against these Adivasi activists, accused them of spreading violence in society and branded them as 'antisocial', 'separatists' and Naxalites. According to these civil society activists and intelligentsia, such struggles endanger peace and harmony in society. However, a few of RCS organizations such as LAS, Navsarjan Trust Surat and the RSSS of Bharuch were an exception. They raised their voice against the repressive measures of the State. The struggle has been diffused since the late 1980s. Unrest and occasional protests continue demanding Adivasi's rights over land and forest. Meanwhile, several HCS NGOs have stepped in the area for carrying out government-sponsored programmes as 'development' work.

The struggles of the Adivasis of the Panchmahal and Sabarkantha districts for land rights have a different trajectory in the last two decades. Incidents of sporadic protests by the tribals against the forest department's eviction of the tribal cultivators from the forestland increased with the new forest bill in the 1970s, empathizing forest conservation and wildlife[3]. The forest department used to destroy the crop cultivated by the Adivasis and started plantation of trees thereon for forest conservation. In order to retaliate against atrocities and to protect tribal rights for cultivation, the Jamin Hit Suraksha Samiti was formed under the leadership of DISHA in 1987. Their major demand was to transfer land for cultivation to forest dwellers who were tilling the same land for several years. After the long state-wide struggle, the government in principle agreed in 1994 that 'no tribal would be displaced from the land he was cultivating' (Jani 2002). In 1998, around 67,000 Adivasi cultivators were promised that they would get the ownership titles for land. But by 2003, after a span of nine years, less than half (32,000) got possession of an average 1.5 acres of land for cultivation. Though it is not enough for subsistence farming without other inputs, the average Adivasi consoles him/herself that 'nothing is better than something'. However, with this and similar struggles as well as Adivasis struggles elsewhere in the country, several CSOs working on human rights launched the all-India campaign demanding forest land rights for the Adivasis, building pressure on the policymakers. Sustained advocacy with other civil society actors and political leaders resulted in the formation of the Forest Rights Act, 2006[4]. With the government notification, Adivasi-rights–oriented organizations and local activists became active for the implementation of the Act. They asserted their right to occupy the land they were cultivating. This resulted into a scuffle between the forest department and the tribals at some places. In Gujarat, a few NGOs such as ARCH-Vahini, Navsarjan (Surat) and DISHA are actively involved in pressurizing the state for the implementation of the Act. But till 2015, only 38 per cent of the claimants could get land rights, as against Tripura (65.97 per cent), Kerala (65.53 per cent), Odisha (56.46 per cent), Rajasthan (48.93 per cent), Maharashtra (41.69 per cent), Chhattisgarh (41.15 per cent) and Andhra Pradesh (41.20 per cent). Though there are localized struggles of the Adivasis to occupy forest land for cultivation, a large-scale struggle for land rights appear to be on the decline.

DALITS' STRUGGLES FOR LAND RIGHTS

Unlike Adivasis, the Dalits are scattered in all parts of Gujarat. They have increasingly moved from rural to urban areas over the last five decades in search of employment in the non-farm sector and freedom from the rural caste structure. Their proportion in rural areas has declined from 72 per cent in 1971 to 57 per cent in 2011. They experience humiliation in their everyday village life. Despite cognizable laws, the practice of untouchability in public sphere—water, education, panchayat, market, etc.—is still widely prevalent (Navsarjan Trust 2010; Shah et al. 2006). There are several cases of the exodus of Dalits from villages to escape from humiliation and social boycott. In the village economy, their traditional occupations have been scavenging, skinning dead animals, weaving and farm labour. Under the land reforms in the early 1950s, sharecroppers and tenants were given the occupancy right to the land that they were cultivating. But the Dalit tenants/sharecroppers hardly got the benefit of that. In fact, they were evicted from the land they were cultivating (Shah 2002). For the first time, the Land Ceiling Act was introduced in 1960, which came into force in 1961. It was later amended in 1974 by lowering the ceiling limit. The land held in excess to the prescribed ceiling as surplus was to be distributed to the SC, ST, OBCs and others, according to the priorities laid down in the Act. From 1961 till 2016, 237,976 acres of land was declared as surplus. Of that, the government acquired 76 per cent of the land, that is 182,447 acres. By 2016, 155,350 acres of land was distributed to 23,204 families. Nearly, 14,000 of SC households received the land title; of them, 43 per cent did not get possession (Dabhi 2017). As they are poor and numerically marginal, they cannot assert and get possession of land.

There is a provision under the Gujarat Land Ceiling Act, 1974, that land may also be given to a group of persons of these communities who were willing to form a co-operative society for farming. One of the reasons for the scheme has been that the members share responsibility for input and labour. There are 130 such co-operative societies. Of them, 121 are of the SCs, 4 of the STs, and 3 of the SCs and STs jointly.

These legislations build hope among the Dalits to get land and improve their economic condition. Wherever possible, they have launched collective struggles to get land as their right under the land reform legislation. Most of their local struggles for land rights do not take off beyond an initial assertion thanks to the indifferent attitude of the government for implementing its own policy. But these attempts indicate the rising aspirations of Dalits. The struggles intensify their social consciousness for rights. A few struggles have succeeded which build confidence to fight.

A few Dalit activists also work to get land from the government either under the Land Ceiling Act and/or the government land. One of them is Valjibhai Patel, a Dalit Panther activist. He has been engaged on the land right issue for Dalits since the late 1960s. He believes that judiciary is the third pillar of democracy which can be meaningfully used to change the socioeconomic condition of the Dalits. In 1979, under the leadership of Dalit Panthers, the Dalits of Jetlapur village got 10 acres of land for co-operative farming for one year. But under the pressure from the local dominant caste, the authority did not renew the lease for the next year. Not only that, but to counter Dalit assertion for their right, a young Dalit Panther activist of the village was also killed in 1980 by a hooligan of the dominant caste. The Dalit activists and other RCS organizations of Gujarat protested against the murder and saw that the criminals got arrested. After a legal battle from the lower court to the Supreme Court, the three culprits got life-imprisonment. This boosted the morale of Dalits. Valjibhai continued his work and formed the Council for Social Justice in 1992 with the community support. He has organized several meetings and *padyatras* (marches on foot) to mobilize Dalits for their rights. He filed individual cases in the court for getting possession of land. With his efforts, 573 Dalit families got land from the government in three districts: Surendranagar, Amreli and Banaskantha (Dabhi 2017).

Like Jetpur, Dalits of Golana and its surrounding villages in Bhal region faced the anger of the dominant castes when they gathered the courage to take the possession of land allotted to them by the government. A Jesuit organization BSC had started activity of conscientization among Dalits with cultural programmes like street plays since the early 1970s. The Dalits first formed a forest co-operative on a 181-acre saline land to produce charcoal and firewood. Later they formed the agriculture co-operative society for cultivation. The co-operative provided them year-round labour: improving the land, trimming trees and making charcoal. The pride of the traditional ruling community was further injured when the Dalit cultivators with their collective efforts improved the quality of land, gained more production and paid higher wages to their own labourers. To teach a lesson to the Dalits for their assertion, goons of the dominant castes killed three Dalits in 1986. The RCS organizations and activists joined hands with the Dalits of Golana in protesting against the murder and pressurizing the state for action against all those who conspired the incident. The CM at that time was from the Adivasis community. Moreover, at that time, the pro-poor faction within the party was very active and built pressure on the government for providing protection to the victims and taking action against the goons of the dominant caste. Police action, in this case, was relatively quick in arresting the accused. At the end of the legal battle of 10 years from the Sessions Court to the Supreme Court, the guilty persons were convicted. As in the case in Jetpur, this was possible because of the meticulous homework and perseverance of the BSC activists, and support from RCS. The message had gone to the dominant castes of the area that they could not get away with violating the law. This raised the confidence of Dalits to assert their dignity.

Martin Macwan was one of the core team members of Golana. He left BSC and formed Navsarjan (Ahmedabad) in 1989. To continue his work to empower Dalits with land rights in the early 1990s, Navsarjan prepared a status report based on the secondary data, focusing on distribution of land to SCs under the Land Ceilings Act to assess land situation among the Dalits. The organization concentrated on one district, Surendranagar, to launch a movement for the land rights. The Jamin Hakk Rakshan Samiti (Land Protection Committee, JHRS) of the local Dalits was formed. With a team of 20 Dalit workers, a survey was carried out inquiring into (a) the number of Dalit households that received land under the land distribution programme of the government and (b) the status of land in terms of actual possession.

Legal Recourse and Collective Struggles of the Subalterns

The survey aroused awareness among the Dalits about their rights, and persuaded them to get united for action to get possession of the land that they received from the government. Later, the report in the form of a memorandum requesting for action was submitted to the district collector. It demanded that in the cases of those beneficiaries who were not given actual possession of land, the allotted land should be handed over to the persons concerned immediately. Having not received a response from the collector, a petition was filed in the high court directing the government for allocation and possession of land to the beneficiaries. The high court ordered the state to ensure that the Dalit landholders get immediate possession of their land. Out of the 6,000 acres of land, the Dalits were able to get land right of almost 4,500 acres in the four talukas. Of them, some did get possession for cultivation, some got a plot of land but not access of road to reach the farm, and some others were prevented from getting possession. The local officers were not willing to carry out the court's directives because of the political clout of the dominant castes. One officer said, 'I am with you in this case, but I am also under pressure'. In a number of villages, Dalits could not dare to take possession of land. They have an apprehension of 'violent retaliation by the non-Dalit encroachers' (Navsarjan Trust n.d., 83). In some cases, Dalits were frustrated with the litigation and gave up the fight (Navsarjan Trust n.d., 83). In a few cases, when Dalits asserted their rights and dared to cultivate land, they were physically assorted by the goons of the dominant castes.

During the recent Una agitation against flogging and dragging of the Dalit tanners by *gau rakshaks* (cow vigilantes) in 2016, the Dalit activists frequently demanded five acres of land for agriculture to every Dalit family for their respectable livelihood. Along with this demand, they asserted that Dalits should be given actual possession of the land which has been already allotted to them by the government (Shah 2017). Though the government promises to meet the demand, the authority avoids taking action against those belonging to local dominant castes who illegally control the land of Dalits. Out of frustration, in February 2018, a Dalit committed suicide for not getting a land title. More than 200 Dalits have threatened to commit suicide on this issue, but it has no impact on the government. As Dalits are numerically few in each village, they are unable to sustain their struggle for a long period against dominant castes. Though urban Dalit activists frequently raise land entitlement issue and protest against atrocities against Dalits, they do not have the patience and perseverance to continue the land struggle for a long period against local dominant castes and the State. They are in a quandary. However, Dalit and other activists irrespective of communities have started united struggles beyond social boundaries for all the oppressed.

FARM LABOURERS

The proportion of agricultural labourers to the total workforce has increased in Gujarat from 30 per cent in 1991 to 35 per cent in 2011. Between 2001 and 2011, the number of landless agricultural workers increased from 5.161 million to 6.839 million. They belong to SC, ST, OBC and Muslim communities. They live below the poverty line. Mahatma Gandhi, the founding father of the textile labour union in 1919, believed in class collaboration. At the same time, he demanded that fair wage include social care provisions. Though the Minimum Wage Act was enacted in 1948, as late as 1966, the Gujarat government accepted that a need to introduce minimum wage legislation for agriculture work. However, it rejected a suggestion that its level should be fixed on the basis of the case needed to meet the day-to-day cost of living. Breman observes,

> The point of departure was then and still is that the proposed wage should not negatively affect agricultural productivity as well as profitability, and moreover, should not be fixed at too high a rate since that would prevent labour, already then massively redundant in the prime sector of the economy, to move out and find a better job in towns and cities. (2016, 15)

With such rationale, an average daily wage paid to agricultural labourers in Gujarat was the lowest among Indian states in 2015. The average daily wage rate was ₹169.32 as against the all-India average of ₹210 and ₹582 in Kerala.

There are frequent sporadic localized protests of agricultural labourers against the local landed class for not adhering to the rules of the

Minimum Wage Act. During the euphoria of 'garibi hatao', a statutory wage of ₹3 per day for farm labour was introduced for the first time by the state government in 1972. But the landed class was not willing to pay this wage. Halpati Seva Sangh (HSS) working among the farm labourers in south Gujarat supported the demand for implementation of the Minimum Wage Act. It professed itself as being Gandhian in its philosophy and approach. Formed in 1961, HSS is an offshoot of the Vedchhi movement that was active among the tribals since the early 1920s. Halpati, also called Dublas, is a tribe that is synonymous in public parlance with farm labourers. In the past, they were bonded labourers, and their condition as semi-bonded labourers continues (Breman 1974). The objective of HSS is to 'uplift' the Halpatis. From its very inception, its work has been focused on social reform, particularly convincing the Halpatis to shun liquor and imparting education to children. It carries out government welfare programmes such as providing government land for shelter and financial support for the construction of houses. In the early 1970s, HSS supported some of the local spontaneous agitations of the Halpatis demanding more wages and it worked as a mediator between the landed class and the labourers (Breman 1974). The landed class could not tolerate even the mediator's role that HSS was performing. Youths of the landed class had publicly beaten the leader of HSS, warning him to stop supporting the labourers (Shah, 1975). Thereafter, the HSS gave up raising the issue of wages. Since then, its activities have been confined to welfare programmes.

In the subsequent period, a few NGOs have expressed their concern on the exploitation of wage labourers. A few initially tried to mediate between labourers and employers, but were threatened by the landed class. Consequently, they avoid a conflicting situation. They confine their activities to welfare. A few have formed trade unions of the labourers and demand to raise the minimum wages. Their demand has been to link the minimum wage for farm labourers with the cost of living index. They mobilize farm labourers and other local like-minded organizations to raise the issue of revision of wages from time to time. These unions occasionally file complaints with the labour commissioner for non-implementation of the Act, but so far the number of such complaints remains negligible—not enough to make an impact.

Several organizations believe that 'conventional union-style work' would never be effective when the landed class is very powerful and the poor labourers have limited bargain power (Rose 1992).

In this scenario, an attempt of Parivartan, an offshoot of Dalit organization Navsarjan, in organizing agricultural workers in Baroda district unfolds the story of the indifferent attitude of the government in the implementation of law. It also reveals how the landed class and political bosses, irrespective of political party and community, join hands against anyone taking a side of farm labourers. During her work for Dalit rights in Vadodara district, Manjula Pradeep a member of Navsarjan, formed Parivartan to focus on agricultural labourers. Its objectives were

> [T]o organize and strengthen local groups of Dalits, tribals and especially women as a collective force to address the local issues and to provide legal support and education to them in order to resist atrocities and other caste practices as well as to protect their rights. (Personal interview with Manjula, see also https://navsarjantrust.org/minimum-wage-implementation-campaign/)

While working for more than a year with agriculture labourers, Parivartan formed the Vadodara Khetmajur Sangathan (VKS), an organization of agricultural labourers, in 1997, covering a hundred villages of three blocks of Baroda district. The VKS organized a rally in Baroda which was attended by more than 1,500 labourers from three talukas on 12 June 1997. Their main demand was the implementation of the Minimum Wage Act. They also demanded that the government should punish labour officers for wilful neglect of duty for not taking action against violators and landed employers. Later, in 1998, another procession was organized demanding minimum wages and the abolition of forced labour against debt, which led to confrontations between the labourers and the landowners in some villages. In June 1998, negotiations were held in Tulsigam village of Savali taluka, where landowners accepted some of their demands, only to renege the next day due to the pressures from landowners from adjoining villages. The labourers then complained to the collector for violation of the Minimum Wage Act and threatened to fast indefinitely at the collector's office. Because of the protests, wages increased, though they remained below the minimum wage rate prescribed by the government.

In order to obstruct the rising awareness and assertiveness of labourers, the landed class resorted to religious communalism—the Vishwa Hindu Parishad (VHP) entered the fray and branded Parivartan as a Christian NGO. It was alleged that the NGO was involved in the conversion of Dalits to Christianity. It stated:

> Parivartan has launched a major network of conversion to Christianity, by exercising undue influence on the poor, helpless women by offering them utensils, clothes, books, sewing machines. This shall at a later stage turn the area into a centre of anti-national activities like Assam, Mizoram and Nagaland. This is a part of the overall conspiracy of converting the entire south Gujarat tribal belt, thus reducing Hindus into a minority. (Leaflet circulated, also reported in Gujarati media)

It was reported in the media that VHP activists ransacked the office and attacked, abused, beat up and dragged out the women activists. When the victims were rushed to the police station for protection and to register their complaint, they were further humiliated by the police. Following this, Parivartan organized a rally in Baroda that was attended by more than 5,000 agricultural labourers from 150 villages, and several NGOs from Gujarat. Several Dalit and non-Dalit activists asserted that the charge of religious conversion that was laid upon Parivartan was baseless, and that the organization worked for the empowerment of the poor; their struggle was against the systems that oppressed the poor. The rally demanded suspension of the police inspector of Padara for not registering the case against the culprits. In May 1999, a public meeting of the representatives of the labourers was organized in Ahmedabad under the auspices of the Gujarat Khet Kamdar Union and DISHA. It was chaired by Kuldeep Nayar, an eminent journalist, where the demands for increasing minimum wages and the implementation of the Act were reiterated.

On the other hand, the leading district-level political leaders of BJP and the Congress shared a consensus that the farm labourers were being paid the minimum wages, and they both opposed the demands of the labourers. They also complained that the labourers were not working full time and were shirking their work. The political leaders accused the 'outsiders', that is, the NGOs, for disturbing the peace and instigating labourers. The dominant class and castes with support from the state succeeded in diffusing the strike of labourers in some villages and in marginalized the organization. Though Parivartan continues to work in the area, often raising an issue of wages and justice, its militancy has been marrow down. The activists feel that it is difficult for an NGO to fight against the dominant castes and classes, political class and the State machinery to get justice for the landless.

MIGRANT SUGARCANE WORKERS

Gujarat has very large interstate migrant population of around 309 million, nearly 30 per cent of the state population. Of them, nearly 3 per cent in rural areas are short-term migrants, working for a few months in Gujarat and returning back to their home state. They are seasonal migrants for agriculture in cotton, sugarcane and tobacco and for construction. Around 150,000 migrant labourers work every year in cutting sugarcane. They are from the neighbouring state of Maharashtra (Shah and Dhak 2014).

The condition of sugarcane migrant labourers came to light by the writings of Jan Breman, a social anthropologist. The focus of his study was to analyse the condition of migrant labourers and the capitalist agriculture development in south Gujarat. Findings of his study were published in a form of an article entitled 'Seasonal Migration and Co-operative Capitalism, Crushing of Cane and of Labour by Sugar factories in Bardoli' in the *Economic and Political Weekly* in 1978. It describes the oppressive condition of sugarcane migrant workers. The study remained unnoticed in the public eye. Later, one of the local organizations, the Socialist Study Centre, published a Gujarati version of the article with a catchy title 'The Crushing of Cane and of Labour'. The booklet was widely circulated and reviewed in the regional press. This drew the attention of some state-level political leaders. The minister who was a socialist and labour leader asked the rural labour commissioner to investigate the situation: wages, work conditions, etc. He noted, 'if some public litigation were to be filed for and on behalf of these migrant workers, the government could be placed in the most embarrassing situation' (Breman 1990, 274). But there was no one in the government to pursue the matter, and eventually it disappeared from the public memory. In fact, the court observed that the district labour officer of Surat was instructed 'not to prosecute "until further" orders' were given to the management of the sugar factories for violation of the Minimum Wage Act (Breman 1990, 274).

Again the issue came to light in 1986 with the publication of two articles 'Mithi Khandani Kadvi Vato' (Bitter tales of sweet sugar) by Indukumar Jani of the Khet Vikas Parishad in the Gujarati journal *Naya Marg* (1 and 15 April 1986). LAS took up the matter by mobilizing public opinion with the support of the media. A series of reports on the condition of the migrant workers in sugarcane farms and factories appeared not only in the state-level Gujarati newspapers but also in English newspapers and magazines. Some MPs raised the issue in the Rajya Sabha. The Commissioner for the SCs and STs visited the area and inquired into the condition of the migrant labourers. He declared that he was shocked at the inhumane treatment that was meted out to the migrant workers.

Girish Patel of LAS filed a petition in the Gujarat High Court. The writ application contended that the sugar factories were not paying minimum wages as per the Minimum Wages Act to more than 100,000 Adivasi workers who were cutting sugarcane. This was a 'clear violation of the Art. 23 of the Constitution', he argued. It was asserted that the Department of Labour was conniving or colluding with the factories and sabotaging the implementation of the Minimum Wage Act. The facts and figures were presented before the court about the living and working conditions of the sugarcane workers which was worse than that of bonded labourers. They were living in concentration camps of the landed class. The LAS demanded an appointment of an inquiry committee into the enforcement of the laws: the Minimum Wages Act and the Migrant Workers Act. Granting the request, the court issued notices to all concerned sugar factory managers to appear before the court and also the Labour Commissioner for violation of the Act. Granting the petition, the court appointed a committee of three persons consisted of advocates and social activists to investigate the living and working conditions of the workers of nine sugar factories, and to submit a report with their recommendations. The committee submitted a report to the court. On the basis of the report and the arguments of the petitioner, the judge passed an interim order directing the sugar factories to pay ₹11 as the minimum wage per day to each worker.

But the question was: How to get the order implemented? The LAS activists had no idea of the ground-level reality. They had no information on the actual number of labourers in different places as the factory owners were not maintaining any register of the workers. There was no data on the quantity of sugarcane cut by each worker each day. However, the records of the tons of sugarcane harvested were maintained because each farmer would have to know the quantity of his produce. The work being done by the teams of *koytas* (a family of two: husband and wife) under *mukadams* (labour contractors) was known. They realized that the time at their disposal was short as the season was to be over within the next few days, and the workers would go home after receiving whatever amount that they would be given. The factory owners would encourage that so that the court would remain ineffective.

In that situation, a quick method had to be worked out so that each worker could get an amount that was somewhere closer to the stipulated minimum wage. At that time, the factory was paying ₹22 per ton of sugarcane harvested. It was calculated that if the workers were paid ₹29 per ton instead of ₹22, it would take care of the minimum wage. Negotiations were made with the management. Accordingly, the LAS approached the High Court, and requested that an ad hoc arrangement for that year might be made, keeping the main order as it was. The court agreed, and it appointed a committee for supervising the payment to each factory, on fixed days. The committee with its assistants went to each factory on an agreed date and personally provided for the payment to the workers on the basis of ₹29 per ton in place of ₹22 per ton. The total production in that year was round about six million tons, and the amount of extra payment would be ₹42 million.

The next year, the same arrangement continued. But in the meanwhile, the factory managements decided to frustrate the whole proceedings by creating a fictitious arrangement, namely, that each farmer would engage migrant workers for his field, would open account in the name of his worker and would directly pay to them. The factory managements submitted before the High Court that they were then no longer employees and were not liable to pay directly to the workers. The labourers would be paid and had been paid by the farmers, they maintained. The LAS opposed the plea, contending that the whole system was bogus and could not work, and that if at all the factories had introduced a change in the system, the change would be illegal under the law without following the legal procedure. The court granted the contention and passed the orders that the factories would directly pay the workers, and the payment, if any, made by the farmers would be ignored on the ground that the change was illegal.

The management went to the Supreme Court, challenging the order of the high court. They succeeded in securing an order from the Supreme Court that if workers had been paid by the farmers that would be taken into account. The Court payment committee fixed the days of payment by each factory, but the factories wound up the work earlier, called the workers, made the payment—of course—at ₹29 per ton and sent them back. When the committee visited the factory, nothing was left. A factory at Vyara sent back the workers after payment even when some crop was standing. The committee's work was frustrated. Though the factories made payment at the factory gates before the due date, they maintained that the farmers, and not the factories, had paid the workers.

During the proceedings, the high court, while admitting the petition, appointed a high-level committee to investigate the working and living conditions of the workers, and submit a report along with its recommendations. After meeting different sections of society including the workers in the camps and factory, other persons and management, the Department of Labour, etc., the committee submitted a detailed report in 1989. A representative of the factory gave a note of dissent. However, the report gave clear findings that the workers were employed by the factories and not by individual farmers, and that the harvesting work was being carried out by the factories themselves on behalf of the farmers who sold the sugarcane to the factory at a price. The high court in its interim order observed:

> We are constrained to observe that measures for the effective implementation of labour welfare legislation in the State need to be tightened because of late we have noticed an increasing tendency to ignore and overlook such statutory provisions intended for the socio-economic uplift of the working class, This Court has had, time and again in the recent past, occasion to impress upon the law enforcing agencies the need to promptly and effectively implement such welfare measures so that the State's commitment to the upliftment of the working classes is translated into action and does not remain on paper. (Cited in Breman 1990, 275)

Before the official submission of the report to the court, the management came to know about its contents and proposed action. One of the recommendations of the committee was that the rate of cutting one ton of cane be treated as equal to three times the minimum wage of agriculture labourer per day. At that time, the prevailing wage was ₹11, but it was to be revised and raised to ₹15. If the formula were accepted, the rate for cutting sugarcane would come to ₹45 per ton. The management built pressure on the government to de-link the wages of sugarcane workers from that of agricultural workers and to fix the wages independently on per ton basis. With their political clout, they succeeded in securing a notification under the Minimum Wages Act for fixing the per ton basis wages at ₹33 separately for sugarcane workers so that if the minimum daily wages of agricultural labour were raised to ₹15, the management would not be required to pay ₹45 per ton. The notification has been challenged, but the petition has continuously remained pending in the court. Meanwhile, LAS' negotiations continue with the management. The minimum wages had continued to be revised, and when the petition came up for hearing in 2002, the minimum wages were ₹65 per ton. At that time, the minimum wage for a farm labourer was ₹50; the minimum wage per ton should have been ₹150 per ton. But except for LAS, there was no NGO at the ground level to organize and mobilize the sugarcane workers for their rights. Their living condition continues to remain as it was before the court case. According to the recent study in 20016–2017, a pair of sugarcane harvesters or koyta (consisted of a husband and wife team) received ₹238 per day after working for 15–16 hours. This is considerably lower than the stipulated minimum wage which comes to ₹425, (₹202 for a female and ₹223 for a male; Prayas

2018). But there is no NGO in the region to fight for their case. And LAS is also inactive as it does not have human and material resources to organize labour and peruse the legal battle. A few activists made efforts to organize these workers, but they have not succeeded partly because of their short-term migration and variation in location from year to year. Moreover, the sugar mill owners constantly keep an eye on the movements of the workers and social activists who interact with them. Thus, despite a long and successful legal battle, the condition of the workers remains the same.

CONCLUSION

Civil society involves people in demanding the enactment of laws and regulations to meet their rights. This is the most important part of the democratization of society. CSOs are engaged in developing awareness of laws and their intricacy. They offer legal support to the poor to fight legal cases to get justice. And some of them also use PILs to protect the rights of the people and get justice. They get success in a few cases, giving hope to the poor that their voice counts in the system. The legal battle boosts up their confidence. With such legal provisions, a few from the deprived communities have been able to get land and some other resources for their survival. Such success builds hope and legitimizes the system. However, a legal battle is not a substitute for mobilization of the victims and their struggles involving confrontations with the State and the powerful dominant classes. The cases of failure in getting benefits of legal entitlement outnumber the success stories. A sizable number of Dalits are unable to get possession of the land allotted to them by the government. This is despite the courts' order. The State fails in protecting the rights of the poor and violates the law that it has enacted. RCS organizations and poor Dalits do not have enough strength to sustain their struggle to get justice. Though there is a law for minimum wages, it is not implemented. The poor labourers on their own and/or with support from the RCS organization launch a struggle with little success for their rightful due. The local dominant class across the social identity, political class across the mainstream parties and the state administration join hands against the labourers. The poor are fragmented and do not have the resources to fight the employers. And RCS organizations are too weak to make a dent in the power structure in favour of the have-nots.

NOTES

1. In the case of *Hossainara Khatun vs. the State of Bihar*, 1979.
2. Public hearing is a process in the environmental clearance process in which stakeholders can interact directly with government officials and the project proponent about the concerns regarding upcoming project.
3. The Wildlife (Protection) Act of 1972 provides a basic framework to ensure the protection and management of wildlife.
4. The Act recognizes land rights:

> To land, they (forest dwellers) have been cultivating prior to December 13, 2005 (Section 4 [3]). Those who are cultivating land but do not have document can claim up to 4 hectares, as long as they are cultivating the land themselves for livelihood (section3[1] [a] and 4[6]). Those who have a patta or government lease, as long as been illegally taken by the Forest Department or whose land is the subject of a dispute between Forest and Revenue Departments, can claim those lands (section 3[1] [f] and [g]).

Social Movements of the Non-poor

Movements in the form of collective actions provide an important arena for discursive discourse on the common good, societal ethical values, obligation of the State, and also immediate and long-term issues that society is facing. They provide an opportunity to negotiate and confront the state and dominant classes in matters concerning the civil, political and economic rights of the citizens in general and of have-nots in particular. As movements mobilize people for participation in collective actions, a consciousness of the participants for their rights, entitlements and also a concern for the common good develop. Social movements are broadly divided into two categories. The first type of movements addresses the idea of a common good, equality for all, against injustice, protection of liberty, etc. This also includes the new social movements such as ecology, feminism, anti-semitism, protection of the rights of immigrants and ethnic minorities, etc. The second type of movements is centred on anti-ethnic-minorities, particularistic primordial identity and interests. These movements are against the common good, and they provide fertile ground for an authoritarian regime. Therefore, it is the prime responsibility of the civil society to counter such movements in all forms.

In the previous chapter, we have examined a few movements of the oppressed for their rights and the role of civil society therein. We shall now analyse some of the movements of the non-poor to understand their character and their modus operandi of mobilization and negotiation with the State for attaining their demands. We shall first briefly narrate two so-called non-class movements which did not raise any class-related issue and made a formidable contribution in the making of Gujarat civil society. We shall then discuss some of the farmers' movements including an environment movement in which peasants played a central role. The farmers constitute 27 per cent (5.8 million) of the workers in Gujarat. In the decade between 2001 and 2011, their number reduced by 355,000, and the number of agricultural workers increased by 1.7 million.

MOVEMENTS OF DOMINANT STRATA: SELF-PROCLAIMED 'COMMON GOOD'

The Maha Gujarat movement in 1956–1960 and the Navnirman movement in 1974–1975 have been considered by the mainstream Gujarati academia and literati as 'popular' and 'mass' movements. They have been projected as movements for the rights of the citizens (Ganguly 2015; Sheth 1977). The former was demand for the formation of a separate state of Gujarat from the bilingual state of Bombay. The main leaders—who formulated demands, devised programmes for action and negotiated with the party in power—belonged to different political parties/ideologies: socialist, communist and liberal. They included litterateurs, social activists and other civil society intellectuals. They belonged to the upper castes. Besides their engagement with cultural identity and regional economic interests, some leaders were concerned with the issues affecting the have-nots and marginalized communities. One of the demands that they articulated was the inclusion of some of the areas with a predominantly tribal population in the north and south of the proposed Gujarat state. But the problems faced by the tribals and other deprived communities and their future in the proposed new state were not addressed. The movement remained essentially of the urban middle class, with the support of the rich farmers and industrialists. Socialists failed to mobilize the working class and marginalized communities in the movement (Shah 2007). The socialists could not retain their influence for a long period on the state and civil society of Gujarat after the formation of the new state.

Though the initial impetus of the student movement in 1974 (later called Navnirman or reconstruction of society) was price rise and other economic issues, it moved to the emotional and individualized issue of corruption. It was essentially a student and middle class movement projecting their notion of 'corruption'. There was, however, a division among the activists, between a few were radical teachers and literati, and many of HRC status quoists as well as socioreligious revivalists. Though the former were vocal, the latter outnumbered them in rank and file and hijacked several programmes and their contents (Shah 1977). The poor were merely onlookers. The movement added to the clout of the middle class in shaping Gujarat politics in the subsequent years. A few of them participated in the anti-Emergency movement in Gujarat against the violation of individual freedom by the state. At the same time, several of the activists of the movement, liberals as well as cultural revivalists, were in the forefront of the 1981 and 1985 agitations against the reservation for deprived communities. The HCS organizations and intelligentsia, barring a few exceptions, supported the agitation by reinforcing the 'meritocracy' of the dominant castes. Subsequently, many of them extended support to the Ram Janmabhoomi agitation for cultural rejuvenation and identity. The middle class was in the forefront in the Somnath to Ayodhya *yatra* (journey) under the leadership of L. K. Advani. They were also in the leading position in an orchestrated hate campaign against Muslims which culminated in a large-scale carnage in 2002. Not only the HCS but also a sizable section of RCS social activists and their organizations either tacitly sympathized with anti-Muslim propaganda or were indifferent to the issue. Fearing a risk of endangering the interests of their organizations by antagonizing the state and dominant majority community, some of the RCS organizations maintained their silence against the inaction of the state and perpetrators of violence but carried out relief work and rehabilitation work for victims. A few others openly opposed the HCS for their silence or for supporting the state's inaction to stop the carnage. The organizations such as PUCL, Lok Samiti, Forum for Secular Democracy, Sarvodaya Mandal, AWAG, Centre for Action and Knowledge (SETU), Sahiyar, Darshan, Jan Vikas, etc., openly raised their voice against the state. They got involved not only in relief work, including legal help and restoring peace, but also in documenting the events and raising consciousness for harmony and secular values.

Anti-SEZ Farmers' Movements

The farmers' (Khedut) movements in Gujarat have a chequered history, with the legacy of the freedom movement. In the 1950s, a small segment of the landed class of mainland Gujarat protested against the land reforms, particularly the Tenancy Act: land to the tillers.[1] They believed that such legislation would lead to the collectivization of agriculture, which was detrimental to the harmony of a village community (Bhalani 1966). However, a large section of the rich and middle peasants, having control over the government did not support the former, successfully sabotaged the tenancy and other land reform legislation. From the mid-1960s, they launched several organized movements against the Land Ceiling Act and Minimum Wage Act; and asserted for infrastructure such as irrigation, inputs, etc., for agricultural development. They along with the farmers of other states called their movement as 'Bharat versus India', highlighting the exploitation of agriculture by industries. In the 1970s and the 1980s, these movements had been around the issues of procurement prices, subsidies on inputs, infrastructure facilities including irrigation, electricity, credit, marketing of their farm produce and transport. But they were silent on the issues specifically affecting small and marginal farmers; distribution of land to the poor, farm wages, and land rights of the tribals and Dalits had not been mentioned (Shah 1988a). According to them, the poverty of the rural areas was not because of the social and agrarian structure. It was due to the pro-urban and industrial policies of the state. The leaders of the agitations then and now often claim of mobilization encompassing all the peasants, irrespective of their social and economic strata. But the main actors of the movements in the past and the present had been of the middle and rich peasants. Since the 1990s, with aggressive neoliberal policy, besides demanding remunerative price, they are up in arms against land acquisition by the state for industry. RCS organizations and activists are now supporting these movements. The central slogan of the farmer movement in contemporary Gujarat is 'Gam Ni Bhumi Gam Ni' (Let land of the village remain with village community).

Anti-port Umbargaon Struggle

The fishing community and poor peasant Adivasis and Kolis of the coastal area of Umbargaon in south Gujarat launched a struggle against SEZ (special economic zone) in 1999. The people got agitated when some of them received government notices informing them of the government's decision to acquire their land for the proposed project to build the port. They were wondering about their alternative source of livelihood. The people of the area were familiar with the land right struggles known as the Warli movement in the 1940s that was led by Godavari Parulekar, the Kashtakari Sanghatana tribal struggle in the adjoining district in Dahanu block, Maharashtra (Parulekar 1975; Prabhu 2002), and the fish workers movement in different parts of the country (Aerthayil 2000). They decided to resist the government's decision and to fight back. The Paryavaran Suraksha Samiti (PSS or Committee for Protection of the Environment) of Sarvodaya and other radical social activists actively working in this area on the issue of industrial pollution supported the initiative of the Umbargaon coastal area people to launch a struggle against the proposed port. After several informal meetings, village committees were formed to save their land. Later, the Kinara Bachao Samiti (KBS or Save the Coast Committee), and Umbargaon Taluka Bandar Hatao Sangharsh Samiti (Umbargaon District Action Committee to Stop the Port) were constituted under the leadership of a local resident, retired Lt. Col. Pratap Save. The KBS organized village meetings and also meetings at the taluka level to protest against the proposed port. Several village councils called panchayats of elected members, and gram sabhas (village council of all adults) passed resolutions opposing the port. They also asserted that under the Schedule VI of the Constitution, the government could not impose any industry or acquire any land without the permission of the gram sabhas. The taluka panchayat too passed a similar resolution. The representatives met the CM with their resolutions against the proposed port. The KBS received support from various CSOs within and outside the state. These organizations include the National Alliance of People's Movements (NAPM), Narmada Bachao Andolan (NBA), Shoshit Jan Andolan, Kashtakari Sanghatana, Samajwadi Jan Parishad, National Fishworkers Forum and Paryavaran Sanrakshana Samiti.

The agitation continued for nearly 15 months. The police broke up the movement by force in April 2000. Several villagers and community leaders were arrested and beaten up. Retired Lt. Col. Pratap Save was picked up from his house at midnight on charges of breaking public order. He was brutally beaten up by the police in the custody, which lead to his death on 20 April 2000. A number of NGOs in Gujarat and outside strongly protested against the police for Save's death. More than 70 RCS organizations organized padyatras from 9 to 15 August from Vedchhi (a centre of Gandhian activities since the 1920s) to Umbargaon to create awareness among the people on the issue of globalization and its impact on the poor. The slogan was 'save freedom, save the country' from multinationals. During the march, the activists stayed in the village and interacted with local people on the issues related to neoliberal economy and its effect on their life. Besides, the activists also protested against the police brutality responsible for Save's death. The PIL was filed in the court demanding an inquiry into his death. The Gujarat High Court appointed a fact-finding committee to inquire into the circumstances leading to the death of retired Lt. Col. Pratap Save. The government shelved the project.

Poshitra Struggle

A similar struggle took place in Poshitra block in Jamnagar district, Saurashtra, in 2001. From 1 April 2000, the government initiated procedures of acquiring land for the proposed SEZ for port and industries in two phases. The project needed 15,000 hectares of land covering 43 villages. Like in Umargaon, the struggle against the government project began soon after the people of the village Poshitra and of other 15 villages from the Okhamandal and 10 villages from the Kalyanpur talukas received notifications related to their land being acquired for development projects. This agitated people who feared that they would be a pauper by losing their land. The area is economically backward and the land is saline. Fishing and agriculture are the main sources of livelihood of the people. Mithapur Tata Chemical Plant established in the 1950s provides employment to a small section of people. Numerically, the Vagher community is the largest in the area. Other major communities are Ahir and Kharva. The Gramya Vikas Trust (GVT), a local NGO, has been working in the area since the mid-1980s. It was founded by D. S. Ker, a college professor, who belonged to the Vagher community. The NGO has been engaged in education, watershade and prevention of salinity in the area. It became the nerve centre of the movement.

Ker took an initiative in forming the organizational network for opposing the SEZ project. Hunger strikes, protests demonstrations and public meetings continued, and the Okha Mandal Bachao Samiti was formed to intensify the struggle. Various RCS activists and organizations such as Aanandi (a women organization for livelihood), Janpath (a network of Gujarat NGOs), Jan Sangharsh Manch (Platform for People's Struggle for Justice), Khet Vikas Parishad (engaged for the rights of agriculture labourers and Adivasis), etc., supported the struggle. They joined the public meetings and demonstrations. In the process, each village formed a land protection committee. A writ petition was filed in the Gujarat High Court demanding a stay on the proceedings of the government. The court asked the respondent company (Larsen & Toubro India) to submit its resettlement and rehabilitation plan for the families. When the company could not submit the plan to the court, the court lifted the ban on developmental activities and on the sale and purchase of land. The company has scrapped the project 'due to environmental reasons' (Pathak 2015).

But the situation is different in Kutch where the government had given common land to industries to develop SEZ. The local people opposed the government's decision. They organized a number of protests: meetings, dharna, rallies and signature campaigns to vent their voice. Several village panchayats passed resolutions opposing the government's move. But all these had no effect on the government. A few protesters were co-opted by the industries. Some were threatened by the vested interests—the state officers, politicians and industries—who accused them of creating hurdles in the development of Gujarat. Gradually, the agitation has fizzled out. Though there are occasional protests against land acquisition in different places, they do not sustain for a long period. By now (2017), Gujarat has set up 27 SEZs; half of them came into existence surreptitiously even before the SEZ Act 2005 was enacted. Till 2014, more than 12,000 hectares of land had been acquired (notified) by the government for SEZ in Gujarat.

Anti-SIR Struggles

To attract investment in industries and infrastructure, the GoG planned 'investment regions as global hubs' of economic activity including industry, commerce, physical infrastructure, transport, housing, etc. For that, the state enacted the Special Investment Region (SIR) Act in 2009. Farmers and RCS organizations and activists consider the SIR as anti-agriculture and anti-farmer. They fear that the farmers would have limited choice in bargaining with the business lobby and the government and that they would lose their fertile land, the source of their livelihood (Ginwala and Rabri 2014). The local cultivators, particularly middle peasants of Olpad in south Gujarat, stalled Hazira the SIR. And thanks to the continuous protest of the farmers of north Gujarat, the government divided Dholera Mandal-Bechraji SIR (into 36 and 8 villages) and de-notified 36 out of the 44 villages in 2013. The protest of the remaining villages under the banner of the Bhal Bachao Samiti continues, demanding 'SIR Act Hatao (remove)' (Rabari 2014). The activists of these agitations have also joined the anti-globalization stir launched by the workers of different industries that have been started in this area. Besides these struggles, there are several local-level agitations against land acquisition. The state and corporate lobby skilfully divide the people, co-opt some and use repressive forces to break the agitations.

ANTI-NUCLEAR PLANT MITHI VIRDI STRUGGLE

In the mid-1980s, Adivasis of south Gujarat under the leadership of Narayan Desai, an eminent Gandhian, struggled peacefully for five years against the proposed nuclear power station at Kakrapar. Located on the banks of river Tapi in Mandvi/Vyara taluk, Kakrapar has a predominantly Adivasi population (nearly eighty percent), around 30 km to Vedchhi Ashram, the centre of Gandhian education activities since 1922. Narayan Desai, following the JP movement in 1975–1976, established Sampoorna Kranti Vidyalaya (Total Revolution University) at Vedchhi in the late 1970s. In 1983, he was upset to learn the news that appeared in the media about the government's plan to locate nuclear plant at Kakrapar. Desai (1984) believes,

> The immediate risks of nuclear activity are faced by the poor Adivasis living in the vicinity of Kakrapar (or at other spots where the nuclear facilities are located) but the benefits of the electricity produced by them are enjoyed by a small minority of bulk consuming industrialists. To help those who

have, by putting at risk those who haven't, goes against the very foundations of justice. A society which cherishes egalitarian ideals, should begin its development by seeking the good of the lowliest and the lost, rather than begin at the top in the hope of benefits trickling down.

He called a meeting of his fellow workers to discuss the project and planned to oppose it. A series of meetings in different villages surrounding Kakrapar were organized, and people were explained in simple language about the plant and its danger on their life. The petitions to the government protesting against the plant that was endangering their life were submitted. The government's argument that nuclear electricity would be cheaper than other energy was countered by the activists with facts. Several demonstrations were organized before the local government offices to express their protests. The work of the engineers and surveyors was peacefully obstructed. However, Desai withdrew the movement after five years following a violent incident involving stone pleating and police firing that killed one Adivasis. He and his colleagues observed a fast, expressing their protest when the plant was inaugurated in 1992.

The campaign against nuclear power energy however did not halt. In the early 1990s, its scope expanded to larger ecological and environmental concerns. It was the time that the anti-Narmada Dam movement was in peak. A small section of Sarvodaya workers supporting the NBA was concerned with environmental issues. They formed the PSS, expanding its span involving like-minded non-Gandhian radicals. One of them is Rohit Prajapati, an engineer by training, who believes in integrating environment issue with class struggle (Chattopadhyay 2009). For him, all local struggles 'against' something are actually struggles 'for' something for social transformation towards an egalitarian non-exploitative social order. The PSS opposed Pokhran nuclear test II in 1998. Kanti Shah, a Sarvodayist, wrote a book *Motnu Vavetar* (ploughing of death). In the course of their grassroots struggles on various environmental issues, a consensus evolved within PSS that while mobilizing masses on a particular issue, a process of building 'environmental consciousness' needed to be carried out. Prajapati is actively associated with the trade union of industrial workers. He along with some other members of PSS have been actively engaged struggling with local industries, the Gujarat Pollution Control Board and the government against industrial pollution created by chemical industries. While doing so, they mobilize industrial workers in the struggle against industrial pollution, and succeeded in a court case against Hema Chemical Industries, Vadodara. The case raised the issues of occupational health hazards, unsafe disposal of hazardous chromium waste, industrial pollution and workers' compensation. The Supreme Court ordered the company to pay ₹170 million towards remediation of the sites.

In 2007, a team of PSS undertook a tour to coastal areas to understand the grassroot socio-economic condition and the government's proposed SEZs. By that time, news in the media appeared regarding the government's proposed 6,000 MW nuclear power plant near Mithi Virdi in Bhavnagar district under the Indo–US civil nuclear pact. The plant was to be set up by the State-owned Nuclear Power Corporation of India Ltd (NPCIL), with technical support from Westinghouse. The government estimated to acquire 777 hectares of land from five villages for the project: Mithi Virdi, Khadarpar, Mandwa, Jaspara and Sosia. According to PSS, the plant would affect 150 villages in the radius of 30 km.

Rajputs and Kolis constitute more than 80 per cent of the population of these villages. Dalits and Muslims comprise less than 5 per cent. The remaining are upper castes, artisan and the fishing community. Though there is occasional tension between Kolis and Rajputs on social issues—status in the caste hierarchy—a small segment (2 per cent) are rich farmers having around 25 acres. A majority of the cultivators of both the communities are small and marginal farmers with less than five acres. Agriculture land is relatively fertile. Currently, the rich alluvial soil of the area supports crops such as groundnut, bajra, cotton, fruits and vegetables.

During the tour, while interacting with people, the PSS activists found that the local residents had heard about the project as 'some industry for generating electricity'. They were, however, not aware of the risks involved in a nuclear power plant. PSS organized a meeting at village Kukar near Mithi Vildi to explain about the nuclear power plant, its history and the dangers of nuclear rays on health. Most of the members of the audience were convinced about the danger and agreed to take the message to other villages (Dhar 2017).

PSS contacted other NGOs working in the area on the issue. One of these was Utthan, which had been working in this area for nearly two decades on the issues of women empowerment and water. Together they organized a meeting of the people of the five villages in April 2007. Inhabitants of other surrounding villages also attended the meeting. The organizers explained the possible dangers of a nuclear power plant on the environment and also on their health. They narrated the destruction by nuclear power to Hiroshima and Nagasaki which some local people were aware of. The recent accident at Chernobyl (1986) was also narrated. At the end, the meeting made a few resolutions: (a) There should not be nuclear plant on any fertile land of the country; (b) Nuclear electricity is a business of loss. It is neither cheap, not clean, 'and, certainly not safe'; (c) If water-shade is developed in the region, it can give employment to many people; and (d) We will not leave land (Krushakant et al. 2010). The same themes had been repeated in subsequent meetings, with pictures and illustrations in simple local language. In these meetings, women organizations such as Sahiyar and Utthan focused on women's participation in the struggle. Hiroshima (6 August), Nagasaki (9 August) and Chernobyl (26 April) days were observed in the area to highlight human destruction caused by nuclear power.

The PSS organized a workshop at Vedchhi on the issue of nuclear power for two days in June 2007. Later, in August, a Hiroshima conference was organized at Bhavnagar, involving local civil society activists. A symposium discussing the advantages and disadvantages of nuclear plants was organized at Bhavanagar in March 2008 (Swati 2010a). To create a wider public opinion, a conference was organized in December 2008 at Gujarat Vidyapith, Ahmedabad, on nuclear electricity. More than 200 activists and scholars from all over the country participated in the conference (Dave 2010). Simultaneously, public meeting in various villages continued repeating the themes of the danger of nuclear power. In February 2010, PSS organized a public hearing on the plant in Ahmedabad in which local people participated by expressing their concern. Students of the Gadhada School of Social Work visited 40 villages and explained the people about the danger of nuclear power.

On 9 June 2010, the district collector informed the village head of Jaspara about the proposed visit of the government officers on 11 June to collect a sample of village land. The sarpanch (elected head of a village) called a meeting of gram sabha (village council of all adults) and conveyed the government's message. The village people unanimously decided that they would not allow the government to take a sample of the land. On 11 June, government troops, accompanied by police and equipped with machinery for drilling, came to take a land sample. When the officers were dumping their machinery, the villagers—women and men—of surrounding areas rushed to Jaspara in very large numbers. They started shouting slogans asking the government officers and police such as to 'go back', 'we will not allow you to take a sample of our land because we do not want nuclear plant', '[we] will give life but not land', etc. The village head told the officers that if they proceed with their work, there would a serious consequence. At last, the government troop had to return back (Swati 2010a).

Thereafter, PSS intensified its work in the area. Some of the activists camped there so as to intensify their interactions with people. A documentary film based on a study of five villages in the vicinity of Rawatbhata nuclear power plant in Rajasthan was shown. The survey has revealed that cancer, physical disability, incomplete mental growth, women becoming sterile and infant deaths had gone up four to seven times among these villagers. Like the earlier phase, local people were involved in discussion and were encouraged to raise questions. The public meetings focused on various aspects of nuclear energy, its possibilities of radiation and their consequences in endangering human health. It was argued that there was no foolproof technology to handle hazardous nuclear waste. Costs and benefits of the nuclear plant for society were explained in detail. People were encouraged to raise questions so that dialogue takes place. The PSS activists believed that '[they were] just informing people. They are free to make their own choices' (Prjapati et al. 2014). In the course of time, all the people of the area, irrespective of their education and occupation, understood the magnitude of the problem. The government's efforts to counter the arguments regarding safety and advantageous did not convince the average villager.

Frequent *khatala* (traditional wooden bed) meetings in villages with people in a sitting/lying down position in the late evenings after supper became a regular feature of dialogue with villagers in different localities. Conscious efforts were made to bring people of different castes and communities together in the deliberations. During these meetings not only the nuclear plant and the government policies and legal procedures for acquiring land and people's power but also contemporary national politics, caste and communalism, secularism, agricultural problems faced, industrial policy, capitalism, etc., were the topics for discussion. One of the objectives of PSS for their dialogue with people was self-learning from the local people. The activists wanted to understand local culture and people's perception of social life, market and the State. In the course of time, some activists felt that they learnt about people's common sense in everyday politics. These meetings served the purpose of making decisions related to the movement. The khatala meetings were organized separately and collectively with all communities: Rajputs, Kolis, Dalits, Muslims, etc. Special efforts were made to organize meetings with farm labourers and also with women of all communities. The major decisions of the meetings were written down, and signatures of males and females of all communities were taken.

The villagers formed the expert group involving PSS and other socially concerned intellectuals to study government reports and represent to the authority on behalf of the people. The PSS meticulously examined the Environment Impact Assessment (EIA) report and had shown the absence of time series data on water, land and many other inadequacies in data. It was pointed out that the EIA report lacked detailed risk assessments and was 'superficial, unscientific, technically not sound and misleading'. On these grounds, the village expert committee objected to the coastal regulation zone (CRZ) clearance by the Gujarat Coastal Zone Management Authority. The expert committee presented their observations in simple language to the villagers.

In March 2013, an EPH of the proposed nuclear power plant was organized at Mithi Virdi. Before that, several meetings in the area were organized focusing a discussion on various aspects of EIA report and people's participation to present their case during EPH. The expert group was ready with a well-researched alternative EIA. The other groups of different organizations were ready with their reports on oceanography, geology and the environment. It was explained to the people that the EPH was a process to take their consent on the project. The villagers were enthusiastically ready with their facts, figures and arguments to present their case. Before the day of the EPH, 5 March, Utthan presented a memorandum to the district collector that EIL did not have an accreditation for writing the EIA for nuclear power stations. A demonstration was also held in front of the collectorate on the same day, opposing the project. It was agreed in the meeting between environmental activists and engineers of the Pollution Control Board that the people's experts will also speak in the public hearing. However, on the 4 March, a day before the event, the district collector announced that only the residents within a 10-km radius of the project will be allowed to speak; the 'outsiders' may submit their written documents.

The venue of the meeting was covered by a huge police force, creating an atmosphere of fear. Over 5,000 women and men from 24 villages came to attend the meeting. When the sarpanch of Jasapara rose to make procedural points about the lapses in the EPH, he was prevented by the authority from doing so. The villagers felt that the hearing was only held to complete a flawed procedure in favour of NPCIL They realized that the public hearing committee was not interested in hearing the issues and grievances of the people. Hence, the community leaders announced that they would boycott the public hearing. And the villagers left the venue peacefully without shouting any slogans.

Moreover, the government attempted to bypass the procedure of mandatory approval of the gram sabha for acquiring forest land. The government asked the sarpanch of Jasapara village to pass a resolution in the village council to handover 81 hectares of forest land under village jurisdiction to the government for the project. The sarpanch called the gram sabha and placed the matter before the people. The gram sabha strongly objected to the unconstitutional method of the government for acquiring the forest land. It unanimously resolved not to hand over the forest land for non-forest use to the NPCIL (Krishnakant 2017).

The movement got momentum with a rally of more than 20 villagers on 23 September 2013, covering 40 km from village Jaspara to the collector's office at Bhavnagar. While walking, the protestors shouted slogans like 'let it go, let it go, let the nuclear power plant go', allow us to eat our hard earned *rotlo* (bread), 'we will give up our lives, not our land', 'let bajra and cotton grow, allow the greenery to flourish' and 'not here, not anywhere; not in any country in the world'. The villagers of 30 villages including adult female and males, agricultural labourers and farmers, signed a petition addressed to the prime minister, opposing the plant.

All the farmers and landless labourers (281 individuals) of these villages submitted an affidavit individually signed that stated: 'I solemnly affirm that I refuse to sell my above-mentioned land at any price to the Government of Gujarat, Government of India or NPCIL'. The labourers mentioned in their affidavit that 'farmlands are their only source of livelihood'. Moreover, they wrote an open letter to the prime minister who was scheduled to visit the USA to sign the nuclear treaty. It pointed out that the Indian government was 'risking citizens' lives even as the crisis in Fukushima (2011) had further deepened over last few weeks. The letter added that, 'it is unfortunate that Indian government is choosing to miss the historic opportunity to go for sustainable, renewable, decentralized and equitable forms of energy and shun nuclear power which contributes less than three percent of its electricity production'.

In March 2014, the gram sabha of the five villages unanimously passed a resolution declaring the entire 'Mithi Virdi-Jaspara region as Nuclear Free Zone'. The statement concludes,

> 'We are opposed to all aspects and parts of the so-called nuclear fuel cycle and expressly forbids the production of nuclear energy, the presence of any equipment and materials related to the carrying out of any part of the fuel cycle and opposes any storage of nuclear waste'. (Prajapati et al. 2014)

A copy of the resolution was sent to the President of India, the prime minister, Gujarat's CM and Secretary-General of the United Nations. Later, in August, the villagers took a pledge that they wished to 'ensure clean air, potable water, fertile lands, nutritious, uncontaminated food and secure life for the future generations...(they) will do all that is possible to save and protect the land, agriculture, agricultural products and seeds'. The determination of people of the area was strong. They remained united despite intimidations and temptations from the government circles to divide the movement.

In between the programmes, regular meetings used to take place in which various political issues and the nature of development in the country affecting their life were discussed. They discussed at length the two ordinances of the NDA government of 2014 and 2015 amending the Right to Fair Compensation and Transparency in Land Acquisition, Rehabilitation and Resettlement (R&R) 2013 (Amendment) Ordinance. They protested against these ordinances considering them as 'anti-farmer'.[2] Simultaneously, the activists involved local farmers for organic farming in the area. They also improved linkages of village farm producers with an urban market to sell their product.

Finally, in May 2017, the government announced its withdrawal of the nuclear plant project from Mithi Virdi area and shifted it to Andhra Pradesh. This was done, according to the government, because 'of delay in land acquisition' in the area. Of course, the announcement brought cheers on the faces of the villagers who had struggled for 10 years. At the same time, they announced that they would extend their support to the people of Andhra Pradesh for their fight against the nuclear plant. The people together celebrated the victory for two days. On the first day, they collectively cleaned the streets. At the government earmarked location of the nuclear plant, they planted an *Abdul vad*, that is, a banyan tree, in the name of a Muslim villager—a symbolic expression of communal unity. Women made a chain of solidarity and played cricket together. Women and men of all castes/communities were at the centre of the function. The next day, local leaders—women and men—occupied a place on the podium in the public meeting. They spoke about their experiences and emphasis for unity. The social activists occupied place in audience. The people reiterated their stand '(Nuclear Plant) Not Here, Not Anywhere; Not in Any Country in the World' (Gelani, Vora and Joshi 2017). The activists of PSS have not withdrawn from the area because they believe that the nuclear plant in Mithi Virdi was not their ultimate objective. Their fight is against capitalist system, communalism and authoritarianism. They continue to develop consciousness for secularism, freedom and equality (Prajapati 2017).

CONCLUSION

In the post-Independence period, the non-class mass movements in Gujarat have been of the middle class, either for the formation of linguistic state and identity or for an emotional issue related to corruption. The marginal communities had been mere onlookers. These movements have reinforced hegemonic values and identities. The farmers' movements were dominated by rich peasants and middle castes till the late 1990s. The situation has begun to change. Since 2000, non-dominant castes launched the struggles against globalization and land acquisition for industries and infrastructure. A few of the movements have succeeded, and the government has been forced to withdraw its projects. These movements have also made efforts to articulate public opinion against a neoliberal economy. RCS activists and organizations actively participate in these movements. The movement against the nuclear plant that continued for a decade has successfully forced the government to withdraw the project. In the course of the movement, the political consciousness of people on different aspects such as the State power, anti-people policies of the government and consequences of a neoliberal economy on their life have been raised. The movements consciously took up issues of secularism and gender equality, and involved women, farm labourers and marginalized communities in the decision-making process.

NOTES

1. At that time, Saurashtra was a separate state. The landed class in Saurashtra was of the feudal landlords. Whereas in Gujarat under the Ryotwari System in which a landholder was recognized as proprietor of land, and paying revenue directly to the government. Peasants of some parts of Gujarat—central and south—developed capitalist farming

since the late 19th century. They were active participants in peasant movements such as Kheda satyagraha and Bardoli satyagraha against a rise in land revenue (Hardiman 1981; Shah 1974). In Saurashtra, feudal class opposed land reforms which adversely affected their interest.

2. The Right to Fair Compensation and Transparency in Land Acquisition, Rehabilitation and Resettlement Act, 2013 (Land Acquisition Act, 2013) defines 'consent' clause as follows: 'land can only be acquired with the approval of the 70% of the landowners for PPP projects and 80% for the private entities'. The amendments dilute consent clause for Industrial corridors, PPP projects, rural infrastructure, affordable housing and defence projects. It also does away the social assessment before a land acquisition, and if any government official conducts any wrongdoing, she/he cannot be prosecuted without prior sanction from the government. The Bill brings provisions for compensation, rehabilitation, and resettlement under other related Acts such as the National Highways Act and the Railways Act in consonance with the LARR Act.

Narmada Dam
Development and Displacement

The Sardar Sarovar Project (SSP) dam on the river Narmada from its conception to completion has involved several CSOs, from international to the local level, with different ideological perspectives. Some of them contested with each other. Some joined hands to intervene in policy discourse and formation as well as the execution of the policy. A few had been engaged in mobilizing immediately project-affected people (PAP) and also a larger public opinion across the regions, raising issues related to nature of development in India and the world.

Construction of dams on a river is not a modern phenomenon. Since time memorial, wherever possible, people used to construct tanks and dams to store water for irrigation and drinking.[1] After Independence, the meaning of dam, particularly large dams,[2] has undergone a change as agriculture has increasingly become capitalist. In this paradigm, dams, particularly large ones, have been considered to provide irrigation for agriculture, drinking water and hydropower for industry. On the eve of Independence, the proposal of the construction of Hirakud dam in eastern India was seen as the only cure for many of the problems of Odisha, namely, floods, droughts, poverty and disease (Baboo 1991). This was the time when Gandhi wrote to Nehru, his political heir, about his vision of India as he elaborated in his book *Hind Swaraj*. Nehru was preoccupied with immediate objectives such as 'a sufficiency of food, clothing, housing, sanitation, etc., which should be the minimum requirement for the country and for everyone. It is with these objectives in view that we must find out how to attain them speedily' (Cited in Chandra 2013, 50). The discourse between Gandhi and Nehru did not take off to a wider scale, though it surfaced from time to time. With the onslaught of globalization, it has revived.

The resistance against Hirakud dam appeared when the process of acquisition of land in 95 villages was initiated in 1946. A satyagraha was organized, but the struggle did not sustain for a long time as the local Congress leaders who were supporting the agitation, in the beginning, withdrew their support after Independence. They alleged a conspiracy of the former rulers of Gujarat against democratic planning and development (Nayak 2010). Local protestors requested Gandhi and the Gandhians for an intervention but, surprisingly, there was no response.[3] While laying the first batch of concrete, Prime Minister Nehru on 12 April 1948 said to the people: 'If you are to suffer, you should suffer in the interest of the country' (Cited in Purohit 2016). He wrote:

> As I threw in some concrete, which was to form the base of the great Hirakud Dam, a sense of adventure seized me and I forgot for a while the many troubles that beset us. I felt that these troubles will pass, but that the great dam and all that follows from it will endure for ages to come. (Gopal and Iyengar 2003, 266)

GUJARAT: DROUGHT, DAM AND DEVELOPMENT

Some parts of south and central Gujarat under the Ryotwari Land System during British rule started the cultivation of cash crops in the late 19th century. It began with cotton and indigo. Later, tobacco and sugar, banana, etc., were added. It was boosted further after Independence. In the first three decades (1961–1980) from its formation, the state constructed as many as 400 dams for irrigation purpose. Except for dams built on Mahi and Tapi, most of the dams do not have the capacity to provide water for irrigation to a large area. Of the total net irrigated area, the canal irrigated area increased from 10 per cent in 1960 to 21 per cent in 1983–1984. Relative prosperity of the middle peasant—mainly Patidars of central and south Gujarat—increased. These areas had become a model of development for the farmers of north Gujarat and Saurashtra. For them, groundwater was the major source of irrigation which they used extensively for cash crops. The number of diesel and/or electric pump-sets on tube wells increased three times from 177,798 in 1979 to 317,403 in 1986. As a result, the groundwater level in north Gujarat had gone down from 100 feet or so in the 1960s to 800 feet in the early 1980s. And ordinary pump-sets became redundant. In the 1970s, on the advice of technical experts, the government decided that no pump-set should draw water beyond 45 metres and there should not be more than one pump-set within certain areas. But under the pressure of farmers' lobby, the government's decision remained on paper. Having exhausted groundwater resources, the middle and rich farmers desperately wanted canal irrigation to prosper. They put their hopes on the Narmada dam (SSP) project.

Moreover, every three years, Gujarat, particularly north Gujarat, Saurashtra and Kutch, witnesses drought. Nearly one-third of the region (43 talukas) is drought prone. Even in a normal year, a large number of villages do not get safe drinking water. The number of villages without any water sources increased from 4,260 in 1963–1964 to 16,351 in 1987–1988 (Hirway and Patel 1994, 21). The state has faced severe famines during 1972–1973, 1980 and 1985 that continued for two subsequent years till 1987. During this period, CSOs were involved in relief work by organizing cattle camps, providing water and fodder, and also managing tension between local population and drought-affected migrants. Simultaneously, they were monitoring government programmes for relief and pressuring the government for finding 'a long-term' solution. In 1986, some of the leading litterateurs and social activists expressed their anguish on the government's inefficiency in implementing plans to solve water problem. They observed that the government had not taken the problem on a war footing. And those with vested interests had taken advantage by commercialization of water, trampling all human values. They believed that,

> *The Narmada project is the only solution for Saurashtra and Kutch. But the project is not in sight and it is likely to be completed in 20 years from now. Should people wait for 20 years? Is it impossible to lay the 300 km pipeline from Narmada (river) to Saurashtra region on a war-footing basis, when thousands of kilometres of pipeline can be laid for petroleum gas?.... We urge the government to consider the situation as an emergency and it should come out of its petty politics in handling the situation. Long-term*

and short-term steps should be taken to solve the problem. (Joshi et al. 1986; emphasis added)

EVOLUTION OF REHABILITATION POLICY FOR PAP

The Narmada dam project, like the Hirakud Dam Project, was conceived in 1947 to control floods and create irrigation facility and hydraulic power. As the river passes through several regions, the planning process of dams involving the distribution of water and power, cost and location of different dams took a long period to prepare. In 1961, soon after its formation, the Gujarat government gave the administrative approval for the first phase of the Narmada dam. Nehru laid its foundation stone, though the exact location of the dam had not been decided. Dispute related to sharing of cost and benefit among the states was under negotiations. In 1969, the central government constituted the Narmada Water Dispute Tribunal (NWDT) to resolve contentious issues raised by the states involved in the project. The tribunal gave its award in December 1979. The award specified a quantum of utilizable waters and power and the cost to be shared by the four states: Gujarat, MP, Maharashtra and Rajasthan.

Following the tribunal report, Gujarat government immediately started the process of planning for the construction of the SSP Dam. The foundation stone was laid near Kevadia in 1980. Policymakers, rich and middle peasants, and the vocal urban middle class and civil society hailed these events as the beginning of a major transformation in Gujarat's economy. They believed that the dam would provide not only irrigation but also drinking water in the remote villages in Saurashtra and Kutch. It was projected as a 'lifeline' of Gujarat. In their quest for 'development', the displacement of the people on the upstream of the dam was not in the lifeworld of the vocal middle class. For the political class, except for a few RCS social activists, displacement of PAP was a non-issue. Majority of them, like Nehru, considered that displacement of some people was inevitable for the 'progress' of the country. A leader like Morarji Desai, once respected as the 'supreme leader' of the Gujarat Congress, the first CM of bilingual Bombay state, said to the PAP of the Pong dam submergence area in

1961: 'We will request you to move from your houses after the dam comes up. If you move, it will be good. Otherwise, we shall release the waters [and] drown you all'.[4] However, the tone of a section of political class towards the oppressed had somewhat changed in the 1970s. The civil society in the 1980s was not callous to tribals who were to be displaced by the dam. But the nature, magnitude and past experiences were beyond their comprehension. The open letter quoted earlier is a case in point. While demanding construction of dam on war footing, these eminent persons expressed their anguishes on the drought situation. At the same time, they insisted on equitable distribution of water and warned against water-consuming industries. However, they did not mention a word for the proposed displaced Adivasis on the upstream of the river. In fact, by that time, resistance of the tribals expected to be displaced by the dam, and discourse on their deprivation and complex issues related to their rehabilitation were already, as we shall see further, in the public domain. Though Gujarat has more than 14 per cent tribal population, these activist intellectuals were not familiar with the wretched condition the tribals were living in. They hardly noted that tribals of some parts of Gujarat have been victims of water scarcity had to travel a long distance every summer to get water to satisfy their thirst and mitigate their hunger by eating beets.[5]

The displacement of people by various development projects though ongoing since Independence in the country and Gujarat, was almost invisible for urban people. Between 1947 and 1985, the GoG acquired for various 'development' works including roads approximately 1.93 million hectare of land that directly affected 280,000 families. Of that, the single largest chunk was for the water resources: small, medium and large dams. This comes to 470,000 hectare land affecting more than 88,000 families (Lobo and Kumar 2009). A majority of the displaced people, particularly those displaced for water resources, were tribals. The government acquired land under the 1894 Land Acquisition Act for 'public purpose'. But till the 1980s, there was no rehabilitation policy. According to the 1894 Act, the displaced get compensation in cash for the land acquired by the government. There is no standardized method for calculating the price of land. Legally speaking, the price has to be guided by 'market' value and the production of land, but the calculation of compensation remains arbitrary. Hence, the amount that the victims receive is more often than not so inadequate that she/he is hardly able to purchase the same amount of land elsewhere. Moreover, since a majority of the tribals who are cultivators but on the government record are not necessarily 'legal' owners, they do not get compensation from the government. They lose not only their sources of livelihood, but are also uprooted from their homes. Gradually they migrate all over the state and become poorer than before.

The adversely affected people due to loss of land, habitat and sources of livelihood everywhere resisted against the authorities. In 1957, the International Labour Organization (ILO) took cognizance of the displaced people and their rehabilitation. It resolved that these displaced people be provided 'with lands of quality at least equal to that of the lands previously occupied by them, suitable to provide for their present needs and future development'. India subsequently ratified the convention on 29 September 1958 (UNHCR 2000). The PAP had invariably resisted against acquisition of their land and habitats. But till the 1950s, except for a few states like Odisha and Maharashtra, civil society of the country hardly expressed its concern over the plight of the displaced population. More often than not, protests were treated as a localized issue of law and order. However, the scenario had begun to change from the early 1970s as the First World faced the environmental crisis. On various international and national forums, concerned scholars and activists got engaged in discourse on 'limit to growth', 'sustainable development' and search for alternative path of development. The issue of the displacement of people by large industries and dams was also raised. In India, protests against the Tehri dam drew the attention of urban sensitive persons. A section of civil society in Maharashtra, Gujarat's neighbouring state, raised the issue of displacement since the 1930s. They had succeeded forcing the government to enact the Rehabilitation Act in 1976. This was the first rehabilitation policy in the country.

Unlike the earlier commissions, the NWDT was not silent on the issue of displacement and rehabilitation. The tribunal recommended that landholders be given land as compensation rather than cash—a major departure from the previous practice of monetary compensation. By this time, in the post-Naxalbari period, the tribals were militantly resisting against the large-scale irrigation projects. In 1980, the Secretary (irrigation) of the GoI wrote to all the state government

> There has, in recent times, been an awakening on the part of the people whose land and property gets submerged as a result of execution of major irrigation power and multipurpose reservoir projects. It is increasingly felt that while the forest and tribal areas usually get submerged, the benefits of the projects go largely to the rich farmers. Unless satisfactory safeguards are kept protecting the interest of the 'oustees'[6] particularly the weaker sections, Government of India might not entertain acceptance of the project since rehabilitation issues might hold up the progress of the projects and result in excessive cost escalation. (GoI 1985)

The NWDT estimated that 6,147 families from 158 villages in MP and 456 families from 27 villages in Maharashtra would be 'project affected people' (PAP) as these villages would be submerged by the construction of the reservoir. Needless to say, these figures were an underestimation. The tribunal laid down detailed provisions regarding compensation. According to the provisions, every displaced family who had more than 25 per cent of its holding acquired by the government, 'shall be entitled to and be allotted irrigable land to the extent of land acquired from it subject to the prescribed ceiling in the State concerned and a minimum of 2 hectares (5 acres) per family'.

The NWDT considered every adult as a separate 'family'. However, it excluded the landless and those who cultivated land without formal ownership—called encroachers—from the compensation package. The GoG had to bear the responsibility for the rehabilitation of the PAP from MP and Maharashtra. These oustees had the option to settle in Gujarat by availing land in the Narmada command areas. The NWDT award did not mention the mode of the rehabilitation of the Gujarat oustees.

By the time the news about the award spread, use of coercive force by the state to displace people in the Srisailam Dam area in Andhra Pradesh was in public knowledge. At the local level, the organizations working among the Adivasis for over two decades, such as

RSSS, headed by Fr. Joseph; and the ANA headed by the Gandhian Harivallabha Parikh, located at Chhotaudepur, opposed the proposed displacement of the tribals caused by the Narmada project. In fact the ANA prevented the construction of a minor dam—Lalpur—that would have adversely affected the Adivasis. At the same time, youths of the Chhatra Sangharsh Vahini (CSV or Vahini), a youth organization of the JP movement, decided to work in the area for the rights of the tribals. They had closely observed the inhuman condition of the tribal oustees of the Ukai dam in the 1960s. They joined ARCH located at Mangrol, close to the dam site. The organization was set up by the husband and wife team of Daksha and Anil Patel—both medical doctors—of the CSV. ARCH focused its activities on the development of Adivasis and the rehabilitation of the Narmada oustees. Its initial aim was to organize the tribals for their rights. At the same time, in MP, on the eve of the publication of the NWDT award, the Nimar Bachao Andolan (Save Nimar—a small town in MP) was formed to protest against displacement (Baviskar 1995; Smith 2010). Thus at the grassroots level, the news of the award and the proposed dam were received with anxiety, distrust on the government and protests.

PROCESS OF REHABILITATION POLICY FORMATION

On the other hand, the Gujarat government was moving ahead in its plan. It approached the WB for a loan of $450 million. This was the time when the WB was facing opposition in different parts of the world for financing large dams. Under mounting pressure from the First World civil society the WB was compelled to give importance to the issue of displacement and rehabilitation. On the basis of the studies on the displaced people by large dams, the bank formulated guidelines for the resettlement of the involuntarily displaced people in 1980. At this stage, the finance minister of GoG was a former socialist and the minister of the public works and irrigation department was himself from an Adivasi community. Both were sensitive to the problems of the deprived communities. The GoG, as required by the WB, formed the Narmada Planning Group (NPG). It was headed by Y. A. Alagh, an eminent economist. The NPG commissioned several socio-economic studies on the project to a few academic and professional consultancy firms. One of these studies was on the sociocultural and economic life of the 19 villages that were to be evacuated. The study was assigned to the Center for Social Studies (CSS), a research institute based in Surat. During the course of the study, the researchers realized that many of the Adivasis cultivate land but are not legal owners, and that most of the households were 'joint' families and land-ownership titles were in the name of the eldest son, father or even a deceased father. Besides cultivation, these villagers depend on forests and the river for their livelihood. The notion of space among the tribals of these villages was different from that of the urban middle class. Because of its leaning towards action research and its commitment to social transformation, the CSS was in contact with ARCH-Vahini and the RSSS. In 1982, the CSS organized a national seminar on the 'Political Economy of Irrigation and the Experiences of Rehabilitation in India', which was attended by researchers, social activists and government officers from different parts of the country, and the NGOs working for the rehabilitation of the Narmada oustees. The thrust of the deliberation was that irrigation was 'not an unalloyed boon, nor was it politically neutral'. Narratives of the experiences of PAP of Ukai dam were presented. In the context of Narmada, several participants argued that

> The contention of the Government of Gujarat was that it was under no legal obligation to provide oustees of Gujarat with land in command area.... Such discrimination offends against Article 14 (of the Constitution), the government of Gujarat's decision not to provide oustees of Gujarat equivalent land in the Narmada Command area is unconstitutional and void. (Shah 1982)

Two more workshops involving political leaders, bureaucrats and social activists were organized in 1982–1983 to discuss CSS's observations in the field and recommendations on rehabilitation. The recommendations included compensatory land to all oustees, including 'encroachers', and also two and a half acres of land to the landless in the command area. Jinabhai Darjee, a radical Gandhian and the chairman of the 20 Points Programme of the GoG, and Amarsinh Chaudhry, the Minister for Irrigation and the in-charge of the Narmada project who belonged to an Adivasis community, were present at one of the workshops. They too endorsed the recommendations. However, government officers present in the deliberations were not of the same opinion. Vidyut Joshi, the study project director, observed:

> Two things are very clear: the tribal oustees do not want to go too far away places where they would have to stay amongst the strangers. And non-tribal land-sellers in nearly by villages are waiting for a chance of entrapping the oustees into buying their land. (Joshi 1983a)

Similarly, 'in the early 1980s, it was estimated that 86 percent of the expected oustees from MP stated their preference to relocate within 50 km of their current homes. In Maharashtra 26 of the 36 villages preferred local resettlement in their home state' (Scudder 2003, 15).

A majority of the government officers (not all) and average political leaders at all levels were not serious about rehabilitation.[7] In the mist, there were a handful of bureaucrats and politicians who were (are) pro-poor and daydreamers. One top-ranking civil servant, the financial advisor, was sensitive and concerned enough to tell the minister in charge that the sum needed for rehabilitation was not very large in the context of the overall cost. He said that, 'good and proper rehabilitation is possible and we should do to improve the condition of the Adivasis with good land, infrastructure related to education and health' (personal interview). But he was an exception; the rest, particularly the engineers and revenue officers, were primarily concerned only with the physical relocation. To them, the oustees were figures—furniture to be shifted from one place to another. Some said without hesitation, 'Give them money (compensation) and then kick them out. Why the fuss?'

In 1982, the revenue officer in charge of rehabilitation prepared a proposal for resettling Narmada oustees in Kutch—nearly 400 km away from their native villages. Kutch is a completely different ecological zone than the tribal area. In fact, he was himself unwilling to live in Kevadiya (a town near the dam site, built for the bureaucrats involved in the Narmada project). The bureaucrats had no idea about tribal society, nor could they understand the problems of the deprived. Most bureaucrats would, in informal conversations, allege that political leaders make 'irresponsible' public utterances for populist politics. The advocacy of a handful of social activists and the academia for better R&R policies had no effect on their mindset.

The government went ahead with its old R&R policy in 1983. The first five villages affected by rock-fill dykes were given notices to evacuate. Unrest simmered in the villages as people wondered where they would go and what they would do. Public meetings and processions protesting against the notices took place in Kevadiya, but to no effect. ARCH-Vahini filed a petition in the Gujarat High Court against the government's notice. The court pronounced a stay order on the government's activities, ordering that relocation should not be done by force. People should be shifted only after the rehabilitation site was equipped with infrastructure. This boosted the morale of the tribals and activists. Having come to know of the possible involvement of the WB in the Narmada project and its concern for the rehabilitation of the PAP, ARCH-Vahini wrote to the WB informing about the plight of oustees. Acknowledging the letter, the WB stated that R&R was 'one of the most important concerns'. This coincided with the WB mission's visit to India. The main agenda of the mission was to sort out the rehabilitation policy and work out a mechanism for effective implementation, focusing on the issue of resettlement. The mission was headed by Professor Thayer Scudder, an anthropologist from the California Institute of Technology who was himself one of the authors of the WB R&R guidelines, and had extensively researched African tribes and effectively pleaded the rights of the indigenous people. Scudder was very sympathetic to the cause of the tribals. At his first meeting in Delhi in September 1983, he found that Indian officials from both central and state governments were very upset by the Bank's sudden interest in resettlement planning. 'Why, I was asked, was the Bank all of a sudden so interested in resettlement which, after all, was strictly an Indian issue and with which Indian officials had many years of experience that had never before been challenged by the Bank' (Scudder 2003, 17). He was told by the Narmada Control Authority (NCA) that the Bank could review what the states intended to do and their plan for action. 'But at this stage *criticism will not be appreciated*' (italics mine). He was also told that the Bank's resettlement guidelines 'represented an ideal situation that would have to be adapted to Indian conditions' (Scudder 2003, 17).

Scudder was struck by the engineers' deep-rooted prejudices towards the tribals. He writes,

> In my case, the depth of prejudice was brought home to me during a discussion with one of Gujarat's four Chief Engineers. At one point, with considerable perplexity, he asked me why I was so concerned about the welfare of Gujarat's tribal resettlers. 'Do you know what they need?' he asked. When I asked 'what', he said 'birth control' by which he meant sterilization. (Scudder 2003, 19)

In his report to the WB, Scudder pointed out that the figures of the expected oustees provided by the GoI were an underestimation. He reiterated the social activists' demands that all oustees (from all three states), including encroachers and the landless, be provided a minimum of five acres of irrigable land; moreover, all adults—18 years of age in 1980—be given five acres of irrigable land.

The Adivasis were meanwhile even more restless and were concerned for the 'encroachers' right to land at the new sites. Though the tribals from the remotest villages—Dungari Bhil—had heard about the dam and reservoir, they were not sure how it would affect them (Joshi 1983). Their imminent displacement was brought home to them by the intervention of Vahini and the CSS researchers. They got angry when they got land acquisition notices. They expressed their anger:

> We cannot be treated like monkeys on trees who will simply climb to a higher level when the water rises. We demand land for all the families. It is no use merely talking in the middle of nowhere in these hills. We will not be heard. We must organize, get out of these hills, and let the outside world know that we are also human beings and that we must get our due before our lands and homes are flooded. (Patel 1997, 73)

ARCH-Vahini organized a protest march of Gujarat and Maharashtra's Adivasi oustees on 8 March 1984 in Kevadiya. The rally got wide coverage in the media. The government was rattled by this as it was negotiating a loan with the WB at the time. It was more so because of Scudder's critical strictures on the authorities' attitude towards the PAP and the WB insistence on a fair R&R policy as per its 1980 guidelines.

Meanwhile, John Clarke, development policy advisor, Oxfam-UK, organized an intensive campaign to pressurize the WB on the issue of R&R, in collaboration with ARCH-Vahini who wrote to Clarke saying, 'there is no doubt in our mind that your intervention from the UK has helped our cause immensely. We need your intervention as strongly as before' (Sen 1995, 17). In 1984, the Survival International Organisation pleaded with the WB that the oustees be given 'real' compensation in terms of land or forest and if this were not possible, to withdraw and suspend funds.

All three state governments and the GoI on one hand, and the WB on the other, signed the agreement in May 1985, agreeing, 'to adhere to implement a carefully monitored resettlement programme in compliance with the requirements of the Tribunal and the WB guidelines on involuntary resettlement of tribal people'.[8] More specifically, in November 1984, Gujarat was obliged to appoint a senior member of the Indian Administrative Service (IAS) with appropriate experience to head and strengthened the R&R wing within the Narmada Development Department, and to form a committee—including social science researchers, representatives of PAP and other NGOs—to advice the R&R wing on resettlement implementation. All three governments were required to appoint 'a qualified' research institution to undertake R&R monitoring and evaluation over the next 10 years (Scudder 2003). But the GoG and the GoI tried to 'abort the resettlement component of the bank mission'. Efforts were also made to see to it that the Bank's consultants Scudder and Mahapatra (an anthropologist from Odisha) did not visit the affected tribal villages and meet NGO activists. When the WB's consultants visited Kevadiya, ARCH-Vahini organized a demonstration by the tribals to present their case; they wanted to meet the Bank's consultants. But both the Bank and the project authorities prohibited such a meeting.

The Gujarat government constantly reiterated its commitment to 'ideal' resettlement and a better deal for the oustees. At the same time, expressing an excuse that there was not enough land in Gujarat for all oustees. CSS informally argued with Scudder and other NGOs that a good deal of surplus land was available in the proposed command area under the Land Ceiling Act. What was needed was the implementation of the law which required the acquisition of land from those who possessed more land above the ceiling. ARCH-Vahini on the other hand, collected information about the availability of land and the owner's willingness to sell. Somehow Vahini managed to pass their research on to Scudder, showing that enough land was available. Scudder recalls,

> As expected, at the meeting in the Ministry of Irrigation, I.M. Shah (Additional Secretary of GoG) told those assembled that no land was available for allowing resettlers to move the clusters of kin and community members. By then I had given the list of land availability to the Bank's lawyer who then handed it over to the meeting's Chair. Not only was I.M. Shah's position discredited, but he must also have lost face since the Chair was furious at both him and the situation. (2003, 22)

Political leaders admitted that the oustees' demands were legitimate and that it was the state's responsibility to improve their condition, but bureaucrats tried to persuade them that if the government agreed to the demand for five acres of irrigable land, this would set a precedent, and people displaced because of other projects would demand the same. Despite their pro-poor stance, the political elite did not have the conviction that the oustees of all projects must get land as their right. Therefore, they did not counter the advice of their officers who were anti-poor.

During the same period, at the international level, Survival International filed a document with ILO complaining about the Indian government's violation of International law with regard to the SSP. Survival International asserted: 'Ownership of land used or occupied by tribals must be recognized. It also emphasized to maintain collective ownership of natural resources; and during the resettlement, villages should be removed as units'. Following the UN Conference on the human environment and the 'green movement', several NGOs in Europe took up the issue of the protection of the environment. In the early 1980s, a number of action groups, research institutes and documentation centres were established everywhere, including India, to study and mobilize public opinion on environmental issues (Capra 1985). In 1983, US environmentalists persuaded the US government to take environmental impact into consideration while financing international development projects (Rich 1994, 113). The

Delhi-based NGO Kalavriksh wrote an article in *The Ecologist* highlighting the environmental dangers of the dam (see Ashish Kothari and Rajiv Bhartari 1985).

RESETTLEMENT AND REHABILITATION POLICY

In the midst of these environmental controversies, the GoG granted gradual concessions in the rehabilitation package. It announced the policy in the form of a government resolution about the rehabilitation of the Narmada oustees that hailed from Gujarat. This policy was in tune with the NWDT's recommendation for MP and Maharashtra oustees. Though the government committed to giving five acres of land to landholders, it was silent on giving land to all adults and encroachers. Therefore, the PAP and ARCH-Vahini rejected the government's policy. And they mobilized international CSOs and activists for building pressure on the WB to persuade the state and the GoI to give land to all adults.

The government yielded to the pressure. On 27 December 1987, the CM of Gujarat called a public meeting of the oustees in Kevadiya where he declared Gujarat's new R&R policy which in principle agreed to provide a minimum of five acres of land of choice to all adult males, irrespective of ownership. Thus, finally, the activists felt that the demands of the Adivasi oustees as formulated by ARCH-Vahini were accepted. The government sought Vahini's co-operation to persuade the oustees to accept its offer and co-operate with the government. It also roped in NGOs such as Shramik Vikas Sansthan (SVS) and the ANA for mediation between the PAP and the government. In collaboration with government officers, SVS and ANA began to organize village meetings to explain the government's offer. ARCH-Vahini, however, was cautious about its involvement in government-sponsored campaigns. It soon realized that the government-supported NGOs were following the bureaucrats who were not in favour of giving land to all adults of displaced households. It was found that these organizations were persuading Adivasis to take up non-farm occupations instead of asking for land (ARCH-Vahini 1988b, 6). Vahini opposed the government approach where, in practice, the government was backtracking from its promise of giving land to all. It dissociated from the government and launched the Rasta Roko (blocking of the road) agitation in 1988 protesting the government's illegal occupation of the private lands of the oustees from the village of Vadgam. The protesters stopped government vehicles from carrying away the black topsoil from their land to build a rock-fill dyke. Vahini filed a PIL in the high court and the Supreme Court, protesting the government's 'wilful violation' of the court's stay order and forcibly acquiring their land. The high court appointed an enquiry commission to investigate the issue. On the basis of the commission's report, the Supreme Court reprimanded the government for its illegal actions (ARCH-Vahini 1988a, 5).

The leaders of the Adivasis from the affected villages met in Kevadiya and decided to launch a struggle for their rights. A convention of Gujarat's oustees was organized on 14 May 1988 in which more than 1,500 oustees, and several social activists from different NGOs and academics participated. The convention unanimously declared: 'If rehabilitation and resettlement not only the oustees of Gujarat but also those of Maharashtra and MP are diluted by the state governments, the oustees of Gujarat will not tolerate this transgression'. Thus the unity among the oustees belong to all the states was emphasized. The participants also declared: 'No rehabilitation and no resettlement, no dam'. The event received wide media coverage, and the Adivasis' stand on R&R was spotlighted. The village leaders then met the chairman of the NCA and protested against the government's turnaround. They then decided to launch several satyagrahas at the government's rehabilitation office at Kevadiya to seek immediate relief and redressal. The government felt a need to pacify the tribals and to accede to their demands as the WB mission was to visit in early 1989. The purpose of the mission was to visit as many communities and resettlement areas as possible. Consequently, in April 1988, the CM of Gujarat announced in a public meeting that each oustee family (included adult sons and also landless) would get a minimum of five acres of land as per their demand.

ARCH-Vahini, the main architect of the movement, and all those who demanded a 'proper' rehabilitation package were happy with the government's announcement. Vasudha Dhagamwar rightly states:

'What Gujarat has been compelled to offer is the best ever resettlement package in our history' (1997). ARCH-Vahini, however, was not complacent. They warned,

> We say again that this (policy) does not guarantee a proper rehabilitation in as fluid a situation as India's, where anything can happen, anything can go wrong, and so could the rehabilitation. Our effort is to help to dispel in some measure this wide-spread pessimism and raise the prospects of possible by degree higher than that was thought possible a few months ago. It is difficult to resist a temptation to say that the situation today would not have been so hopeless, if this tendency of viewing all efforts to fight the domination of all kinds of power, especially that of the State, which so thorough-going scepticism as to deny them even a fighting chance of success, was kept in check! (1988c, 15)

This policy and the subsequent movement led by NBA had triggered off the formation of the national-level rehabilitation policy. A number of NGOs and intellectuals pressurized the government not only for scrapping the colonial 1894 Land Acquisition Act and formulating national rehabilitation policy but also for a need for people's participation in deliberation for preparing the policy. As a result, for the first time, the Ministry of Rural Development, GoI, drafted a National Rehabilitation Act in 1993. It was revised in 1994. Various provisions of the draft were widely discussed in different forums. In 1995, several groups and concerned citizens collectively prepared a critique of the government draft, and also prepared an alternative draft policy for rehabilitation. At last, the Right to Fair Compensation and Transparency in Land Acquisition, Rehabilitation and Resettlement Act, 2013 was enacted which came in force in 2014.

POLEMICS AND UNCIVIL WAR

While the confrontations and negotiations with the Gujarat government for 'proper' rehabilitation policy and its implementation were in motion, Medha Patkar also joined the process in 1985. At that time, she was working with the SETU, an Ahmedabad-based NGO. In her early career as a student at TISS, she was influenced by Gandhian socialists in Maharashtra who were already involved in the struggle on the issue of the displaced people of the Godavari project. And their agitation successfully forced the Maharashtra government to form the Rehabilitation Act in 1976. They then articulated a demand for 'a proper and timely rehabilitation, before acquiring land or before starting work on the project' (Vora 2002, 385). Embedded in this lifeworld, Medha started work in the villages of Maharashtra which were to be submerged under the Narmada dam. She undertook a 14-day padyatra protest march that covered 26 villages, so as to get acquainted with the local people and mobilize them for collective action against the government. The Narmada Dharangrast Samiti (NDS) was set up in Akkalkuwa and Akrani/Dhadagaon talukas in Dhule district, Maharashtra, in 1986 to fight for the rights of the oustees. By this time, as mentioned earlier, similar unrest was simmering in the villages of the MP located on the banks of the river. They opposed the large dams on the river Narmada: Sardar Sarovar in Gujarat and Narmada Sagar in MP. Local people formed organizations such as Narmada Ghati Nav Nirman Samiti and Narmada Ghati Sangharsh Samiti. In 1987, various organizations from Maharashtra and MP submitted a memorandum to the NCA with 38 demands. One of them was to release forest land for the rehabilitation of the PAP. They pointed out that the Narmada project had not fulfilled the basic environmental conditions, and the people of the villages likely to be affected by the dam were not consulted. Various organizations working in MP and Maharashtra on the issue of the rehabilitation of Narmada Dam oustees formed an umbrella organization called the Narmada Bachao Abhiyan (Save Narmada Campaign or NBA) in 1988. They opposed the dam on environmental, economic and social grounds. On the basis of the evidences form the earlier projects, the activists were convinced that not only do the poor people get uprooted from their culture they also do not get enough compensation in cash or land which can improve their life. They argued that 'just' rehabilitation of the affected people under the present 'development' paradigm was impossible. A slogan '*Vikas Chahiye, Vinash Nahi*' (Want development and not destruction) was floated. NBA articulated an alternative model of development based on Gandhi's philosophy of decentralization, and critiquing high technology and big dams (Vora 2002, 359). It begun to argue that there was no point in fighting the battle on the issue of rehabilitation. 'The rehabilitation centred struggle', NBA pointed out, 'has not been able to achieve the objective after all these years. Now, it is time when the movement must question the very logic of having big dams anywhere in the country. The movement should challenge the development model itself' (Vora 2002, 389–390). NBA took unequivocal position against the Narmada dam per se. Medha Patkar argued that the struggles and demands of the PAP were not confined to only the aspect of resettlement. The people had begun to question the development paradigm:

> [T]he displacement itself: why displacement? For whom? What is the public purpose? Who decides the public purpose, and the propriety of displacement? Can a financial evaluation of the resources of the affected people, which includes their sociocultural and other aspects of life could compensate them adequately? Thus, the struggles regarding displacement and resettlement are directly linked with development policy and projects. (Patkar 1998, 2433)

It was asserted that the construction of big dams helps engineers, contractors, industrialists and rich farmers.

ARCH-Vahini and some other social activists in Gujarat had no substantial disagreement with NBA's arguments. Conceding the importance of technology, in this case dams, they were bothered about who does and does not benefit from the dam. ARCH-Vahini articulated its response publicly,

> Our short answer [is] 'yes, we do' (oppose the present style of development). A little longer answer is: the activists and public-oriented intellectuals and professionals must not only criticize and denounce the present mode of development from the conference rooms and seminars. The point is to oppose it actively by forging and activating the democratic alliances, organizations and institutions—national and international. The development projects, harmful to the poor people, must be opposed in their entirety or in part, depending on our strengths and weaknesses. (Patel 1988)

The difference between NBA and ARCH was in strategy and perception of one's strength. In its given strength, ARCH-Vahini believed that while fulfilling the demands that they have put, the state would realize that it would think twice before planning gigantic projects in the future because of the huge cost for rehabilitation. While putting this argument, Vahini had a faith in the state's benevolence. And they assumed that CSOs would be able to oversee the state's implantation of the policy in letter and spirit. There was hardly any discussion on this position. The commitment of the state and dominant classes for the well-being of the PAP was taken for granted by ARCH without interrogation.

The NBA had no patience to dialogue on the issues raised by ARCH-Vahini and/or to assess the strength of the state, dominant classes and also of its own to resist and confront the adversary forces. There was no one to mediate between the two. They considered each other as persona non grata, though there was a large common ground between the two on the issue. The NBA took a stand of opposing the dam per se, and declared that people would not leave their villages under any circumstances. They said, 'We will ask these oustees to drown themselves in the rising waters of the dam rather than accept rehabilitation'. Opposing this position, Anil Patel of ARCH argued:

> The oustees of Maharashtra and MP have now reached a crossroad, where they have to make an unexpected choice: Whether to fight the dam on environmental grounds or to fight for the R and R policy analogous to Gujarat and fight for its fair implementation, *so as to set into motion the process that will in all probability help all the displaced persons in future and thereby put a powerful break on the reckless and mindless development project.* (Patel 1988, emphasis mine)

In order to intensify the struggle, the NBA organized a rally at Harsud, a small town on the banks of the river in MP, in September 1989. It was attended by more than 20,000 people and more than 150 NGOs from different parts of the country. The participants included villagers who were to be displaced, human right activists, environmentalists, academicians, filmmakers, Sarvodaya workers, etc. Some highlighted that the present paradigm of 'development' was '*poisoning the earth with chemicals and impoverishing the planet*'. The participants demanded a halt to the 'disastrous effects of the development projects'. The protestors took a pledge, administered by Baba Amte, a Sarvodaya leader from Maharashtra, not to be displaced by the project, and asked the government to alter its development policies or face the 'people's wrath'.[9] Similar rallies were organized in more than 20 cities, including Delhi.

The GoG headed by Chimanbhai Patel started a counter campaign. He was the one who was forced to resign as CM by the 1974 student movement on the issue of corruption. He managed to become the CM in 1990 with BJP support. During this time, Gujarat's middle class, as well as rural middle peasants, were under the spell of the Ayodhya Ram Janmabhoomi movement. A large segment of the HCS—literatures, media and development NGOs—was also soft to the Ayodhya movement (Shah 1990). All of them were for the Narmada dam. A discourse on the nature of development did not find a place in their agenda. They formed the Narmada Abhiyan (campaign) or NA in 1988, and mobilized not only religious and caste associations but also economic interest groups such as farmers and business organizations like the Gujarat Chamber of Commerce and Industry. A section of the Sarvodaya workers and NGOs concerned for drinking water also joined the pro-dam campaign without raising questions on the nature of development. Like the dominant wasted interests, they put a faith in the state that it would serve common interests.

As the NBA raised environment issue on the dam, in the early 1990s, the NA, on the other hand, in collaboration with the government organized several demonstrations in Delhi for early clearance of the SSP from the Ministry of Environment, Forest and Climate Change. An aggressive campaign against NBA activists was simultaneously launched. At this juncture, the activists of the RCS in Gujarat split into two factions on the question of the Narmada dam: pro and anti. There were, however, different shades of opinion within each group.

A few of the pro-dam NGOs, already involved in fighting with the government for 'proper' rehabilitation, continued to peruse the cause for proper rehabilitation. They developed a faith that by pressuring the government, 'proper' rehabilitation of all the oustees was possible. On that premise, many of them not only opposed NBA's anti-dam position but also eventually joined the pro-dam lobby whole hog, and unwittingly joined hands with the dominant classes. A few among them, however, revisited their position and kept a distance from the pro-dam groups. But they did not support the anti-dam movement because they were not against the dam per se, and did not find an immediate alternative for drinking water and drought in Gujarat. For them, technology is not neutral. A dam can be used for irrigation, drinking water and hydraulic power with the least displacement and humane rehabilitation. On the other hand, there were some activists who believed that 'modern science' and technology were the panacea for growth and development. They argued that the West has exploited nature and prospered, and wanted to prevent India from development in the name of environment for using high technology. At the same time, a small segment of the RCS—a section of Gandhians, liberals and leftists—was sympathetic to NBA's no-dam position. All of them were not against the dam per se and did not share Gandhi's economic philosophy, but they were questioning the nature of development.

NA represented the mainstream society being hand-in-glove with the government. It mobilized various religious, caste, professional, business and industrial organizations such as the Gujarat Chamber of Commerce as well as Sarvodaya and other CSOs, litterateurs and public figures. Sarvodaya and liberal activists who were hitherto a part of the RCS became spokespersons of the pro-dam civil society. They were instrumental in preparing the literature on positive aspects of the dam with the government's data. They ridiculed NBA activists as hypocrites, a stooge of the Western power and anti-people. Medha and her co-activists were accused of 'throwing bones in the holy fire of this project'. Religious symbols and idioms were invoked to arouse sentiments of the people. They directly confronted the NBA at Ferkuva in December 1990 when the NBA organized a *Sangharsh Yatra* (SY), that is, an agitation march, from Rajghat in MP. The purpose of the NBA for the march was to raise awareness among the people on the issue and also to pursue the Gujarat government for reviewing and stopping the project. To counter NBA, the NA organized a *'Narmada Agey Badhao Shanti Yatra'* (Move Narmada forward peace march). Its purpose was to prevent NBA's SY from entering Gujarat (Patel 2010, cited in Ganguly 2015). After a tug of war for 33 days, NBA had to wind up its march as they were not allowed to enter Gujarat. Vahini and pro-dam Sarvodaya workers were in the forefront of the show to counter NBA.

Even before this episode, the government and the HCS created an environment of terror and fear in which pro-dam activists were hooted out from public platforms for dialogue on the dam. For instance, in May 1990, a workshop to discuss various aspects of the issue was disrupted by pro-dam hooligans. The workshop was organized by like-minded pro- and anti-dam activists. A majority of the anti-dam activists were from Gujarat. They were Sarvodayists and liberals. Around six activists, all from Gujarat, represented the anti-dam position. It was reported in the media,

> [The disrupters] had come on the instructions of chief minister Chimanbhai Patel and the minister of the state for home affairs, Narhari Amin.... They shouted slogans vowing to complete the Narmada project and prevented even pro-dam participants...from expressing their views. They stormed the meeting hall and tore papers, damaged furniture and manhandled participants.... They went on to threaten that no discussion would be allowed anywhere in Gujarat on the Narmada Project. (Sanghvai et al. 1990)

Some of the leaders of the NA defended the hoodlums and said that 'non-Gujarati activists should not "poke" their noses in the affairs of Gujarat'. The pro-dam liberals rationalized hooligans' action as a part of political tactics. However, a few Sarvodaya pro-dam activists did not approve the disruption by the pro-dam activists. But they did not maintain a distance from such rowdy pro-dam activists. They maintained silence when the NBA's offices in Baroda and Ahmedabad were ransacked, and Medha Patkar was physically hurt in Ahmedabad. There were, however, isolated voices of protest against the behaviour of the pro-dam activists.

In the midst of such an atmosphere, isolated attempts were made by some public-spirited persons to create a space for dialogue between different points of views on the issue. With such concern, a few concerned citizens, litterateurs, journalists and NGOs such as Mahiti, Utthan, Viksat and the Centre for Environmental Education jointly organized Pani Parishad (assembly on water) in May 1993 at Ahmedabad. Many of the organizers concerned with the problem of drinking water in Saurashtra and Kutch were in favour of the dam. The organizers invited presidents of all the district and taluk panchayats, and social activists and experts for a wider discussion. A senior Sarvodaya leader Chunibhai Vaidya, an ardent supporter and activist of NA, was invited to chair the meeting. As soon as the first speaker started speaking, a crowd from the outside entered and started anti-Medha slogans with abusing words. The miscreants ransacked the dais, broke the furniture and the mike, and manhandled the delegates. The organizers called the police and tried to contact several political leaders for protection. Three constables came after one hour and did not do anything. A police complaint was filed with video-footages showing violent destructive actions of the hooligans. One of the organizers of the dialogue Ashwini Bhatt, a well-known litterateur, wrote a letter to all the members of Gujarati Sahitya Parishad (Gujarat Literature Assembly) describing the event and its background. He mentioned that after ransacking, the miscreants had gone to Chiman Patel's residence and had a lunch with him. He sent the letter dated 10 May 1993 to various persons, office bearers of Gujarat Sahitya Parishad and social activists, in which he raised questions:

> [H]ave we lost a right to speak and express our dissent voice in this state? I demand your reaction from you as a sensitive creative writer. Can the Gujarati Sahitya Parishad do anything to a person who among you had such experience? Or we have to move by putting bandage on our mouth?

He hardly received any response from his fellow litterateurs. One of the literati, Rajnikumar Pandya, however, shared his agony and wrote that what he had experienced was a miniature of the national picture. '[T]his country, people who are morally degenerated...you are in illusion that you are fighting for the people whose values are for the national interests...in reality we do not have a courage to walk with you even for a single step'.[10]

RCS organizations and activists got divided. A few radicals such as Lok Adhikar Manch, Indian Social Action Forum (INSAF), Jan Sangharsh Manch, Savendan Sanskritik Manch, etc., openly supported the NBA and raised questions against the pro-dam euphoria. A few did not support NBA openly nor did they join the pro-dam CSOs. Once in a while, they protested against the chauvinism created by the dominant classes and the Gujarat government. While critiquing the Gujarat government and pro-dam NGOs in general and the Gandhians in particular, Madhusudan Mistry of DISHA pointed out that instead of helping the Adivasis of MP, the Gujarat government used and divided the NGOs and Adivasis against each other. He observed,

In a way, the Narmada's water will not be available to the Adivasis of Chhotaudepur taluka. Not only that, none of Adivasis areas located in the upper-stream of the 14 big dams of Gujarat gets water. Their water problem remains as it was in the past. Yet pro-government NGOs try to show that big dams are also in the interests of [the] Adivasis.... Many leaders of the Gandhian organizations which proclaim the ideology of 'Sarvodaya' joined hands with the business houses against the interests of the Adivasis of the submerging villages.... By this, the Sarvodaya ideal had become against the ideal of Antyodaya (Poorest of the poor).... Thus the poor are pitted against poor.... As it happened in other irrigated areas, cash crops like sugarcane, cotton, etc., will flourish which will make the rich farmers more prosperous.... We will go on fighting for minimum wages to labourers and the Labour Minister would be some rich farmer. This class would claim to represent all classes of Gujarat. This is Asmita (identity) of Gujarat. (*Naya Marg* 1991, 29–31)

The arguments between the pro-dam and anti-dam activists remained bitter and acrimonious. Both often indulge in personal allegations. They have sometimes come to blows directly or by proxy.

The liberals and Sarvodaya pro-dam activists expressed their faith in the government and declared that the government would implement its plans and promises. Chunibhai Vaidya, who did not trust the government on the other issues, said that the government had already given several times more benefits in advance to the oustees. He defended the government's facts and figures as sacrosanct. Except for Vahini, most of the pro-dam Sarvodaya and liberal activists had put faith in the government and almost behaved as the government's spokespersons. Some articulated their position in opposing the anti-dam position by arguing that the anti-dam is anti-development and anti-Gujarat, giving primacy to the environment over the people. On the other hand, anti-dam activists expressed distrust in the government and also produced counter figures and facts. The battle between the two was drawn, left with very little space for dialogue.

NGOS AND THE IMPLEMENTATION OF THE POLICY

As mentioned earlier, while announcing the rehabilitation package incorporating all the demands of the NGOs, the CM asked the NGOs for their co-operation in the implementation of the same. The chairman of the Sardar Sarovar Narmada Nigam, a former socialist, was keen to implement the R&R policy sincerely. NGOs were involved in (a) persuading the PAPs to accept the government's offer and move to the new sites; (b) assisting them to select land—its quality and size for agriculture and houses; and (c) negotiating with the land sellers. ARCH-Vahini, CSS and a few others were made members of the Rehabilitation Advisory Committee and asked to assist the Director of Rehabilitation. ARCH-Vahini was also involved in the land purchasing committee and played a very significant role in the rehabilitation. The crucial difference between ARCH-Vahini and the other NGOs was that the former was critical of the government and did not hesitate to point out lapses and corruption in the process of implementation of the programme; the rest more or less toed the government line, only criticizing the officers behind their backs.

Though the CM declared that rehabilitation would remain a priority; the administration of Gujarat relaxed when the WB was out of the project, and the attitude of officers at all levels towards the demands and complaints of the oustees began to change. The Director of Rehabilitation who was considered 'accessible and honest' was replaced by an 'unknown' senior IAS officer; middle-level officers were changed, and then the officer in charge of the Land Purchasing Committee—who according to Anil Patel was known for his integrity—was removed. The time is taken to resolve the oustees' complaints increased. Many complaints brought to the notice of the R&R Director by Vahini and the CSS researchers remained unattended. Patel observed that the land given to the MP oustees was of poor quality and uncultivable; the usual practice of inspecting the land with the NGO before allotment had not been observed. Vahini's protest had no effect. Several instances of the bad quality of the land led the MP oustees to decide not to settle in Gujarat. Amita Baviskar in her study of an MP village observed,

> If there is one thing that Anjanvara is sure about, it is this: they don't want to go to Gujarat. They have visited resettlement sites there and they have seen the misery. Waterlogged fields, no livestock, fragmented families, hostile neighbours, no commons to collect fuel or fodder–this sums up the experience of most Adivasis from MP who were given land in Gujarat. (Baviskar 1999)

The GoG, however, was bent on projecting an image of a flawless rehabilitation. It roped in litterateurs and media persons to paint beautiful pictures of the resettled Adivasis. Rigorous monitoring of the resettlement of the oustees became increasingly sluggish thanks to the indifferent attitude of the authority towards rehabilitation. Moreover, Vahini found that the newly formed NGOs involved in rehabilitation were more interested in getting funds, and were neither sensitive nor experienced enough to work among the displaced Adivasis. Disgusted by both the government and some of the NGOs, ARCH-Vahini publicly protested the way the rehabilitation work was being carried out, and it resigned from the Land Purchasing Committee and the Executive Committee of Rehabilitation. An anguished Dr Anil Patel observed in 2001.

> The Gujarat government, in the post-1993 phase, had mindlessly and arrogantly undermined the R&R the carefully nurtured, nascent, from which it had still not fully recovered. Corruption was given free hand.... The ultimate bankruptcy of the state of Gujarat became visible when the Supreme Court, apparently unable to make up its mind about the claims and counter-claims of the two sides, forced the state of Gujarat to accept the Grievance Redressal Authority[11] (GRA), headed by a retired Chief Justice of the High Court. The aim of the GRA was to set Gujarat's R&R house in order and worked with exemplary focus and perseverance. The huge backlog of the problems was finally recognized by the GRA, as it toned up the indolent and negligent R&R machinery. The Supreme Court had to impose its authority to redress major lapses in the R&R. This is unprecedented. All the problems anticipated by the international experts in the R&R have paled into insignificance in the face of the unfolding reality. (Patel 2001, 326)

According to the state government's report, all the PAFs from the 19 affected villages of Gujarat have been resettled in over 141 villages, mostly in Vadodara and Narmada districts. About 6,037 oustee families from MP have been rehabilitated in 111 villages, and the 807 PAFs from Maharashtra have settled in 25 villages in different parts of Gujarat. Most of the villages are not in the Narmada command area. Though most of them have received agricultural land and housing plots, there are some complaints regarding the quality of land and its size. On the basis of the studies carried out by CSS, D. C. Sah observes,

The success stories of rehabilitation are based on [the] experiences of PAPs who were exposed to non-tribal institutions and markets. The Bhil, Nayaka and Vasava PAPs of Zone II and III (remote areas) who are not exposed to markets and modern production technology are unable to adjust with the mainstream as quickly as Tadavi and Rathava. (2002, 433)

However, on the whole, thanks to pressures from all sides, the rehabilitation of the oustees in Gujarat is not far from satisfactory. The compensation package is comparatively not bad, though several avoidable and unavoidable shortfalls remain. The oustees from MP and Maharashtra who have settled in Gujarat have not received the same advantage and treatment as that of the Gujarat oustees. As a result, a few of them had returned back to MP.

The height of the dam has been increased up to the level of 163 metres. In 2017, the government declared the completion of the dam and the rehabilitation of all the 32,684 the PAFs: Gujarat (4,763), Maharashtra (4,307) and MP (23,614). According to the activists, a large number of PAFs in MP have not yet been fully rehabilitated. All of them have not received irrigable land. Moreover, the MP government has violated the Tribunal Award and Supreme Court's judgments (2000 and 2005) and had given cash as a substitute for land to many oustees (Jain et al. 2015). Moreover, the pro-dam RCS activists of Gujarat have been disappointed as most of their dreams are increasingly getting shattered on several counts such as delay in construction of canals, water scarcity, salinity and soil degradation in downstream villages on the bank Narmada, government's priority to industry over drinking water, control of dominant castes and muscular power in village-level water committee depriving the poor for getting their share of water, etc. Gradually, many of the RCS activists, once divided between pro and anti-dam camps, are now coming nearer to each other and joining hands against the present mode of development.

CONCLUSION

The Narmada dam has triggered several micro and macro social movements, making a far-reaching impact on civil society, not only of Gujarat and India but also of the world. These movements have raised several questions not only on the neoliberal development paradigm but also on limitations of science and technology in human development. The CSOs of Gujarat and also the NBA have forced the Indian state to enact a rehabilitation policy providing irrigable land not only to those whose land was acquired but to landless labourers dependent on land for livelihood. With the long struggle for over three decades involving local and regional as well as international civil society, most—not all—PAP are entitled to land and other benefits. Of course, the implantation of the R&R policy is beyond the level of satisfaction of most of the concerned activists and policymakers. The situation would have been more effective had the activists of NBA and others developed an organic relationship with the affected people, and could have mobilized them. This would have also helped the activists to understand changing social reality and consciousness of the common people. Of course, it is easier said than done at a ground level with the middle-class character of the activists and the might of the state as well as of the dominant classes. Be that as it may, the struggle has positively contributed in compelling the state to accept relatively better than the earlier land acquisition and R&R policy, incorporating the provisions of impact assessment of the project, 'public hearing' and 'consent' of the affected people as a legitimate right of the people. It has also contributed in reinterpreting Indian jurisprudence in the context of human rights, and eminent domain in the context of common resources and environment.

NOTES

1. Under the colonial rule, following the recommendation of the first Irrigation Commission, the number of dams was increased to mitigate the problems of famine. Between 1901 and 1950, 304 dams were constructed primarily for canal irrigation.
2. A large dam is generally classified as one with a minimum height of more than 15 metres from its deepest foundation to the crest. The storage exceeds 1 million m^3 or the maximum flood discharge exceeds 2,000 cumecs, with length of crest not less than 500 metres, or capacity of the reservoir formed by the dam not less than one million cubic metres or the maximum flood discharge dealt with by the dam is not less than 2,000 cumecs or National Register of large Dams. See http://www.cwc.nic.in/main/downloads/New%20NRLD.pdf, accessed 31 July 2018.
3. Arun Kumar Nayak, who had studied the agitation, informs me,

    So far as my readings on Hirakud dam and protests and movements is concerned, the people of the region had registered a massive protests and they too had given letter to Gandhiji to intervene in this matter. However, Gandhiji was silent on this matter. He had not replied anything to protesters.

I have not found any reference on Hirakud dam in the volumes of CWMG between 1946 and 1947.

4. See https://contemplatingme.wordpress.com/tag/morarji-desai/, accessed 8 July 2018.
5. This is not evident from their writings.
6. According to NWDT, an oustee is a person who since one year prior to the date of publication of the notification under Section 4 of the Act has been ordinarily residing or cultivating land or having any other occupation or caring or working for gain in the area, likely to be permanently or temporarily.
7. One of the ministers said, 'the government didn't have to move a finger to resettle the tribals, who would [automatically] leave their habitat like rats from their holes when the water would rise' (Patel 1995).
8.
   The major elements of the WB policy on R&R were:

   (1) All involuntary resettlements should be conceived and executed as development programmes with re-settlers provided with sufficient investment resources and opportunities to share in project benefits. Displaced persons should be compensated for their losses at full replacement cost prior to the move; assisted with the move and supported during the transition period in the resettlement site; and assisted in their efforts to improve their former living standards, income-earning capacity, and production levels, or at least to restore them. Particular attention should be paid to the needs of the poorest groups to be resettled.
   (2) Community participation in planning and implementing resettlement should be encouraged.
   (3) Re-settlers should be incorporated socially and economically into host communities so that any adverse impact on the host communities is minimized.

   Land, housing, infrastructure, and other compensation should be provided to the adversely affected population, indigenous groups, and ethnic minorities who may have customary rights to the land or other resources taken for the project. The absence of a legal title to land by such groups should not be a bar to compensation. (S. Parsuraman, in Dreze, Samson and Singh 1997, 36–37).

9. See https://www.ucanews.com/story-archive/?post_name=/1989/10/02/thousands-protest-against-narmada-dam-project-in-madhya-pradesh-state&post_id=38633 access on 17 October 2017.
10. Rajnikumar Pandya. I thank Urvish Kothari for sharing Ashvini Bhatt's letter and Rajni Kumar's response to this letter.
11. Following the PIL by the NBA in 1994, the Supreme Court gave an interim stay order on the construction of the dam based on issues of the environment and rehabilitation. The Court maintained that 'without effective R&R facilities no further construction of the dam would be permitted by the NCA' (Supreme Court 2000). Hence, the government set up a high-level authority called the Grievance Redressal Authority (GRA) to

look into the grievances of the oustees; Justice P. B. Desai, retired chief justice of the Gujarat High Court, was appointed its chairperson. The GRA was authorized to,

> [E]nsure that the oustees already settled and the oustees settled hereinafter in the R&R sites created for resettlement and rehabilitation of the oustees from the State of MP and Maharashtra receive all the benefits and amenities in accordance with the Award and the various Government resolutions from time to time; and ensure that oustees resettled in Gujarat have received all the benefits and amenities due to them.

The GRA became an effective monitoring and implementing agency as far as the relief and rehabilitation of the PAFs in Gujarat was concerned. The judge was keenly interested in resolving the grievances of the oustees, and the GRA took the bureaucracy to task and ensured implementation.

EPILOGUE

A core concern of civil society as well as of the State is the common good with universalistic values. Theoretically, they are complementary to each other to attain the objectives enshrined in the Indian Constitution to build an egalitarian social order embedded with liberty and fraternity. While enlarging its circumference by involving subalterns on equal footing, civil society democratizes itself in its functioning. It also inculcates democratic egalitarian values in different sections of society in everyday life. Simultaneously, it also builds pressure on the State for formulating policies to translate rights into reality and to deepen democracy with people's participation in decision-making. In the process, civil society also intermittently participates in governance at different levels to make it more participatory and transparent.

The modern civil society in India is the legacy of the Western education system and governance. The first generation of Western-educated elite adhering to their lifeworld initiated public discourse on rationality, and the relationship between society and man, science and religion, State and citizenship, etc. They formed public associations for discourse related to the common good and also undertook activities for spreading formal education and 'modern' values, and reforming social customs and structure. The space of modern civil society then was primarily occupied by the upper strata of society traditionally engaged in trade, business and knowledge production. In South India, rural peasant castes (non-*dwij*) entered civil society by the turn of the 19th century and contested the hegemony of the upper castes. But this was not the case in Gujarat. The scale of civil society in Gujarat gradually enlarged by the early 20th century with the expansion of higher education coupled with the emergence of urban industrial centres. The freedom movement accelerated the process with the entry of a small section of peasant castes and Muslims. It grew at a faster rate with the growth in economy and education in post-Independence India. The expansion, however, has so far remained largely horizontal than vertical in terms of social composition of upper caste and middle castes. It has gradually taken a backward step by alienating Muslims from its circumference. Over the past six decades, a few activists and organizations belonging to Adivasis, OBCs and Dalit communities have entered civil society, particularly its RCS segment. They are not fully integrated because of their different approach and priorities of activities. Though these activists are organically rooted in the milieu of their communities, as most of them are educated and have attained a middle class status, they get more interested in the issue of identity than in the economic marginalization and exploitation of the vast majority of their communities. Women activists and their organizations for gender equality also have a visible presence.

At a normative level, CSOs and social activists are committed to a democratic political system for the common good. They also affirm democratic principles in the decision-making and functioning of the CSOs to which they are associated. Except for a few, these organizations have been formed within the administrative-political structure. Since they are formed by one or a few individuals and are registered under the government's Trust or Societies Act, membership of these organizations is limited. In many organizations, the founder-trustees enjoy tenure for life. They also fear that open membership would endanger the working of their organizations. More often than not, the working of these organizations is confined to a small number of activists. And the relationship between the head executive and the grassroots activists is more of employee–employer relationship rather than of the comrades. This is also partly because the former has a responsibility to raise and manage funds, whereas the latter joins the organization at a later stage as an employee. This delimits its democratic spirit and hampers its sustainability for a long-term struggle against the dominant forces and the State. Most of these organizations are not mass-based, except at the time when they get involved in social movements. However, there are quite a few organizations, often offshoots of social movements, that are voluntary in the true sense of the term. They are not registered under the government rules; hence, they enjoy more freedom in their functioning than other registered organizations.

All of them at the normative level are in favour of a democratic political system and constitutional values; their commitment to their maintenance and advancement is not strong. Most of the HCS often declare themselves as apolitical and avoid taking a position on contentious political issues. The intelligentsia and activists, though often talk about freedom of expression, are susceptible of getting co-opted by the State and dominant classes. At the same time, a few of the social activists and organizations of HCS, championing for a neoliberal economy, stand for bourgeois democracy. And whenever the political authority and/or sectarian groups sabotage established democratic procedures and norms impinging on basic individual freedom, some of them register their protest. On the other hand, activists of RCS invariably get perturbed when the State and dominant castes violate or ignore adherence to the core democratic components. They openly express their opinion, protest and even confront the State, as many did during the Emergency. They continue to do so, though they are not large in number. They are under State surveillance and are subject to harassment.

Civil society as a whole is concerned and actively involved in philanthropic work, in providing relief to all in the eventuality of natural and human-made disasters such as earthquakes, floods, fires and ethnic conflicts. Many of the social activists were involved in the rehabilitation of the earthquake victims between 2001 and 2004 in Gujarat. They did impressive work, though it was not free from their caste and communal bias. In fact, the work with 'noble' purpose had reinforced social hierarchy and divisions in new resettlement habitats (Simpson 2015). Their social bias against the minority community and/or fear of the State and majority community kept many away from the relief and rehabilitation work for the victims of the 2002 communal carnage. And many of them had been lukewarm in the resettlement and rehabilitation work of the people affected by the Narmada Project, not only of MP and Maharashtra but also of Gujarat tribals.

Civil society reproduces hegemony and the way of life of dominant upper castes. The hegemonic values, however, are not monolithic and one-dimensional. Dominant caste values are embedded within the hierarchical caste system in which all social groups are conceived of as having an organic and holy relationship. During the freedom movement, these values were reiterated. There is more of an element of compassion than of empathy in their work among the have-nots. They have a paternalistic mindset. A sense of guilt is often inculcated among the deprived people, that they themselves were responsible for their plight: their lifestyle, lack of education and 'ignorance'. At the same time, market and capitalist states in the last five decades invoke competition, profit, achievement, merit, etc. which also work in favour of the hegemonic classes. The conflicting nature of social hierarchical and modern market values coexists with tension and generates their new dynamics. Both these value systems are reinforced by formal and informal education and public discourse as well as by interpersonal relationship in public spheres. The subaltern communities with their own experiences and aspirations often contest hierarchical norms, assert and reinvent their cultural autonomy, and confront and rebel against dominance. They strive for equality and dignity. A large segment of the RCS activists is not free from these hegemonic values because of their social orientation of being from the upper strata. These activists have imbibed hegemonic values without self-reflection. The received values have been treated by them as 'normal' universal. Because of their preoccupation with economic and political issues, they have not questioned the received cultural norms. For instance, formal education in West Bengal ruled by a Left government over three decades continues to reproduce *bhadralok* hegemonic values. Timothy Scrase observed in 1993 that although the ideological position of the West Bengal government was radically different from the regimes of other states' governments,

> [I]n practice it can be seen that reflections of ideological bias exist within specific social and cultural institutions (like education) and so serve to legitimate power of the ruling class. In this way, political hegemony is maintained in West Bengal and a corresponding cultural hegemony is preserved in the social and cultural institution. (Cited in Chakravarti 2009, xi)

Over and above, though the present formal education system raises aspirations among the subalterns as the only way to break shackles of poverty and injustice, it perpetuates their exclusion. of the education system, occasionally expresses resentment against the way in which the education system functions. Most of the social activists either do not know how to improve it, and/or they find a way for the children of their upper and middle class to get a 'better quality' education. A change in the education system is not on the agenda of CS. A tiny section of RCS has been campaigning since the early 1970s for a common school as recommended by the first Education Commission for good quality education for everyone. But its voice is increasingly getting mute within civil society itself. Ironically, social activists of the subalterns, though protesting against exclusion in education institutions, are not actively supporting the movement for common schooling. Granting the importance of education, a large section of RCS finds that the piecemeal changes in the education system would not work. These activists and organizations frequently protest against privatization of education. Social activists and organizations, particularly women, subaltern communities and radicals, irrespective of the social background, are in the forefront in interrogating these values. They also raise their voice against the contents of school curricula and textbooks which reinforce hegemonic values. A few isolated literati, including playwrights, poets, social organization and activists, make conscious efforts to evolve counter-cultural values, symbols and forms in the course of social movements.

Equality, dignity and social justice are the stated goals of several RCS as well as HCS organizations. They are critical of globalization and liberalization, and are perturbed by the ever-widening inequality in society. There is almost a consensus amongst these social activists that poverty, unemployment and the absence of social security are interwoven into the one major problem that the vast majority of the people in Gujarat face. A sizable section of RCS believes that the whole structure of the economy is anti-poor, based on exploitation and injustice. Consensus prevails among them, including most of the HRC activists, regarding the necessity of State intervention to provide social security to the poor. They believe that people cannot be left to the market alone. Empowerment and capacity building of vulnerable sections of society are often mentioned in their project planning. In practice, these notions are limited to raising the household income. Social transformation is not on the agenda of the HCS organizations. Security and rights of religious minorities—particularly Muslims and Christians—are not their concern. In fact, several of them share a majoritarian outlook with a sectarian ideology. They have a specific, tangible goal for their target groups. With the paternalistic approach, they undertake welfare programmes for the betterment of the poor.

On the other hand, social transformation towards a secular egalitarian social order is on the agenda of the RCS activists and organizations. They are worried about their inadequacy to counter the widespread majoritarian tendency in the social fabric with State connivance. They are concerned with the emancipation of women, Dalit, Adivasis and all the toiling masses. They often invoke their agenda for the annihilation of caste, patriarchy, capitalism, majoritarian culture, moral degeneration, etc. Women's organizations aim at fighting for women's rights and achieving an equal status in society. Organizations that focus on the Dalits also strive for equality and social justice. Some women and Dalit organizations have gradually expanded their notion of equality for all, and they join hands with all the oppressed and marginalized groups for equality. At the same time, many of them hardly reflect critically on the political economy of the State and its relationship with culture in general, and patriarchy and contemporary caste conflict in particular.

With the financial support from international organizations such as the WB, UNDP, DFID (Department for International Development, UK) and other funding organizations, a large number of NGOs have entered in the civil society arena for 'development' work and for good governance. They believe that professional expertise and participation of stakeholders with accountability and transparency in governance is the royal path for development. Besides support from the international funding agencies, some NGOs collaborate with the union or the state governments in the form of PPP. They work at different levels and segments, including infrastructure such as roads and transport, water management, solid waste management, skill development, vocational training, agro-business, credit, sanitation, health, education, shelter, etc. The parameters of 'good governance' have been actualized in a few cases where the stakeholders are from the rich and middle class. Participation of poor stakeholders and accountability of the government have remained on paper. More importantly, PPP has sidelined political leaders and has legitimized the depoliticization process (Ghosh et al. 2009). These NGOs do assist the poor to add some income and to sustain life so that cheap labour remains available to the propertied classes. Not only that, they make the poor feel guilty if they are unable to develop their skills and capacity to meet the needs of the market. Thus, large segments of the pro-poor civil society engaged in welfare programmes unwittingly socialize the poor to the market, 'by promoting the acquisition of certain behavioural patterns and decision-making preferences and by supporting the functional social networks needed for markets to operate smoothly' (James Busumtwi-sam 2002). As these activists and their organizations, including of RCS, carry out the welfare programmes unreflectively, despite their dislike of capitalism, they inadvertently promote a capitalist culture and legitimize the neoliberal economic system.

However, the organizations with a rights-based perspective use these programmes to develop consciousness among the poor for their rights as citizens. They develop local leadership among the deprived communities who develop the confidence to negotiate with political leaders and bureaucrats for their rights. These grassroots activists encourage and lead collective actions of local residents and in some instances have successfully obtained basic services such as drinking water and shelter, and prevented eviction from their settlement by the authority (Desai 1995; Mitlin 2001; Van Eera 2008). Such success stories boost the morale of the poor for collective actions to get amenities. Such struggles do contribute to developing a consciousness for citizen's rights.

With sustained efforts of radical social activists, the notion of 'right' is not merely confined to universal franchise but is extended to social and economic aspects. Article 21, Right to Life, has been legally accepted as 'the procedural *magna carta* protective of life and liberty'. On several SALs, the Supreme Court has interpreted that the right to life includes the right to live with dignity, right to livelihood, right to health and so on. With continuous struggles of the people at the grassroots, public discourse at various levels, lobbying with policymakers and legal battles in the courts, the colonial policy of land acquisition has been replaced with the Right to Fair Compensation and Transparency in Land Acquisition, Rehabilitation and Resettlement Act, 2013. The Act has provisions to provide fair compensation to those whose land is taken away, bring transparency to the process of acquisition of land to set up factories or buildings and infrastructural projects, and assure rehabilitation of those affected. In the case of the SSP, the State has been forced to enact a relatively better rehabilitation policy, promising land to all PAFs and other infrastructure. Simultaneously, thanks to environment movements in India and abroad, the Environment Protection Act came into existence in 1986. Later, in 1994, the EIA became mandatory, and in 1997, public hearing was recognized as an essential element in the EIA. This involves public consultation and participation. Though these provisions have several limitations, and the powerful dominant forces have the capacity to sabotage people's rights, nonetheless, they provide a legal right to social activists, compelling the State to negotiate with people. With intensive sustained mobilization of people coupled with political consciousness, social movements can halt anti-people projects. In fact, a few people's struggles such as Mithi Virdi, Umargaon, Poshina and Mahuva in Gujarat; POSCO in Odisha; Singur and Nandigram in West Bengal; etc., have compelled the State and industrial tycoons to withdraw their plans. Such struggles and legal provisions have opened up opportunities for democratizing the decision-making process.

The Indian Constitution directs the State to protect citizens' rights and to take welfare measures for their well-being. In the period before economic liberalization, the State proactively enacted several legislations towards that objective. The Minimum Wage Act is one of those legislations, which was passed in 1948. In the late 1960s and 1970s, a number of legislations such as equal remuneration, the abolition of bonded labour, interstate migrant labour regulation, contract labour regulation, etc., found a place in the statute book. In recent years, with a sustained campaign of RCS in mobilization of public opinion, the court's intervention and advocacy with policymakers, some important pro-poor legislations, such as the National Rural

Employment Guarantee Act (NREGA), 2005, renamed the Mahatma Gandhi National Rural Employment Guarantee Act (MGNREGA) in 2009, the Right to Information (RTI) Act, 2005, the Forest Rights Act, 2006, the RTE Act, 2009; and the National Food Security Act (NFSA) 2013, have been enacted. But in the past and the present, implementation of these legislations has been lackadaisical. At the ground level, the State machinery in collusion with the dominant classes remains indifferent in the implementation of the law. Most of the HCS organizations consider that monitoring the implementation of these laws is beyond their brief. They do not wish to confront the State machinery and dominant classes who flout the law. RCS organizations, though often actively take up the issues related to wages, food security, land, etc., are numerically small and weak in human and financial resources to withstand for long against the local power structure. They could make some impact wherever they have a local network and mobilization of the people.

The poor people are increasingly becoming conscious of their rights and are asserting themselves to attain those rights. Sometimes, they collectively launch a struggle to get justice. But these are fragmented and do not have the wherewithal to sustain their confrontation with the dominant classes. The organizations of the deprived communities dominated by the middle class are more preoccupied with issues of identity than with the wretched condition of their brethren. Nevertheless, grassroots struggles of the oppressed people resisting and confronting the State and the dominant classes for their rights to protect natural resources, land, wages, etc., and also against atrocities and injustice, are frequent and innumerable. Their forms and nature vary. They are isolated and are missing a larger political perspective that relates their issues with the political economy of the land. Hence, their strength to sustain these struggles is limited. Some RCS organizations do play a role in co-ordinating and sustaining these struggles. Their involvement in the people's struggles helps them to identify them with the oppressed and to become more reflective in their understanding of social reality.

RCS activists are relatively well articulated than HCS on public issues. These organizations and activists are actively engaged in raising their voice on the issues related to violation of public morality, injustice to poor, freedom of expression, etc., by the State and the political class, irrespective of party and dominant strata. They write articles in media providing facts and analysis, collectively submit petitions and give memoranda to authorities demanding an inquiry into incidents, organize public discussions, stage demonstrations, etc. In some cases, they file PILs to the court for justice. These activities influence public opinion. Though the presence of RCS organizations is quite visible and the State is often compelled to take cognizance of their demands, their capacity of mass mobilization so far is limited. In terms of space, RCS is on the periphery of the CS. But with unfolding contradictions of the neoliberal economy, the circumference of RCS organizations in civil society is expanding. A few of the socially sensitive activists and groups of HCS are coming closer to RCS.

Different segments of RCS have different ideological positions on the nature of power relations in society, the character of State and political class, political economy in general and neoliberal economy in particular. Their premise on Indian culture and tradition and their strategies for transformation vary. But, more often than not, they work in alliance with each other on most of the issues related to inequality and deprivation, violation of human rights, shrinking democratic space, etc. All of them increasingly realize the limitations of their ideological framework in comprehending changing social realities. But either because of their constant engagement in the field and/or because of their lack of aptitude and/or arrogance about their ideology, many of them are not inclined to engage in a reflective analysis of their own experiences and to unlearn their pet theories. This is a major stumbling block to meet the increasing challenges of rising sectarian forces and the neoliberal political economy which is in crisis. It is a time for different organizations of RCS to critically interrogate their ideological framework, and evaluate their own trajectory of struggles to locate their achievements and failures. Simultaneously, there is a need felt among many activists to interrogate hegemonic cultural values and perspectives, and to evolve a counter-culture around the principles of justice and equality.

BIBLIOGRAPHY

Aerthayil, M. 2000. *Fishworkers Movement in Kerala (1977–1994)*. New Delhi: Indian Social Institute.
AISES. 2006. *Seventh All India School Education Survey*. Delhi: National Council of Educational Research and Training.
AISHE. 2016. *All India Survey of Higher Education*. Delhi: Ministry of Human Resource Development.
———. 2017. *All India Survey on Higher Education (2016–17)*. Delhi: Ministry of Human Resources.
Ambedkar, B. R. 1982. *Dr. Babasaheb Ambedkar Writings and Speeches*, vol. 2. Bombay: Department of Education, Government of Maharashtra.
———. 1993. *Dr. Babasaheb Ambedkar Writings and Speeches*, vol. 12. Bombay: Department of Education, Government of Maharashtra.
Antony, M. J. 1993. *Social Action through Courts: Landmark Judgements in Public Interest Litigation*. New Delhi: Indian Social Institute.
ARCH-Vahini. 1988a. 'The 14th May, 1988 Vadgam Convention Before and After' (Mimeo). Mangrol: ARCH-Vahini.
———. 1988b. 'Displacement in Sardar Sarovar (Narmada) Project: A Gujarat Experience' (Mimeo). Mangrol: ARCH-Vahini.
———. 1988c. 'Sardar Sarovar Oustees—Which Way to Go: Activists' Dilemma' (Mimeo). Mangrol: ARCH-Vahini.
ASER. 2013. *Rural Annual Status of Education Report (Rural)*. Delhi: ASER Centre.
———. 2017. *The Annual Status of Education Report (Rural)*. Delhi: Pratham Education Foundation.
Austin, Granville. 1966. *The Indian Constitution: Cornerstone of a Nation*. Oxford: Clarendon Press.
Baboo, Balgovind. 1991. 'State Policies and People's Response Lessons from Hirakud Dam'. *Economic & Political Weekly*, 12 October.
Baviskar, Amita. 1995. *In the Belly of the River: Tribal Conflicts over Development in the Narmada Valley*. Delhi: Oxford University Press.
———. 1999. 'A Grain of Sand on the Banks of Narmada'. *Economic and Political Weekly*, 34 (32, 7 August), pp. 2213–2214.

Berliner, D. 2011. 'Rational Responses to High Stakes Testing: The Case of Curriculum Narrowing and the Harm that Follows', *Cambridge Journal of Education*, 41 (3), 287–301.

Bhatia, Bela. 1992. *Lush Fields and Parched Throats: The Political Economy of Ground Water in Gujarat*. Annankatu, Finland: UNU World Institute for Development Economic Research.

Baxi, Upendra. 1988. 'Taking Suffering Seriously: Social Action Litigation in Supreme Court of India', in *Law and Poverty: Critical Essays*, edited by Baxi Upendra. Bombay: N.M. Tripathi Pvt Ltd.

Breman, Jan. 1974. 'Mobilisation of Landless Labourers'. *Economic and Political Weekly*, 9 (12, March), 489–496.

———. 1978. 'Seasonal Migration and Co-operative Capitalism, Crushing of Cane and of Labour by Sugar Factories in Bardoli'. *Economic and Political Weekly*, 13 (31–33, August special number), 1317–1360.

Berryman, Phillip. 1987. *Liberation Theology: Essential Facts about the Revolutionary Movement in Latin America—and Beyond*. Philadelphia, PA: Temple University Press.

Bhalani, Ashmita. 1966. *Karma Yogi Bhaikaka*. Vallbah Vidyanagar: Charotar Gramodhar Sahakari Mandli.

Bhargawa, Rajeev, ed. 2008. *Politics and Ethics of the Indian Constitution*. Delhi: Oxford University Press.

Bhatt, Ela. 2006. *We Are Poor But So Many: The Story of Self-Employed Women in India*. Delhi: Oxford University Press.

Bhatty, K. 1998, 11 July. 'Educational Deprivation in India'. *Economic & Political Weekly*, 33 (28), 1731–1740.

Borooah, V., and Nidhi S. Sabharwal. 2017. *English as a Medium of Instruction in Indian Education Inequality of Access to Educational Opportunities*. Delhi: NUEPA.

Bourdieu, P. (1986). 'The Forms of Capital'. In *Handbook of Theory and Research for the Sociology of Capital* (241–258), edited by J. G. Richardson. New York: Greenwood Press.

Bourdieu, Pierre, and Jean-Claude Passersion. 1977. *Reproduction in Education, Society and Culture*. London: SAGE Publications.

Breman, Jan. 1974. 'Mobilisation of Landless Labourers'. *Economic and Political Weekly*, 9 (12), 489–496, March.

———. 1990. 'From Cane Fields to Court Rooms: Legal Action for and Against Rural Labour in Gujarat', in *Capitalist Development: Critical Essays*, edited by Ghanshyam Shah (pp. 270–288). Bombay: Popular Prakashan.

———. 2007. *Labour Bondage in West India: From Past to Present*. Delhi: Oxford University Press.

———. 2016. *On Pauperism in Present and Past*. Delhi: Oxford University Press.

Buci-Glucksmann, Christine. 1980. *Gramsci and the State*. London: Lawrence and Wishart.

Busumtwi-sam, James. 2002. 'Development and Human Security'. *International Journal Canada's Journal of Global Policy Analysis*, 57 (2, 1 June), 253–272.

CAG. 2012. 'Performance Audit on Commercial of Government of Gujarat'. Available at: http://saiindia.gov.in/english/home/Our_Products/Audit_Report/Government_Wise/state_audit/recent_reports/Gujarat/2011/Civil/overview.swf (accessed on 1 September).

———.2014. *Report of the Comptroller and Auditor General*. Gandhinagar: State Legislative Assembly.

Cammack, Paul. 2002. 'Making Poverty Work', in *A World of Contradictions Socialist Register*, edited by P. Leo and L. Colin. Delhi: Leftword Books.

Catanach, I.J. 1970. *Rural Credit in Western India: Rural Credit and the Co-operative Movement in the Bombay Presidency, 1875–1930*.

Chakravarti, Paromita. 2009. *West Bengal: Textbook Regimes*. Delhi: Nirantar.

Chandhoke, Neera. 1995. *State and Civil Society. Explorations in Political Theory*. Delhi: SAGE Publications.

Chandra, Sudhir. 2013. 'Hind Swaraj: A Lost Discourse?', in *Re-reading Hind Swaraj: Modernity and Subalterns*, edited by Ghanshyam Shah. Delhi: Routledge.

Chandru, K., Ghanshyam Shah, and Govardhan Wankhede. 2016. *Report of the People's Tribunal on Caste Discrimination & Police Action in University of Hyderabad*.

Chattopadhyay, Kunal. 2005. 'Class Struggle and Environmental Activism'. Available at: http://www.radicalsocialist.in/articles/environment/57-class-struggle-and-environmental-activism (accessed on 12 September 2017).

Chaudhari, Priti. 2012. *Impact of KGBV on Girls' Education and Retention*. Vadodara: M.S. University.

———. 2009. 'Class Struggle and Environmental Activism'. *Radical Socialist*, 13 October Available at: http://www.radicalsocialist.in/articles/environment/57-class-struggle-and-environ (accessed on 12 September 2017).

Chauhan, N. 2018. 'Schedule Castes and Higher Education in Gujarat' In *Education of the Scheduled Castes: Uphill Task*, edited by Ghanshyam Shah, Kanak Kanti Bagchi and Vishwanatha. Surat: Centre for Social Studies.

Chavada, Vijaysingh. n.d. *Modern Gujarat*. Ahmedabad: New Order.

Citizens for Democracy. 1978. *Education for Our People. A Policy Frame for the Development of Education (1978–87)*. Bombay: Allied Publishers.

Club of Rome's report on *The Limits to Growth* (1972). Available at https://www.clubofrome.org/report/the-limits-to-growth/ (accessed on 10 October 2018).

CWMG. (1969). *Collected Works of Mahatma Gandhi*, 98, vols. IX and XIII. New Delhi: Publication Division Ministry of Information and Broadcasting.

CSWI (Committee on Status of Women in India). 1975. *Towards Equality*. Delhi: Ministry of Education and Social Welfare.

Dabhi, Manjula. 2017. *Surplus Land Distribution Impact on Dalit's Economic Status*. Ahmedabad: Gujarat Vidyapith.

Das, Biswaroop. 2000. *Micro Finance Institutions and Social Intermediation* (A Case of Sewa Bank in India [Mimeo]). Ahmedabad: Taleem Research Foundation.

Bibliography

Das, Biswaroop. 2005. *Micro Finance and Rural Credit Markets*. Ahmedabad: Friends of Women's World Banking.

Dave, Kapil. 2013. 'Gujarat Clears Mithivirdi Nuclear-Power Project'. *Times of India*, 9 July.

Dave, Rajni. 2010. 'Anu Vijali Sasti Nathi, Swachhch Nathi, Salamatto Nathij Nathi–Samelan'. In *Rudhai Rahyo Che Bharatno Atma*, edited by Rajni Dave and Parul Dandekar, 96–100. Vadodara: Yagna Prakashan.

de Wet, Chris. 2003. *Contested Spaces: An Outside Perspective on Debates on Development-Induced Displacement and Resettlement (DIDR) in India* (Mimeograph). South Africa: Rhodes University.

Delige, R. 1997. *World of Untouchable*. Delhi: Oxford University Press.

Desai, A. R. 1997. 'Rural Development and Human Rights of Agrarian Poor in India'. In *Social Transformation in India*, edited by Ghanshyam Shah. Jaipur: Rawat Publications.

Desai, I. P. 1977. *Vedchi Andolan*. Surat: Centre for Social Studies.

———. 1979. 'The Concept of Desired Type of Society and the Problems of Social Change'. *Sociological Bulletin*, 28 (1–2), 1–7, 1 March.

Desai, A. R., and Wilfred D'Costa. 1994. *State and Repressive Culture: A Case Study of Gujarat*. Bombay: Popular Prakashan.

Desai, Kiran. 2002. 'Land Reforms Through People's Movements'. In *Land Reforms in India: Performance and Challenges in Gujarat and Maharashtra*, edited by Ghanshyam Shah and D.C. Shah. Delhi: SAGE Publications.

Desai, Narayan, ed. 1984. *Vedchchi no Vadalo*. Vyara: Gram Seva Samaj.

Desai, Narhari Karuna. 1910. 'Deshnu Majuriaat, karkhana ane khetinu Jivan'. *Buddhi Prakash*, 57 (9, September), 266–273.

Desai, Narhari Karunaram. 1910. 'Labouring Class in Our Country: Their Conditions in Factories and Agriculture'. *Buddhiprakash* (May), 12–14.

Desai, Neera. 1983. *Gujaratma Oganimi Sadima Samajik Parivartan*. Ahmedabad: University Granth Nirman Board.

Desai, Neera, Vina Mazumdar, and Kamalini Bhansari. 1998. *From Women's Education to Women's Studies*. Delhi: Indian Association for Women's Studies.

Desai, V. 1995. *Community Participation and Slum Housing: A Study of Bombay*. New Delhi: SAGE Publications.

Dhagamwar, Vasudha. 1997. 'NGO Movements in the Narmada Valley: Some Reflections)'. In *The Dam and the Nation: Displacement and Resettlement in the Narmada Valley* (pp. 92–101), edited by Jean Dreze, Meera Samson, and Satyajit Singh. Delhi: Oxford University Press.

Dhanagare, D. N. 2005. 'Civil Society, State and Democracy: Contextualizing Discourse'. In *On Civil Society: Issues and Perspective* (pp. 43–66), edited by N. Jayaram. New Delhi: SAGE Publications.

Dhar, Damayantee. 2017. 'The Mithivirdi Movement: The Untold Story of a Struggle Against a Nuclear Power Plant in Gujarat'. *The Wire*. Available at: https://thewire.in/152914/mithivirdi-movement-gujarat/ (accessed on 8 August 2018).

Draper, Hal. 1977. *Karl Marx's Theory of Revolution*. New York, NY: Monthly Review Press.

Dreze, J., and A. Sen. 2003. 'Basic Education is a Political Issue'. In *Education, Society and Development: National and International Perspectives*, edited by J. Tilak, 3–49. New Delhi: APH.

Dreze, Jean, Meera Samson, and Satyajit Singh, eds. 1997. *The Dam and the Nation: Displacement and Resettlement in the Narmada Valley*. Delhi: Oxford University Press.

Dubey, Amaresh. 2009. 'Determinants of Post-Higher Secondary Enrolment in India'. In *Higher Education in India: Issues Related to Expansion, Inclusiveness, Quality and Finance*, edited by UGC, 139–198. Delhi: University Grants Commission.

Dumount, Louis. 1980. *Homo Hierarchicus*. Chicago, IL: Chicago University Press.

Edwards, M. 2004. *Civil Society*. Cambridge: Polity.

Farrington, John, Cathryn Turton, and A.J. James, eds. 1999. *Participatory Watershed Development: Challenges for the Twenty-First Century*. Delhi: Oxford University Press.

Foucault, M. 1987. 'Truth and Power'. In *The Faucault Reader*, edited by P. Rabinow. Harmondsworth: Penguin.

Frankel, Francine R. 2005. *India's Political Economy, 1947–2004: The Gradual Revolution*. Delhi: Oxford University Press.

Freire, Paul. 1970. *Pedagogy of the Oppressed*. New York: Continuum.

———. 1972. 'The Banking Model of Education'. In *Critical Issues in Education: An Anthology of Readings*, edited by Eugene F. Provenzo. Thousand Oaks, CA: SAGE Publications.

Fromm, Eric. 1967. *Marx's Concept of Man*. London: Routledge & Kegan Paul Ltd.

Gandhi, M. K. 1938. *Hind Swaraj or Indian Home Rule*. Ahmedabad: Navjivan Publishing House.

———. 1962. 'Naitalim Education Objectives'. *Village Swaraj*. Ahmedabad: Navjivan Press (Compiled by Vyas).

Ganguly, Varsha Bhagat. 2006. *Legal Intervention, NGOs' Efforts and Poor in Gujarat*, (Mimeo). Delhi: CSDS, IDPAD project [5.1.17].

———. 2015. *Protest Movements and Citizens' Rights in Gujarat (1970–2010)*. Shimla: Indian Institute of Advanced Studies.

Gelani, Dipali, Reshma Vora, and Sejal Joshi. 2017. 'Mithi Virdi Jaspara Andolan: Itihasma Umeru Navu Panu'. *Bhumi Putra*. 1 October.

Ghosh, Archana, Loraine Kennedy, Joel Ruet, Stephanie Lama-Rewal, and Marie-Helene Zerah. 2009. 'A Comparative Overview of Urban Governance in Delhi, Hyderabad, Kolkata, and Mumbai', In *Governing India's Metropolises*, edited by Joel Ruet and Stephanie Lama-Rewal. New Delhi: Routledge.

Ghosh, Suresh Chandra. 2013 (1995). *The History of Education in Modern India 1757–2012*. Hyderabad: Orient BlackSwan.

Ginwala, Persis and Rabri Sagar. 13 May 2014. 'Gujarat's SIR Act Seeks to Corner All of Government Land and 50% of Privately-held Agriculture Land for

Bibliography

'Land Pooling Purpose'. Available at https://counterview.org/2014/05/13/gujarats-sir-act-seeks-to-corner-all-of-government-land-and-50-of-privately-held-agriculture-land-for-land-pooling-purpose/ (accessed on 14 May 2014).

GoG. 2003. *Investment Incentives in the Industrial Policy.* Gandhinagar: Department of Industries and Mines.

GoG. 2009. *Gujarat Government Industrial Policy.* Gandhinagar: GoG.

———. 2011. *Socio-Economic Survey.* Gandhinagar: Bureau of Economics and Statistics.

Gopal, S. 1976. *Jawaharlal Nehru: A Biography Vol. I 1889–1947.* Delhi: Oxford University Press.

Gopal, S., and Uma Iyengar, eds. 2003. *The Essential Writings of Jawaharlal Nehru.* New Delhi: Oxford University Press.

Government of India (GOI). 1985. *Report on the Committee on Rehabilitation for Displaced Tribals Due to Development Project* (Mimeo). Delhi: Ministry of Home Affairs, Government of India.

———. 2009. *The Right of Children to Free and Compulsory Education Act, 2009.* New Delhi: GoI/MHRD. Available at http://mhrd.gov.in/rte (accessed on 13 August 2018).

———. 2014 *Statistics of School Education 2011–12.* Delhi: Ministry of Human Resource Development, GoI.

———. 2015. *All India Report on Agriculture Census 2010–11.* New Delhi: GoI.

———. 2016a. *Report on Fifth Annual Employment–Unemployment Survey (2015–16),*Vol I. Chandigarh: Ministry of Labour & Employment, Labour Bureau.

———, 2016b. *Report on Fifth Annual Employment Survey (2015–2016),* Vol. 1. Delhi: Ministry of Labour and Employment, GoI.

———. 2017. State of Indian Agriculture 2015–16. Delhi: Ministry of Agriculture and Farmers Welfare, GoI.

Gramsci, A. 1978. *Selections from the Prison Notebooks.* New York, NY: International Publishers.

Hardiman David. 1981. *Peasant Nationalists of Gujarat, Kheda District 1917–1934.* Delhi: Oxford University Press.

———. 1987. *The Coming of the Devi: Adivasi Assertation in Western India.* Delhi: Oxford University Press.

———. 1990. 'Penetration of Merchant Capital in Pre-colonial Gujarat'. In *Capitalist Development: Critical Essays. Felicitation Volume in Honour of Prof. A.R. Desai,* edited by Ghanshyam Shah. Bombay: Popular Prakashan.

———. 1981. *Peasant Nationalists of Gujarat: Kheda District 1917–1934.* Delhi: Oxford University Press.

Haynes, Douglas. 1991. *Rhetoric and Ritual in Colonial India: The Shaping of a Public Culture in Surat City, 1852–1928.* Delhi: Oxford University Press.

Hirway, I., and D. Mahadevia. 2004. *Gujarat Human Development.* Ahmedabad: Mahatma Gandhi Labour Institute.

Hirway, Indira, Amita Shah, and Ghanshyam Shah, eds. 2014. *Growth or Development: Which Way is Gujarat Going?* Delhi. Oxford University Press.

Hirway, Indira, and P. P. Patel. 1994. *Water Dynamics in Rural Gujarat*. Ahmedabad: Centre for Development Alternative.

Hulme, David, and Thankom Arun. 2011. 'What's Wrong and Right with Microfinance'. *Economic & Political Weekly*, 46 (48), 26 November.

Indorewala, Hussain. 2017. 'Behind Our Prejudice Against Street Vendors'. *The Wire*, 26 October. Available at https://thewire.in/society/street-vendors-urban-public-spaces (accessed on 7 May 2018).

IRMA. 2000. *White Paper on Water in Gujarat*. Anand: Institute of Rural Management.

Isaka, Riho. 2002 'Gujarati Intellectuals and History Writing in the Colonial Period'. *Economic and Political Weekly*, 37 (48, 30 November).

———. 2004. 'Language and Education in Colonial and Post-colonial India', in *Nature and Human Communities* (pp. 28–42), edited by Saski Takeshi. Tokyo: Springer.

ISID. 2018. *Quality in School Education for Quality Council of India*. Delhi: Institute for Studies in Industrial Development.

Iyenger, Sudarshan. 2005. *Gandhian Economic Thought and Modern Economic Development: Some Reflections*, Working Paper No. 1. Surat: Centre for Social Studies.

———. 2014. 'Education in Gujarat'. In *Growth or Development: Which Way Is Gujarat Going?* edited by Indira Hirway, Amita Shah, and Ghanshyam Shah. Delhi. Oxford University Press.

Jain, Panachanad, V. D. Gyani, N. K. Mody, and Nagmohan Das. 2015. *Sardar Sarovar Claims and Realities of Development and Rehabilitation, Madhya Pradesh India*. Delhi: National Alliance of People's Movement.

Jain, Sampat. 2002. *Public Interest Litigation*. Delhi: Deep and Deep Publications.

Jani, Indukumar. 2002. 'Land Struggle in the Eastern Belt of Gujarat'. In *Land Reforms in India: Performance and Challenges in Gujarat and Maharashtra*, edited by Ghanshyam Shah and D.C. Sah. Delhi: SAGE Publications.

Jeffrelot, Christophe, and Narender Kumar. 2018. *Dr. Ambedkar and Democracy: An Anthology*. Delhi: Oxford University Press.

Jongeward, Carolyn. 2002. 'A Route to Self-reliance: Interview with Ashoke Chatterjee'. Available at: www.india-seminar.com/2003/523/523%20interview%20with%20ashoke%20chatterjee.htm (accessed on 13 August 2018).

Joshi, Umashankar, et al. 1986. 'Gujarat Government and Drought Relief'. *Economic and Political Weekly*, 21 (18, 3 May), pp. 761–762.

Joshi, Vidyut. 1983. *Aapan Gujarat Chhe Dosto* (This Too is Gujarat Friends). Surat: CSS.

———. 1983a. 'Dubata jata Gamona Punh Vasvat na Abhyaso (Studies of submerging villages)'. In CSS *Workshop papers on rehabilitation*. Surat: Centre for Social Studies.

———. 2004. *Sahitya Ane Samaj*. Ahmedabad: Parshva Publications.

Juneja, N. 2003. *Constitutional Amendment to Make Education a Fundamental Right*. New Delhi: National Institute of Educational Planning and Administration.

Kalathil, Mathew. 1978. *Free Legal Aid in a Tribal Area*. Surat: Centre for Social Studies.
Kantavala, Hargonid and Nathashanlkar Sahsty. 1890. *Prachinkavyamala*. Vadodara: Author.
Karim, Lamia. 2011. *Microfinance and Its Discontents: Women in Debt in Bangladesh*. Minneapolis, MN: University of Minnesota Press.
Karnik, V. B. n.d. *A New Path: Manifesto and Constitution of the Radical Democratic Party*. Bombay: Radical Humanist.
Kingdon, Geeta Gandhi. 2016. *The Emptying of Public Schools and Growth of Private Schools in India*. London: Department for International Development (DFID).
Kochanek, Stanley. 1974. *Business and Politics in India*. Berkeley, CA: University of California Press.
Kothari D. S. 1966. *Education and National Development: Report of the Education Commission, 1964–66*. Delhi: Ministry of Education.
Kothari, Daulat Singh. 1966. *Report of the Education Commission, 1964–66*. Delhi: NCERT.
Kothari, Rajni. 1969. 'Political Consensus in India: Decline and Reconstruction'. *EPW*, 11 October.
———. 1970. *Caste in Indian Politics*. Hyderabad: Orient Longman.
———. 1970. *Politics in India*. Hyderabad: Orient Longman.
———. 1972. 'Political Economy of Garibi Hatao'. *EPW* Special Number, 7 (31–32–33), 5 August.
———. 1975. *Footsteps in Future, Diagnosis of the Present World and Design for an Alternative*. New York, NY. The Free Press.
———. 1984. 'Non-party Political Process'. *Economic and Political Weekly*, 19 (5, 4 February), 216–224.
———. 1988. *State Against Democracy: In Search of Humane World Order*. Delhi: Ajanata.
Kothari, Rita. 2004. 'Avoiding Poverty: The Case Against Gujarati Literature', Paper presented in the seminar on 'Condition of Poverty in Gujarat: Looking Back and Looking Forward', organised by CSDS, Delhi, at Ahmedabad on 26–27 November.
Kulke, Eckehard. 1978. *The Parsees in India: A Minority as Agent of Social Change* (p. 69). Delhi: Vikas Publication House.
Kumar, Rajesh. 2010. 'Indian Constitution: Sixty Years of Our Faith'. *Indian Express*, New Delhi, 2 February.
Krishnakant. 2017. 'And We Pushed Out Westinghouse Nuclear Plant from Mithi Virdi Area'. *PUCL Bulletin*, XXXVII (6, June).
Krushakant, Lakhan, Gadekar and Virmagami. 2010. 'Mithiviradima Motna Vavetar na Khape-anuurja Same Andolan'. In *Rudhai Rahyo Che Bharatno Atma*, edited by Rajni Dave and Parul Dandekar, 88–90. Vadodara: Yagna Prakashan.
Kulke, Eckehard. 1978. *The Parsees in India: A Minority as Agent of Social Change*. Delhi: Vikas Publication House, 69.

Kumar, B. L. 2004. 'Schools and Schooling in Tribal Gujarat: The Quality Dimension'. Working Paper No. 150. Ahmedabad: Gujarat Institute of Development Research.

Ladson-Billings, G. 2006. 'It's Not the Culture of Poverty, It's the Poverty of Culture: The Problem with Teacher Education'. *Anthropology and Education Quarterly*, 37 (2), 104–109.

Lakha, Salim. 1988. *Capitalism and Class in Colonial India: The Case of Ahmedabad*. Delhi: Sterling Publishers.

Lemos, Ramon. 1977. *Rousseau's Political Philosophy: An Exposition and Interpretation*. Athens, GA: The University of Georgia Press.

Lobo, Lancy and Kumar Shashikant. 2009. *Land Acquisition, Displacement and Resettlement in Gujarat 1947–2004*. Delhi: SAGE Publications.

Locke, John. 1966. *Two Treaties of Civil Government*. Montreal: Delta.

Macpherson, C. B. 1973. *Democratic Theory: Essays in Retrieval*. Oxford: Clarendon Press.

Macwan, Martin. 2004. 'Gijubhai Badheka: Mucchari ma ke Muccharo Brahman?' *Dalit Shakti*, November.

Mahajan, Vijay. 2005. *From Microcredit to Livelihood Finance* (Mimeo). Hyderabad: BASIX.

Mahajan, Gurpreet. 1999. 'Civil Society and Its Avatars: What Happened to Freedom and Democracy?' *Economic & Political Weekly*, 15 May, 1188–1196.

Maharaj Ravishankar. 1984. Gita Pravchano. Ahmedabad: Sarvoday Mandal.

Maheriya, Chandu. 2011. 'Umashankar Joshi Ane Samajik Naya: 'Mathanmanoni n Mana Hajo Mane'. In *Umashankar Joshini Vichar Yatra*, edited by Chandu Maheriya, Manishi Jani, and Swati Joshi, 192–204. Ahmedabad: Gurjar Granthartan.

Manjrekar, Nandini, T. Shah, J. Lokhande and N. Choudhury. 2010. *Gujarat. Text Books Regimes: A Feminist Critic of Nation and Identity*. Delhi: Nirantar.

Marriott, McKim. 1955. *Village India*. Chicago, IL: University of Chicago.

Mathew Kalathil, S. J. 1978. Free legal Aid in a Tribal Area. Surat: Centre for Social Studies.

Macwan, Martin. 2004. 'Gijubhai Badheka: Mucchari ma ke Muccharo Brahman?' *Dalit Shakti*, November.

Mehta Babalbhai. 1955. *Ravishankar Maharaj* (pp. 19–20). Ahmedabad: Kamal Prakashan.

Mehta. Makrand. 1986. *Sampradayaki Sahitya ane Sumajik Chema Swaminarayan Sam-pradayano Abhyas 1800–1840* (*Arthat*, Vol. 5, No. 4, October–December, pp. 12–20).

———. 2005. 'Gandhi and Ahmedabad'. *Economic and Political Weekly*, 40 (4, 22 January), 291–299.

Matthai, Ravi. 1985. *The Rural University, The Jawaja Experiment in Educational Innovation*, 24. Bombay: Popular Prakashan.

Meadows, D. H., D. L. Meadows, J. Randers, and W. W. Behrens. 1972. *The Limits to Growth: A Report to the Club of Rome*. Potomac Associates—Universe Books.

Mehta, Bharat. 2011. 'Pragatishil Sahitya Andolan and Umashankar Joshi'. In *Umashankar Joshini Vichar Yatra*, edited by Chandu Maheriya, Manishi Jani, and Swati Joshi, 98–110. Ahmedabad: Gurjar Granthartan.
Mencher, Joan. 1975. 'The Caste System Upside Down or Not-so-Mysterious East'. *Current Anthropology*, 15 (1), 469–493.
MHRD. 2011. *Statistics of School Education 2009–2010*. Delhi: MHRD, Bureau of Planning, Monitoring and Statistics.
Mistry, Madhusudan. 1991. 'Narmada bandh ane Adivaiso'. *Naya Marg*, 14 (3), 29–31, 1 February.
Mitlin, D. 2001. 'Civil Society and Urban Poverty: Examining Complexity'. *Environment and Urbanisation*, 13 (2), 151–173.
Mody, Chunibhai. 1881. *Niti ni shikhamano*. Ahmedabad: Gujarat Vernacular Society.
Moffatt, Michael. 1979. *An Untouchable Community in South India*. Princeton, NJ: Princeton University Press.
Mudaliar, A. Lakshmanaswami. 1957. *Report of the Secondary Education Commission*. Delhi: GoI.
Mudaliar Commission. 1953. Report of the Secondary Education Commission, October 1952 to June 1953. Delhi: Ministry of Education, Government of India.
Mudrakartha, Srinivas. 2012. *Ground Water Recharge Management in Saurashtra: Lessons for Water Governance*. PhD thesis. Suresh Gyan Vihar University, Jaipur.
———. 2004. 'Ensuring Water Security through Rainwater Harvesting: A Case Study of Sargasan, Gujarat, India'. *Water Nepal*, 11 (1), August 2003–January 2003.
NABARD. 2014. *Status of Microfinance in India 2012–2013*. Delhi: NABARD.
Naik, J. P. 1974. *Policy and Performance in Indian Education (1947–74)* (First Saiyidain Memorial Lecture, 1974). New Delhi: Dr. K. G. Saiyidain Memorial Trust.
———. 1975. *Policy and Performance in Indian Education 1947–74*. New Delhi: Orient Longman.
———. 1982. *The Education Commission and After*. New Delhi: Allied Publishers.
Nambissan, Geetha B. 2012. *Low-Cost Private Schools for the Poor in India: Some Reflections*. Available at http://www.idfc.com/pdf/report/2012/Chapter_8.pdf (accessed on 16 March 2018).
National Centre for Advocacy Studies. 2002, July–September. 'Campaign for the Right to Education'. Advocacy Update No. 17. Available at http://www.doccentre.net/ eldoc/n00_/campaign_right_education.pdf (accessed on 14 July 2018).
Navsarjan Trust. n.d. *The Story of Land Reforms in Gujarat*. Ahmedabad: Navsarjan Trust.

———. 2010. *Understanding Untouchability: A Comprehensive Study of Practices and Conditions in 1589 Villages*. Ahmedabad: Navsarjan Trust.
Nayak, Arun Kumar. 2010. 'Big Dams and Protests in India: A Study of Hirakud Dam'. *Economic & Political Weekly*, 45 (2), 9 January.
NCAER (National Council of Applied Economic Research). 1994. 'Non Enrolment, Drop Learning Materials'. In *India Education Report*, edited by R. Govinda, 153–166. New Delhi: Oxford University Press.
NCF. 2000. *National Curriculum Framework*. Delhi: NCERT.
Nilkanth, Mahipatram Rupram. 1905. *Gujarati Kavyadohan* (expurgated and revised). Mumbai: Government Central Book Depot.
———. 1879. *Mehtaji Durgaram Manchram Charitra*. Ahmedabad: Author.
Nilsen, Alf Gunvald. 2010. *Dispossession and resistance in India: The River and rage*. New York: Routledge.
NUEPA. 2014. *Education for All Towards Quality with Equity INDI*. Delhi: National University of Educational Planning and Administration.
NSSO. 2014. *Social Consumption Education Survey 2014, 71st Round*. Delhi: Ministry of Statistcs and Programme Implementation (MOSPI), Government of India
Nururllah, Syed and J.P. Naik. 1943. *History of Education in India: During the British Period*. Available at https://www.slideshare.net/2sadanand/history-of-education-in-india (accessed on 10 October 2018).
Oliver-Smith, Anthony. 2010. *Defying Displacement: Grass Root Resistance and Critic of Development*. Austin: University of Texas Press.
Oza, Dankesh, ed. 1983. *Narmad no Jamano: Ek Vivad-Ek Sankalan*. Gandhinagar: Samvad Prakashan.
Paliwal, Ankur. 2013. *Mithivirdi: Nuclear Shadow Over Gujarat Village*. Available at: https://www.downtoearth.org.in/blog/nuclear-shadow-over-gujarat-village–40631
Palshikar, Suhas. 2008. 'Indian Sate: Constitution and Beyond'. In *Politics and Ethics of the Indian Constitution*, edited by Rajeev Bhargawa. Delhi: Oxford University Press.
Pandya, Rohit. 2000. *Gujarat Na Gramin Samaj Nu Parivartan and Gandhiwadi Netrutva*. Ahmedabad: Parshva Publications.
Pandya, Umiyashankar Harishankar. 1884. *Apana Kartya karma*. Ahmedabad.
Chakravarti, Paromita. 2009. *West Bengal: Textbook Regimes*. Delhi: Nirantar.
Parulekar, Godavari. 1975. *Adivasis revolt: The story of Warli peasants in struggle*. Calcutta: National Book Agency Pvt Ltd.
Patel, Anil. 1995. 'What Do the Narmada Valley Tribals Want?' In *Toward Sustainable Development? Struggling over India's Narmada River*, edited by William F. Fisher. Armonk, NY: M.E. Sharpe.
———. 1997. 'Resettlement Politics and Tribal Interests'. In *The Dam and the Nation: Displacement and Resettlement in the Narmada Valley*, edited by Jean Drèze, Meera Samson, and Satyajit Singh. New Delhi, India; New York: Oxford University Press.
———. 1988. 'The Resettlement Problem'. *The Indian Express*, 1 October.

———. 2001. 'Resettlement in the Sardar Sarovar Project: A Cause Vitiated'. *Water Resources Development*, 17 (3), 315–328.
Patel, Girish. 2009. *Public Interest Litigation and the Poor in Gujarat: Experiences of the Lok Adhikar Sangh*. Ahmedabad: Girishbhai Sanman Samiti.
Patel, J. C. 2018. 'Under the Shadow of Prosperity: Scheduled Tribe Students in Gujarat', in *Education of the Scheduled Tribes: Uphill Task*, edited by Ghanshyam Shah and Joseph Bara. Surat: Centre for Social Studies.
Patel, Krushnaprasad Z. 2010. *Jay Ho Maiya Narmada: Narmada Ladatni Gauravgatha*. Ahmedabad: Gurjar Granthratna Karyalaya.
Patel, Mangubhai. 1988. *Ravbahdur Bechardas Ambaidas Laskari*. Ahmedabad: Gujarat University.
Patel, Sujata. 1987. *The Making of Industrial Relations: The Ahmedabad Textile Industry 1918–1939*. Delhi: Oxford University Press.
Pathak, Maulik. 2015. 'L&T Scraps Gujarat Port Project Citing Environmental Reasons'. *Livemint*, 21 August. Available at https://www.livemint.com/Companies/hdh72vL6fLo1mlPkQcsCSP/LT-scraps-Gujarat-port-project-citing-environmental-reasons.html (accessed on 8 August 2018).
Pathak, D., H. Spodek, and J. Wood. 2011. *The Autobiography Indulal Yagnk*, vol. 2. Delhi: Manohar.
Patkar, Medha. 1998. 'The People's Policy on Development'. *Economic & Political Weekly*, 33 (38), 19 September.
Pinto, Stany. 2002. 'Land Alienation and Adivasi Assertion in Bharuch District', in *Development and Deprivation in Gujarat*, edited by G. Shah, M. Rutten and Streefkerk. Delhi: SAGE Publications.
PND (Policy and Development Initiatives). 2002. 'Assessment of Watershed Development Programme in Gujarat'. Ahmedabad Gujarat Institute of Development Research. (Mimeograph).
Potter, D. 1986. *India's Political Administrators, 1919–1983* (pp. 250–251). Delhi: Oxford University Press.
Prabhu, Pradip. 2002. 'Land Alienation, Land Reform and Tribals in Maharashtra'. In *Land Reforms in India: Performance and Challenges in Gujarat and Maharashtra*, edited by Ghanshyam Shah and D.C. Sah. Delhi: SAGE Publications.
Prajapati, Rohit, Krishnakant and Trupti Shah. 2014. 'Villagers' Struggle Intensifies in Gujarat Against the American Nuclear Project'. Available at http://www.dianuke.org/villagers-struggle-intensifies-in-gujarat-against-the-american-nuclear-project/ (accessed on 20 April 2018).
Prajapti, Rohit. 2017. 'Implementation of Supreme Court Order Dated 22 February 2017 Will Be Tested in Coming Days', *PUCL Bulletin*, XXXVII (6, June).
Prajabndhu, 23 June 1935.
Pratham. 2015. *Annual Status of Education Report (Rural) Beyond Basics*. Available at: http://www.asercentre.org (accessed on 1 November 2018).
———. 2017. *Annual Status of Education Report (Rural) 2016 Beyond Basics*. Available at: www.asercentre.org (accessed on 2 August 2018).

Pratham. 2018. *Annual Status of Education Report (Rural) 2017 Beyond Basics.* Available at: www.asercentre.org (accessed on 8 August 2018).
Prayas. 2018. *'A Bitter Harvest: Seasonal Migrant Sugarcane Harvesting Workers of South Gujarat'.* Ahmedabad: Prayas Centre for Labour Research and Action (PCLRA) and Surat Centre for Social Studies. Available at *https://counterview. org/2018/04/25/why-migrant-labourers-are-employed-as-sugarcane-harvesters-by-south-gujarat-coop-sugar-factories/* (accessed on 25 April 2018).
Priyolkar, A. K. 1945. 'Swagrastha, Durgaram Mehtaji and Manavdhram Sbano Uday and Vikas', *Forbas Gujarati Sabha*, 10 (1–2). Reprinted in *Sitanshu Yaschandra, Aaporakhani Mathaman, Forbas Gujarati Sabha*, 71 (2–3).
Purohit, Makarand. 2016. 'Damn the Dams, Says the Displaced'. Available at http://www.indiawaterportal.org/articles/damn-dams-say-displaced (accessed on 7 July 2018).
Rabari, Sagar. 2014. *Gujaratma Kheti ane Khedut: Taki Rahevani Mathaman.* Vadodara: Yagna Prakashan.
Radhakrishnan, S. 1950. *The Report of the University Education Commission (December 1948–August 1949)*, Vol. I. Delhi: Government of India.
Rai, Shivkrit, and Deepanshu Mohan. 2017. 'Gaps in Implementation of Street Vendors Act Are Making Delhi's Merchants Invisible'. *The Wire*, 1 November. Available at https://thewire.in/economy/street-vendors-act-implementation-gaps (accessed on 7 May 2018).
Rajalakshmi, T. K. 2001. 'A Regressive Bill'. *The Frontline*, 18 (26), 8–21 December.
Rajora, R. 2002. *Integrated Watershed Management: Field Manual for Equitable, Productive and Sustainable Development.* Jaipur: Rawat Publication.
Ramaswamy, Uma. 2017. *Creating Spaces Nurturing Leadership.* Ahmedabad: Janvikas.
Rao, Srinivasa S. 2013. 'Structural Exclusion in Everyday Institutional Life'. In *Sociology of Education in India*, edited by Geetha Nambissan and Srinivasa S. Rao. Delhi: Oxford University Press.
Rao, Sudhakar N. 2001. 'The Structure of South Indian Untouchable Caste: A View'. In *Dalit Identity and Politics*, edited by Ghanshyam Shah, 74–96. Delhi: SAGE Publications.
Rathore, M. S. et al. 2003, October. 'Groundwater Recharging in Saurashtra: A Community Effort towards Groundwater Management'. Ahmedabad: VIKSAT, Nehru Foundation for Development.
Raval, R. L. 1987. *Socio-Religious Reform Movements in Gujarat during the Nineteenth Century.* New Delhi: Ess Publications.
Ravitch, D. 2010. *The Death and Life of the Great American School System: How Testing and Choice are Undermining Education.* New York: Basic Books.
Rich, Bruce. 1994. *Mortgaging the Earth: The World Bank, Environmental Impoverishment, and the Crisis of Development.* Boston, MA: Beacon Press.
Rose, Kalima. 1992. *Where Women Are Leaders: The SEWA Movement in India.* Delhi: Vistaar Publications.

Rose, P., and C. Dyer. 2008. 'Chronic Poverty and Education: A Review of Literature'. Working Paper No. 131. Manchester: Chronic Poverty Research Centre.

Rudolph Lloyd and Rudolph Susanne. 1960. 'The Political Role of India's Caste Association'. *Pacific Affairs*, XXXIII (1), March.

Rudolph Susanne Hoeber. 2000. 'Civil Society and the Realm of Freedom' *Economic and Political Weekly*, 35 (20), 13 May: 1762–69.

Rupera, Ketan, ed. 2015. *Agnipushpa: Chunibhai Vaidya Smurti Granth*. Ahmedabad: Lok Samiti.

Sadgopal, A. 2002. 'A Convenient Consensus'. *The Frontline*, 18 (26), 22 December 2001–04 January 2002.

Sah, D.C. 2002. 'Crop Commercialisation and Migration: Evidences from Sardar Project'. In *Land Reforms in India: Performance and Challenges in Gujarat and Maharashtra*, edited by G. Shah and D. Shah Delhi: SAGE Publications.

Sangvai, Sanjay, Nandini Oza, Mahesh Patel, Udit Shah, and Himanshu Thakkar. 1990. 'Attacks on Anti-Narmada Activists'. *Economic and Political Weekly*, 25 (20, 19 May), 1060–1061.

Saravanan, M. 2016. 'The Impact of Self-Help Groups on the Socio-economic Development of Rural Household Women in Tamil Nadu—A Study'. *International Journal of Research–Granthaalayah*, 4 (7: SE 2016), 22–31.

Savur, Manorama. 1990. 'Relations Between in Indian Capitalist Class and the State in IRDP (A Case of Mafatlals in Rural Areas)'. In *Capitalist Development: Critical Essays*, edited by Ghanshyam Shah. Bombay: Popular Prakashan.

Scott, J. 1998. *Seeing Like the State*. New Haven, CT: Yale University.

Scudder, T. 2003. 'India's Sardar Sarovar Project (SSP)'. Available at http://www.its.caltech.edu/~tzs/Sardar%20Sarovar%20Project%20Case.pdf (accessed on 7 August 2018).

Seal, Anil. 1971. *The Emergence of Indian Nationalism*. Cambridge: Cambridge University Press.

Seethalakshmi, S., and M. Seshagiri. 2006. 'Private Schools Have the Last Laugh'. *The Times of India*, 8 August. Available at http://timesofindia.indiatimes.com/articleshow/1874504.cms (accessed on 14 August 2018).

Sekhar, Vundru Raja. 2013. 'Political Representation: Ambedkar and the Electoral Method'. NMML Occasional Paper (History and Society New Series 12). Delhi: Nehru Memorial Museum and Library.

Sen, A. 2001. *Development as Freedom*. Oxford: Oxford University Press.

Sen, A. C. 1985, January–February. 'A Case Study of Voluntary Action in India'. *Voluntary Action*. Nos. 7–8.

Sen, Jai. 1995. *Chronology of Events Related to Local, National and International Movements Around the Narmada Dam Projects in India* (Mimeo). Surat: Centre for Social Studies.

Shah, Amita. 2001. 'Who Benefits from Participatory Watershed Development? Lessons from Gujarat, India'. Gatekeeper Series No. 97. London, International Institute of Environment and Development Policy and Development Initiatives.

Shah, Amita, and Bilab Dhak. 2014. 'Labour Migration and Welfare in Gujarat: Recent Evidences and Issues'. In *Growth or Development: Which Way is Gujarat Going?* edited by Indira Hirway, Amita Shah, and Ghanshyam Shah, 301–349. Delhi. Oxford University Press.

Shah, Bhagirath. 1982. 'Legal Aspect of Rehabilitation', In *CSS Political Economy of Rehabilitation seminar papers*. Surat: Centre for Social Studies.

Shah, Ghanshyam. 1974. 'Traditional Society and Political Mobilization: The Experience of Bardoli Satyagraha'. *Contribution to Indian Sociology* (NS) (8), 89–108.

———. 1975a. *Caste Association and Political Process in Gujarat*. Bombay: Popular Prakashan.

———. 1975b. *Politics of Scheduled Castes and Tribes*. Bombay: Vora & Co. Publishers.

———. 1977. *Protest Movements in Two Indian States*. Delhi: Ajanta Publications.

———. 1988a. 'Kheduts in Gujarat'. *Seminar 352 (352)*, pp. 25–27. December.

———. 1988b. *Mid-day Meals Scheme in Gujarat: An Evaluation* (Mimeo). Surat: Centre for Social Studies.

Shah, Ghanshyam. 1988c. 'Grass Roots Mobilisation in Indian Politics', in *India's Democracy: An Analysis of Changing State-Society Relations* (pp. 262–304), edited by Atul Kohali. Princeton, NJ: Princeton University Press.

———. 2002a. 'Caste and Land Reforms in Gujarat'. In *Land Reforms in India: Performance and Challenges in Gujarat and Maharashtra*, edited by Ghanshyam Shah and D.C. Sah. Delhi: SAGE Publications.

———. 2002b. 'Education and Backward Castes in Gujarat'. In *Education and the Disprivileged*, edited by Sabyasachi Bhattacharya. Delhi: Orient Longman.

———. 2004. *Social Movements: A Review of Literature*. Delhi: SAGE Publications.

———. 2005. 'Gijubahi Badheka Nu Bal Sahitya', *Niriskshak*, 1 February.

———. 2007. 'Rachantamak Ka Mane Sangarsh: Indulalni Darshtie'. In *Indulal Yagnik*, edited by Oza Dingant. Ahmedabad: R. R. Sheth.

———. 2008. *Civil Society and the Poor* (Mimeograph). Delhi: Indian Council of Social Science Research.

———. 2011. 'Goebbel's Propaganda and Governance: The 2009 Lok Sabha Elections in Gujarat'. In *India's 2009 Elections*, edited by Wallace Paul and Roy Ramashray. New Delhi: SAGE Publications.

———. 2013. *Re-reading Hind Swaraj: Modernity and Subalterns*. Delhi: Routledge.

———. 2014. 'Governance of Gujarat: Good Governance for Whom and for What?' In *Growth or Development: Which Way is Gujarat Going?* edited by Indira Hirway, Amita Shah, and Ghanshyam Shah, 517–556. Delhi. Oxford University Press.

Shah, Ghanshyam. 2017. 'Neo-liberal Political Economy and Social Tensions Simmering Dalit Unrest and Competing Castes in Gujarat'. *Economic and Political Weekly*, Lii (62, 2 September), 62–70.

———. 2018. 'Social Democrat Nehru: Vision, Praxis and Dilemma'. In *The Legacy of Nehru: Appraisal and Analysis*, edited by Lobo Lency and Shah Jayesh. Delhi: Manohar.

Shah, Ghanshyam, and Biswaroop Das. 1985. *Voluntarily Organisations and Development*. Surat: Centre for Social Studies.
———. 1988. *Voluntary Organizations in Gujarat, An Exploratory Survey*. Surat: Centre for Social Studies.
Shah, Ghanshyam, Harsh Mander, Sukhadeo Thorat, S. Deshhpande, and Amita Bavishkar. 2006. *Untouchability in Rural India*. Delhi: SAGE Publications.
Shah, Ghanshyam, and H.R. Chaturvedi. 1983. *Gandhian Approach to Rural Development*. Delhi: Ajanta Publications.
Shah, Ghanshyam, Sujatha Kalimili, and Sukhadeo Thorat. 2018. *Still Long Way to Go: Educational Status of Scheduled Castes: Attainment and Challenges*. Surat: Centre for Social Studies.
Shah, Kalpana. 1984. *Women's Liberation & Voluntary Action*. Delhi: Ajanta Publication.
Shah, Kantilal. 1955. *Thakkarbapa*. Delhi: Thakkarbapa Smarak Samiti.
Shah, Neha. 2003. *Institutional Credit, Employment Generation and Poverty Alleviation: A Comparative Analysis*. PhD Thesis. Sardar Patel Institute of Economics and Social Research, Ahmedabad.
Shah, Rajeev. 2014. NSSO Report Suggests that Indebted Rural Households in Gujarat are More Dependent on Informal Moneylenders than Other States, 17 December. Available at https://counterview.org/2014/12/27/nsso-report-suggests-that-indebted-rural-households-in-gujarat-are-more-dependent-on-informal-moneylenders-than-other-states/ (accessed on 18 December 2014).
Shah, Tushaar. 1998. 'The Deepening Divide: Diverse Responses to the Challenge of Groundwater Depletion in Gujarat. IDE-Ford Foundation Supported Irrigation Against Rural Poverty Research Programme'. IWMI-Tata Policy School Working Paper.
Shani, Ornit. 2018. *How India Became Democratic Citizenship and the Making of the Universal Franchise*. Cambridge: Cambridge University Press.
Shankardass, Rani Dhavan. 1988. *Vallabhbhai Patel: Power and Organisation in Indian Politics*. Hyderabad: Orient Longman.
Sheth, D. L. 2013. 'Civil Society, Movements, and the Democratic Theory'. In *Democracy on the Move?* edited by Mahindra Nath Thakur and Dhananjay Rai, 190–203. Delhi: Aakar Books.
Sheth, Pravin. 1977. *Navnirman and Political Change in India*. Bombay: Vora & Co.
Shivali, Tukdeo. 2015. 'Class Divided: Global Pressures, Domestic Pulls and a Fractured Education Policy in India'. *Policy Futures in Education*, 13 (2), 205–218.
Simpson, Edward. 2015. *The Political Biography of an Earthquake: Aftermath and Amnesia in Gujarat, India*. Delhi: Oxford University Press.
Singer, Milton. 1959. *Traditional India: Structure and Change*. Philadelphia, PA: American Folklore Society, 1959.
Sinha, Assema. 2005. *Regional Roots of Developmental Politics in India: A Divided Leviathan*. Delhi: Oxford University Press.
Singh, Yogendra. 1973. *Modernization of Indian Tradition*. Faridabad: Thomson Press.

Smita. 2006. *Locked Homes Empty Schools: The Impact of Distressed Seasonal Migration on the Rural Poor*. New Delhi: Zubaan.
Sodhan, Amrita. 2001. *A Question of Community: Religious Groups and Colonial Law*. Calcutta: Somya.
Singh, S. 2006. 'Right to Education Only on Paper'. *The Statesman*, 22 October.
Singh Yogendra. 1973. *Modernization of Indian Tradition*. Faridabad: Thomson Press.
Sitanshu, Yshachandra. 2006. 'ur antar lidho jan: AAp orakhani mathaman', *Farbas Gujarati Sabah*, 71 (2), 6–19.
SMC. 2000. *Varshik Vahivati Aheval (Annual Report) 1999–2000*. Surat: Surat Municipal Corporation.
Sodhan Amrita. 2001. *A Question of Community: Religious Groups and Colonial Law*. Calcutta: Somya.
Soni, Raman. 2005. '"Sachu Kam" Etale Balvu Ke Samjvu?' *Nirikshak*, 1 February.
Spodek, Howard. 2011. *Ahmedabad: Shock City of Twentieth Century India*. Bloomington, IN: Indiana University Press.
Spretnak, C. and F. Capr. 1985. *Green Politics: The Global Promise*. London: Paladin.
Srivastava, Alka. 2004. *Self-help Groups and Civil Society: A Preliminary Study*. Delhi: Indian Social Institute.
Srivatsan, R. 2006, 4 February. 'Concept of "Seva" and the "Sevak" in the Freedom Movement'. *Economic & Political Weekly*, 41 (5), 427–438.
SSE. 2014. *Statistics of School Education 2011–12*. Delhi: Ministry of Human Resource Development.
Suhrud, Tridip. 2009. *Writing Life: Three Gujarati Thinkers*. Hyderabad: Orient BlackSwan.
Sulek, Marty. 2010. 'Civil Society Theory: Aristotle'. In *International Encyclopedia of Civil Society*, edited by Helmut K. Anheier and Stefan Toepler. Available at https://www.researchgate.net/publication/271212659_Civil_Society_Theory_Aristotle (accessed on 31 July 2018).
Supreme Court. 2000. Available at: http://www.narmada.org/sardar-sarovar/sc.ruling/nba.comments.html (accessed on 5 February 2012).
Swaan, Abram. 1988. *In Care of the State*. Cambridge: Polity Press.
Swati. 2010a. 'Bhavnagarma Anuurja Jagruti Ane Hiroshima Divas Milam'. In *Rudhai Rahyo Che Bharatno Atma*, edited by Rajni Dave and Parul Dandekar, 92–94. Vadodara: Yagna Prakashan.
———. 2010b. 'Sabda Rahejo'. In *Rudhai Rahyo Che Bharatno Atma*, edited by Rajni Dave and Parul Dandekar, 111–112. Vadodara: Yagna Prakashan.
Teltumbde, Anand. 2011. 'From the Underbelly of Swarnim Gujarat'. *Economic & Political Weekly*, 46 (14), 2 April.
———. 2013. 'Keep off Education'. *Economic & Political Weekly*, 48 (23), 10–11.
Thakar, Javer Ranji. 1899. 'Chhpaniya Dukar vishe kavita'. *Buddhi Prakash*, 46 (4), 11–15.

Thakar, Gauttam, ed. 2014. *Char Dayka Ni Safar: Gujaratma Manav Adhikar Ane Nagaril Swatntra Chalval*. Ahmedabad: PUCL.
Thakkar, Amritlal. 1926. 'Pahadio ma Dharmantar'. *Navijivan*, 7 (31), April 4, 242–243.
Thakore, D. 2011. 'Affordable Schools Gold Rush'. Available at http://www.educationworldonline.net/index.php/page-article-choice-more-id-2776 (accessed on 12 February 2012).
Thakor, Vaikunthlal and Sumant Mehta. 1918. *Ambalal Charitrani Samagri*. Ahmedabad: Authors.
The Economic Times. 2006. 'Private Schools in India Wriggle Out of 25% Seats for the Poor'. *The Economic Times*, 8 August.
Thorat, S., K. Shyamprasad, and R. Srivastava. 2010. *Report of the Committee to Enquire into the Allegations of Differential Treatment of SC/ST Students in all Indian Institute of Medical Science*. Delhi: All India Institute of Medical Science.
ToI. 2014. 'India witnessing NGO boom', 23 February.
———. 2016. 'Gujarat Government releases check dam figures'. *The Times of India*, June 16. Available at: http://timesofindia.indiatimes.com/articleshow/52772475.cms?utm_source=contentofinterest&utm_medium=text&utm_campaign=cppst
Tooley, J. 2009. *The Beautiful Tree: A Personal Journey into How the World's Poorest People Are Educating Themselves*. New Delhi: Penguin/Viking.
Tripathi, Govardhanram. 1894 (1958). *Classical Poets of Gujarat and their Influence of Society and Morals*. Bombay: Forbes Gujarati Sabha.
Trivedi, Navalram Jaganath. 1934. *Samaj Sudharanu Rekhadarshan*. Ahmedabad: Gujarati Sahitya Parishad.
UNDP. 2006. *Governance for Sustainable Human Development: A UNDP Policy Document Good Governance and Sustainable Human Development*. Available at http://mirror.undp.org/magnet/policy/chapter1.htm (accessed on September 10, 2014).
UNHCR. 2000. *Assessment Report*. Aviable at https://www.iom.int/jahia/webdav/shared/shared/mainsite/microsites/rcps/cis-conference/IOM_UNHCR_Assessment_of_CIS_2000.pdf (accessed on 21 July 2011).
Van Eedrd, Maartje. 2008. *Local Initiatives in Relocations: The State and NGOs as the Partners?* New Delhi: Manohar.
Vasava, Anand. 2017. 'Pthyapustakma Adivaso'. *Naya Marg*, 40 (18), 19 June.
Vijaliwala, Sharifa. 2005. 'Aapane Ketalu Balishu? Todishu?' *Nirikashak*, 1 February.
VOICE. 2008. *A Report on the Success and Failure of SHG's in India: Impediments and Paradigm of Success*. Delhi: Voluntary Operation in Community and Environment.
Vora, Rajendra. 2002. 'Land Grabbing and the Struggles of the Displaced in Maharashtra'. In *Land Reforms in India: Performance and Challenges in Gujarat and Maharashtra*, edited by G. Shah and D. Shah. Delhi: SAGE Publications.
Vyas, V. S., Ranjit Gupta, T. K. Moulik, and B.M. Desai. 1976. *Rural Development for Rural Poor*. Ahmedabad: Centre for Management in Agriculture, IIM.

Yagati, Chhina Rao. 2002. 'Education and Identity Formation Among the Dalits in Colonial Andhra', in *Education and the Disprivileged*, edited by Sabyasachi Bhattacharya. Hyderabad: Orient Longman.

Yagnik, Achyut, and Kirit Bhavsar. 2004. *Gujarati Adimudrit Granthoni Suchi*. Ahmedabad: SETU.

Yagnikm, Achyut, and Suchitra Sheth. 2006. *The Shaping of Modern Gujarat*. Delhi: Penguin.

Yagnik, Indulal. 1971. *Atamkatha*, Part V. Ahmedabad: Gurjat Granthratna.

Zelliot, Eleanor. 1969. 'Dr. Ambedkar and Mahar Movement'. PhD dissertation: University of Pennsylvania, Philadelphia, PA.

INDEX

Aanandi (a women organization for livelihood), 159
acharyas (priests/gurus), 32, 43
Action Research in Community Health and Education (ARCH), 178
Adivasis, 27, 38–40, 52, 56
  compared with *sabhaya*, that is, civilized communities, 103
  land rights of, 135–138
Aga Khan Rural Support Programme, 121
Age of Consent Bill, 1892, 26
agribusiness, 53
agricultural or farm labourers exploitation in Gujarat, and role of NGOs, 142–146
agro-based industry, 53
Ahmedabad Association, Ahmedabad, 35
Ahmedabad Mill-owners Association, 36
Akrosh journal, 68
Alagh, Y. A., 178
Ambedkarist Dalits, 42
Anand Niketan Ashram (ANA), Vadodara, 56, 178, 185
Anarde Foundation, 121
anti- SEZ Farmers' Movements, 155–156

anti-ethnic minority social movement, 153
anti-nuclear plant Mithi Virdi struggle, in Gujarat, 160–169
anti-port Umbargaon struggle, 156–159
anti-special investment region struggle, in Gujarat, 160
Antyanj Seva Mandal, 39
Antyodaya Mahila Sangh (AMS), 115
Antyodaya Mahila Sangh of the Ahmedabad Study Action Group (ASAG), 115
ARCH-Vahini, 179, 181–183, 185, 189, 196, 197
Arya Samaj, 29
Aryan Brotherhood, 31
Ashram school, 38
Ashram Shala Yojana, 93
Asiatic Registration Bill, 35
atyanjs (Dalit) school, 36, 44
Atyanj Seva Mandal, 40
avoidance of conflict, 49
AWAG, 155
Ayodhya Ram Janmabhoomi movement, 191

Baba Amte, 190
Bahiskrut Hitkarini Sabha, 41
Balika Vidyalaya, 91

Bardoli Satyagraha (1928), 39
Baviskar, Amita, 196
Baxi, Upendra, 131
Bhal Nalkantha Prayogik Sangh, 56
Bhatt, Ashwini, 194
Bhatt, Ela, 118
Bhil Seva Mandal (BSM), 38
Bhumihin Kisan Hakka Sangharsh Samiti, 136
Bhumiputra, Gandhian journal, 67
Bombay Code of 1827, 25
Bourdieu, Pierre, 71
Brahmo Samaj, 29
Breman, Jan, 146
British administrators/ethnographers, encouragement to native intellectuals to write about history, 28
Buddhi Prakash, 32

caste
    -based discrimination, 30, 133
    -based hierarchy, 30
    as self-governing community, 25
Center for Social Studies (CSS), 179
Central Board Secondary Education (CBSE), 91
Centre for Action and Knowledge (SETU), 187
Centre for Social Justice (CSJ), Ahmedabad, 132
Chapaniyo Dukar, 34
Chaturvarna, 41
Chhatra Sangharsh Vahini (CSV or Vahini), 178
child marriage, prevention of, 29
Chaudhry Amarsinh, 179
Citizens for Democracy, 78
civil society organizations, 35–36, 69
    objectives of, 51
Clarke, Amarsinh, 183
Co-operative Societies Act 1904, 35
Coastal Regulation Zone (CRZ), 165

Committee on the Status of Women in India (CSWI), 78
communication technology, 27
Community Development Projects, 76
Companies Act 2013, companies to undertake corporate social responsibility, 54
comprehend classroom teaching, 99–101
Compulsory Education Act 1916 and 1930, 73
Constitution of India
    Article 14 of, 131
    Article 39 A of, 131
contents and language, role in school teaching, 101–104
cross-cultural learning, 100
cultural level, of backward communities, 75

Daduba, 32
Dalit Harijan Samaj (DHS), 42
Dalit Panthers, 139
Dalits, 36, 40, 55
    Gandhian, 42
    Gujarat, 42
    struggles for land rights, 138–142
    vocal section caught between Ambedkar and Gandhi, 42
Dalpatarai, 31
dams development, in Gujarat, 172–174
dan, 26
daridranarayan, 37
Dariyapur Navyuvak Mandal, 41
Darjee, Jinabhai, 179
Darshan, 155
Dave, Jugatram, 39
democratic egalitarian values, 71
Depressed Class League, 31
Depressed Classes Hostel, 42
Desai, A.R., 109
Desai, Morarji, 174

Desai, Narayan, 160
Desai, Niru, 46
Deshmukh, Durgabai, 76
Development Alternatives Information Network (DAINE), 52
Dharmshala (rest house for travellers), 33
discrimination(s), 45, 49
　among students, in educational institutions, 104–106
DISHA, 137, 145
District Primary Education Programme (DPEP), 79
District Rural Development Agency (DRDA), 114
drought and famines, in Gujarat, 172–174
drought-prone area programme (DPAP), 120
Dukha Nivaran Mandali (An organization to resolve pain and unhappiness), Bharuch, 34
Durgaram, 26

Education Commission, first (1964), 76
education in India, post-independence policy, 75–80
education of girls, 29
Education Policy of 1904, 73
Elphinstone College, 27, 29, 72
enacted Special Investment Region (SIR) Act 2009, 160
enrolment in schools and institutions
　students by institutions, 96
Environmental Protection Act (EPA) 1986, 133
Environmental Public Hearing (EPH), 165
ex-untouchables, 40–42

Fadke, Mama, 40
fakirs, 43
Forbes, 27

Ford Foundation, 132
Foreign Contribution Regulation Act, 1976 (FCRA), 52
Forest Rights Act, 2006, 137
formal education in India
　access to, 81
　agenda of political and social leaders for social transformation, 71
　colonial legacy, 71–75
　segregation of students by school types, 84–92
Forum for Secular Democracy, 155
Free Legal Aid (FLA), 132
Friends of Women's World Banking (FWWB), 115

Gandhi, Kasturba, 91
Gandhi, Mohandas (Mahatma Gandhi), 35, 142
　compassion to work for poor and deprived class, 37
　constructive work, notion of, 37
　priority to uplife ex-touchables, 40–42
　radical approach adopted to resolve workers and owners conflict, 45–46
　work for deprived communities, 42–45
Garibi Hatao (remove poverty) slogan, 130
GoG Gunotsav (or Celebrating Quality programme), 98
Gokhale, G. K., 37, 73
government-aided schools, 92–95
governmentalization, 94
gram swaraj (village republic), 56
Gramya Vikas Trust (GVT), 158
gram sabha (village council of all adults), 164
Gujarat Chamber of Commerce and Industry, 191
Gujarat Coastal Zone Management Authority, 165

Gujarat College, 28
Gujarat Ecology Commission, 123
Gujarat Khet Kamdar Union, 145
Gujarat Land Ceiling Act, 1974, 138
Gujarat Pollution Control Board, 161
Gujarat Sabha, 35
Gujarat State Tribal Development Residential Educational Institutions Society, 91
Gujarat Vernacular Society, 27, 28
Gujarat Vidhya Sabha, 28
Gujarati literature, 28
　shift in tone and subject matter of, 28
Gujarati Sahitya Parishad (GSP), 47, 194
Gyan Prasarak Mandali, 27

Halpati Seva Sangh (HSS), 143
Hansa Mehta Committee (1961), 76
Harijan, 40
Harijan Sewak Sangh, 40
Hind Swaraj, 35, 171
Hindu nationalists, 57
Hindu trading community, 25
Hindutva, 49
Hirakud dam project
　objectives of, 174
　rehabilitation policy for project adversely affected people, 174–178
　resistance against, 172
　solution of problems of Odisha, 171
human rights organizations, 66–67
humiliation, 49

ideology for public work, necessity of, 65
Income Tax Act, 1961, 54
Indian National Anti-revolutionary Party, 41
Indian National Congress
　and social reform, 31
　formation in 1885, 34

inequality, 31–34, 49
injustice, 49
INSAF, 194
Integrated Wasteland Development Programme (IWDP), 120
inter-community relationship, 25
International Labour Organization (ILO), 176
Iyer, Krishna, 131

Jain trading community, 25
Jalkranti Trust, 121
Jamin Hakk Rakshan Samiti (JHRS), 140
Jamin Hit Surkasha Samiti, 137
Jamindari system, 130
Jan Sangarsh Manch (Platform for people's struggle for justice), 159, 194
Jan Vikas, 132, 155
jangali, 38
Janpath (a network of Gujarat NGOs), 159
Jat-Pat-Torak Mandal, 31
Jawahar Navodaya Vidyalaya, 90
Joshi, Umashankar, 47

Kalavriksh NGO, 185
kaliparj, 38
Kashtakari Sanghatana, Samajwadi Jan Parishad, 157
Kendriya Vidyalayas (KVs), 90
Khadayata Vaniyas, 29
Khatala (traditional wooden bed) meetings, 165
Khedut movements in Gujarat, 155
Khet Vikas Parishad (engaged for the rights of agriculture labourers and Adivasis), 159
Kinara Bachao Samiti (KBS), 157
Kisan Sabha, 46
Kothari, Kakkalbhai, 46
Kothari, Rita, 47

Index

Lalbhai, Chimanbhai, 35
Land Acquisition Act 1894, 175
Land Ceiling Act 1961, 135
land grab movements, of socialist, 130
land reforms, first phase of, 130
lattas, 25
lawmaking process, 129
Legal Aid and Human Right Centre (LAHRC)
    establishment of, 132
    objective of, 132
    programmes of, 132
literay scenario, post-Independence, 48–49
Lok Adalat (people-oriented court), 133
Lok Adhikar Manch (LAM), 66, 194
Lok Adhikar Sangh (LAS), 134, 136, 146
Lok Samiti, 155
Lotwala, Ranchhod Das, 45
low-fee private (LFP) schools, 95

Maha Gujarat movement (1956–60), 154
mahajans, 25, 26
Maharaj, Ravishankar, 42
Majmudar, Parikshitlal, 40
Majoor Mahajan, 45
Manav Dharm Sabha, 30
manpatra (felicitation letter), 41
Mathai, Ravi, 121
Medhavi, 121
Mehta, Babalbhai, 56
Mehta, Chunibhai, 39
Mehta, Dinkar, 46
Mehta, Durgaram, 32
Mehta, Makrand, 68
Mehta, Sumant, 45
Microcredit Year (2005), 114
migrant sugarcane workers, in Gujarat, 146–151
Minimum Wages Act 1948, 130, 142

Ministry of Agriculture, 120
Ministry of Human Resource Development (MHRD), 90
Ministry of Urban Development and Poverty Alleviation, 127
Mistry, Madhusudan, 194
modern education in India, 27, 28
    genesis of, 72–73
    spread to bring social change, 28
Mudaliar Commission, 90
Muknayak fortnightly magazine, 41
Muslim trading community, 25

Nabhubhai, Manibhai, 31
Nagar Club, 29
nai talim education system, 93
Nandy, Ashish, 68
Naoroji, Dadabhai, 29
Narayan, Jayaprakash, 78
Narmad, 30
Narmada Abhiyan (campaign) (NA), 191, 192
Narmada Agey Badhao Shanti Yatra, 192
Narmada Bachao Abhiyan (Save Narmada campaign, NBA), 157, 161, 187, 188, 190, 192–194, 198–201
Narmada Control Authority, 188
Narmada Dharangrast Samiti (NDS), 188
Narmada Forward Peace March, 192
Narmada Ghati Nav Nirman Samiti, 188
Narmada Ghati Sangharsh Samiti, 188
Narmada Planning Group (NPG), 178
Narmada Water Dispute Tribunal (NWDT), 174, 177
Narmadashankar, 28
National Alliance of People's Movements (NAPM), 157
National Alliance of Street Vendors, India (NASVI), 127

National Bank for Agriculture and Rural Development (NABARD), 114
National Committee on Women's Education, 76
National Council for Civil Liberties, 69
National Curriculum Framework (NCF), 101
National Educational Policy (NEP) 1968, 78
National Fishworkers Forum, 157
National Legal Services Authority (NALSA), 133
National Policy on Education (NPE) 1986, 101
National Policy on Urban Street Vendors (2009), 127
National Rural Livelihood Mission (NRLM), 114
National Social Conference, 29
National Social Reform Conference, 34
National Watershed Development Programme, 120
nationalization, 94
native intellectuals, 27
Native School Book, 26
Native School Society, 27
natural or moral rights, concept of, 129
Navnirman movement (1974–1975), 154
Navodaya Vidyalaya (NV), 90
Navsarjan Trust Surat, 136
Naxalbari movement, of CPI (ML), 130
Naya Marg, Gujarati journal, 147
NGOs in India
  as delivery agency, 109
  Governing Council social profile, 60
  in Gujarat, 52
  objectives of, 54–56
  organizational structure, 60
  period of formations, 53–54
  survey on registered organizations in 2008, 51–52
  welfare and development programmes for poor, 109
Nimar Bachao Andolan (Save Nimar), 178
Nuclear Power Corporation of India Ltd (NPCIL), 162

Operation Blackboard, 79
ORPAT trust, 120
Oxfam-UK, 183

Pardi Ghasia (grassland) Satyagraha, 135
Pandya, Kamlashankar, 45
Paramhansa Mandali, 30
Parikh, Harivallbha, 56
Parikh, Rasiklal, 48
Parivartan, offshoot of Dalit organization Navsarjan, 144
paryavaran, 56
Parsi trading community, 25
Paryavaran Samrakshana Samiti, 157
Paryavaran Suraksha Samiti (PSS), 157, 161
Patel, Chimanbhai, 94, 191, 193
Patel, Girish, 134
Patel, Vallabhbhai, 44
Patkar, Medha, 187, 189, 192, 193
Phule, Jotirao, 72
Pokhran nuclear test II (1998), 161
*pole*s, 25
Policy and Development Initiatives (PDI), 123
Poshitra struggle, 158–159
poverty, 31–34
  causes of, 62–63

Praja Hitvardhak Sabha (Society for the Advancement of People's Welfare), 34
Praja Socialist Party, 135
prakhar gram sevak, 56
Prarthana Samaj, 29
Pratham Education Foundation, 98
prayashchitta ceremony, 31
primary schools, medium of instruction in, 98
printing press, 27
private schools and colleges, rise after economic liberalization, 95–96
problems, management of, 65
Progressive Literature Sangh, 47
project affected people (PAP), 171
 rehabilitation policy evolution for, 174–178
project spirited families (PAFs), 197, 198
Public Interest Litigation (PIL), 131
Public Union of Civil Liberty (PUCL), 67
public-spirted intelligentsia, role in voice on public issues, 67–69
public
 deliberation, 129
 institutions, 34–35
 life, 49
 space, 49
punya (or God's blessings), 32, 33
Pushtimargiya Vaishnav Parishad (PMVP), 67

quality of education, 98–99

Rajpipla Social Service Society (RSSS), 131, 136, 177, 179
Ram Janmabhoomi agitation, 155
Rehabilitation and Resettlement (R&R) Policy 1983, 181
religious communities, 25
Reserve Bank of India (RBI), 114

Right of Children to Free and Compulsory Education Act (RTE), 80
Right to Fair Compensation and Transparency in Land Acquisition, Rehabilitation and Resettlement 2013 (Amendment) Ordinance, 168
rural development, Gandhian approach to, 56–57
Ryotwari Land System, 172

Sadguru Water and Development Foundation (SSST) Trust, 121
Sahajanand, 30
Sahiyar, 155
Sampoorna Kranti Vidyalaya (Total Revolution University), 160
sannyasis, 43
Sardar Sarovar Nigam, 196
Sardar Sarovar Project (SSP) dam project on Narmada river, 171
 NGOs role and rehabilitation package policy, 195–198
 polemics and uncivil war on Gujarat government by activists, 187–195
 rehabilitation policy formulation process, 178–185
 resettlement and rehabilitation policy, 185–187
Sarthee, 121
Sarva Shiksha Abhiyan (SSA) or Total Literacy Campaign, 79
Sarvodaya Mandal, 155
Saurashtra Jaldhara Trust, 121
Saurashtra Lok Manch Trust, 120
Secondary Education Commission (SEC), 75
self-employed groups, 112
Self-Employed Women Association (SEWA), 112–113
self-help groups (SHGs), 112, 113–119

Servants of India Society (SIS), 37
SETU, 155
SEWA Trade Facilitation Centre (STFC), 113
sewa, notion of, 37
SEZ Act 2005, 159
seths (wealthy merchants), 32
Shivaraman Committee, 53
Shoshit Jan Andolan, 157
Shramik Vikas Sansthan (SVS), 185
Shri Dariyapur Atyanj Hitvadhak, 41
Shri Mahila SEWA Shakari Bank Ltd., 113
social action litigation (SAL), 79, 131, 134–135
social discrimination, 59
social morality, 129
social movements
　aims and objectives of, 153
　categories of, 153
　of dominant strata, 154–155
social reform, 29, 31
social relationship, 49
social services, market and role of state in, 65–66
Societies Registration Act, 1860, 51
Sri Sailam dam, in Andhra Pradesh, 177
Street Vendors (Protection of Livelihood and Regulation of Street Vending) Act 2014, 127
street vendors, SEWA role to organize, 123–127
Subodhak Mandali, 41
Sudharo (social reform), 28
Surat mahajan, protest against Bengal standard weights and measures on trading community, 26
Surat Praja Samaj, 34
Survival International Organisation, 183
Swa-sudharak mandali, 31
Swadhyay Parivar, 121
Swami Vivekananda, 37
Swaminarayan Sampraday, 121

Swaraj, 64
Swarnjayanti Gram Swarozgar Yojana (SGSY), 114

Tata Company, 37
Tehri dam project, protest against, 176
test litigation, 131
Textile Labour Association (TLA), 45
Thakkar, Amritlala, 37
Times of India, 69
Tod, James, 27
Tripathi, Govardhanram, 28

Ujaliyat (white people), 38
Umbargaon Taluka Bandar Hatao Sangharsh Samiti, 157
Una agitation, 141
University Education Commission (UEC), formation in 1948, 75
urban places, neighbourhoods in, 25

Vadodara Khetmajur Sangathan (VKS), 144
Vaidya, Chunibhai, 194, 195
Vanvasi Kalyan Ashram (VKA), 57
Varnashrama dharma, 31
Vedchhi Intensive Area Scheme (VIAS), 56
veth, 30
Vidyabharati, 57, 93
Vishwa Hindu Parishad (VHP), 145
voluntary poverty, concept of, 57
Vruksh Prem Seva Trust, 120

Warli movement, 157
watershed programmes, in Gujarat, 119–123
western education, introduction by Christian missionaries, 26–27
widow remarriage, 29
World Bank (WB), 53, 178, 181, 183, 185

Yagnik, Indulal, 44, 45, 46

ABOUT THE AUTHOR

Ghanshyam Shah is an independent researcher, based in Ahmedabad. He is a retired professor of Jawaharlal Nehru University (JNU), New Delhi. He was earlier a Fellow-in-Residence, the Netherlands Institute for Advanced Study in Humanities and Social Sciences, Wassenaar; and National Fellow, Indian Institute of Advanced Study, Shimla, and Indian Council of Social Science Research, New Delhi. He was also Director, Centre for Social Studies, Surat, and Dr Ambedkar Chair Professor (1995–1996) at LBS National Academy of Administration, Mussoorie. He was a Visiting Professor at the University of Chicago, Illinois; Banaras Hindu University, Varanasi; M.S. University of Baroda, Vadodara; and S.G. University, Surat.

He has authored/co-authored and edited more than 20 books, including *Social Movements in India* (1981 and 2004), *Protest Movements in Two Indian States* (1977), *Public Health and Urban Development: The Study of Surat Plague* (1997), *Untouchability in Rural India* (2006), *Dalit Identity and Politics* (2001), *Re-reading Hind Swaraj: Modernity and Subalterns* (2012) and *Growth or Development: Which Way Is Gujarat Going?* (2014). He is a recipient of several academic awards.